The Mind of a Market Gambler

This book is your STOP-LOSS

Mental and Financial Traps
That Destroy Traders

Thomas P. Wysler

Publisher: https://sherlocktrades.com/
Design and layout: SherlockTrades.com
Contact: info@sherlocktrades.com

This book is intended for informational purposes only. It does not constitute financial, legal, or investment advice. Always consult a licensed professional before making any financial decisions.

This book is for educational purposes only and does not replace psychological, therapeutic, or medical advice.

The author is not liable for any consequences resulting from the improper use of the material presented herein.

This book is for educational purposes only and presents the author's personal experiences.

Stylistic and language editing: the author, with the support of text editing tools.
ISBN: 978-83-976140-1-7

To my wife, Joanna.

No words could ever capture
the depth of what I feel.

I love You, I thank You…
You are my Angel.

You bought my book — thank you.

I hope it helps you become an effective and happy Trader.

Check out my YouTube channel.

Shortly after the book is released, I'll start posting regular videos with detailed chart analyses and insights into "**Smart Money" activity**. [1]

If I can keep the pace, I'll aim to share at least five case studies of interesting market setups each week. I'll give you the exact instrument and date so you can pull up the same chart and see if you spotted what I did. These videos will be purely educational.

YouTube Channel

https://www.youtube.com/@SherlockTrades

https://www.facebook.com/sherlocktrades/

https://www.instagram.com/sherlock.trades/

https://www.tiktok.com/@sherlock.trades

Until now, I've stayed away from social media, so I'll be building all these channels from scratch. This will be my next challenge. Just like writing this book, it will probably take me quite a while — so I'm asking for your patience. :)

1 Introduction

This book **isn't** the story of my life — it's about the lessons I've drawn from it on my journey to becoming a Trader and making a living from trading. It's the distilled essence of my experience and the knowledge I've gathered over the years, tested in countless "battles with the charts."

I'm sharing my thoughts and principles as if I were talking to a friend, so you can avoid costly mistakes and reach success as a Trader faster.

Remember — you are 100% responsible for your own life and decisions. The value you get from studying this book depends entirely on you.

This isn't a strategy manual or a step-by-step guide on how to enter and exit the market.

> *It's a story about what lies inside a Trader's mind — what can be destructive, and* ***what can give you strength.***

A Trader is ready for stable, profitable, long-term trading when their approach is built on two solid foundations: the "trading technique — Technical Analysis" and the "mental game — Trader Psychology." [2]

In this book, I'll tell you everything I know about the mental game — how your mind works and reacts, and how to train it.

I also lay out the rules of risk management, i.e., Money Management [3], because it's inseparably tied to psychology.

The mental game, discipline, and risk management are the toughest parts of the Professional Trader's craft.

This book won't guarantee you success — but if you study it diligently, **your odds will rise dramatically**.

Whether you succeed is entirely up to you.

Approach this material without rushing, in quiet and calm.

Think through each chapter. Take notes.

Do it once, do it well — then revisit it later.

Got your pen and paper ready to take notes?

That's important.

Some images don't show well on e-readers or phones, so I've put the important ones on a webpage for readers of this book.

http://www.sherlocktrades.com/books/mental/photos

The images are organized by chapter number.

Table of Contents

2 Why Should You Read This Book?

2.1 In Short?

Because you want to become a Trader — and I already am one.
Because I know the demons you'll have to defeat within yourself.

Most aspiring Traders start by learning how to trade because they want to jump into the market and make money as quickly as possible.
That's the quickest way to blow up your first account — almost a sure thing. [4]

The purpose of this book is to make you aware of **the factors that can defeat you and** to show you practical solutions.
Becoming a Trader means shaping yourself into someone with traits most people will never have.
It sounds like training a superhero — and in a way, that's exactly what it is.
A Trader needs to have two fundamental areas firmly developed:

2.1.1 Technical Analysis

Technical Analysis (TA) is the art of reading charts and using tools that help you decide when to enter the market and when to exit.
This is what most beginners focus on — because it's usually where they start. What they don't realize is that it's not the analysis that will beat them, but their own psychology.

2.1.2 Trader Psychology

This is the toughest part of the craft. Each of us is different; we all have our own demons and weaknesses.
I'll help you grasp the core of the problem and how to handle it.
Your job is a deep self-audit — to find what you need to improve or reshape.

Get ready for a lot of work on yourself, because in this book we're tackling a tricky, trap-filled territory — your mind.

I'll show you the tough sides of this profession so you can become a conscious Trader faster and avoid being a source of capital for others.
It's cheaper to learn from other people's mistakes, but unfortunately, the lessons that stick best are usually the ones we make ourselves.
Especially the really painful ones.

So don't overdo it with the studying.

Learn, and at the same time start trading.

Start out on a demo account first!

Starting your trading journey on a demo account is crucial.
In later chapters, I'll explain why.
Remember: you'll get as much value from any book as you're ready to take in. When you read the same thing six months or a year from now, different words will hit home — because you'll already be a different person.
Learn, try, learn again, and try again until you become a master.

We're all different, and we all have our weaknesses. I'll show you what I discovered in myself, and what my friends and fellow Traders discovered in themselves...
Everyone has their own unique battle to fight. Fortunately, as humans we share many recurring flaws and weaknesses, so you'll definitely find topics here that fit you perfectly. :)

Not everything will be handed to you on a silver platter. The solutions that fit you best are often the ones you must find yourself.
Think of this book as a set of signposts and prepare for serious self-work.
Many topics will be worth exploring on your own.
If you take full responsibility for yourself, you gain power and control. You become the master of your destiny.
If you expect someone else to do it for you... you'll lose.

Be 100% honest with yourself at every stage.
If you don't fool yourself, you'll find your weaknesses and turn them into your strength.
That's half the battle — to me, it's even more than half.
I'm sharing my story with you, along with what I've learned about the nature of a Trader through years of experience and self-development.

The role of a good teacher isn't just to pass on knowledge, but above all to teach independent analysis and how to find information. It's better to hand someone a fishing rod and teach them how to fish than to just give them a fish.
The more you take in and put into practice from this book, the faster you'll grow into a profitable Trader — and the smoother your learning curve will get.
The task is hard, but achievable.
High rewards aren't paid out for easy wins.

2.2 How It Was for Me...

I'm 52 years old, living a pretty typical life, wrestling with plenty of problems like any ordinary person.
For more than half my life, I ran small businesses and know all too well what it's like to fight for every cent just to keep bread on the table.
Over 20 years ago, after watching the movie Wall Street again — and later its 2010 sequel Wall Street: Money Never Sleeps — I realized that if I didn't change something, I'd spend the rest of my life just struggling to survive and end up old with nothing but unfulfilled dreams.
I found a trading course, paid for it, and traveled halfway across the country to learn the craft.
I came back with knowledge, fired up with enthusiasm — and soon after, I blew up my trading account. I took a break.
Then I came back to the market and... blew up my account again.
Another break. **Another attempt. Another lesson.**

Finally, in 2018, I sat down to trade again — this time supposedly wiser after so many failures. Unfortunately, not wise enough, because I blew up my account yet again.
Maybe just a little later than I used to. :)
I focused only on technique, convinced that being smart and experienced meant I didn't need to work on my Trader's mindset anymore.
I was very wrong.
Trading isn't easy. It's not a profession for everyone.
Reading one manual isn't enough, and neither is attending a good webinar.

Trading is a profession you have to commit yourself to.
It's a brutal game — no feelings, no mercy. [5]

For a long time, I thought I could dabble in trading on the side — squeezing it in between one task at my business and the next — and it never worked.
Eventually, I reached the point where I told myself I'd either stay stuck in the same routine for the rest of my life, running my business and making small money, or I'd take one more shot at fulfilling my dream.

From 2018, for over three years, I took part in two serious mentoring programs [6] as well as additional technical analysis training. Every two to three weeks, I joined online meetings with people who move millions in the market.
It cost me a small fortune (for my means) and a huge amount of self-work. Many times, I thought it just wasn't for me.
But I didn't quit — I stubbornly kept moving toward my goal.

I might be boring you with all my comebacks and failures, but I want you to know this: if you don't succeed the first time, it's no big deal... I wasn't sharp enough to start winning right away either. Success usually goes not to the smartest, but to the most persistent and determined.

2.3 Success Is the Reward for the Persistent

Finally, in 2019, things started to click. I began making money consistently. Suddenly, everything made sense — as if someone had taken the blinders off my eyes. In truth, I took them off myself by putting together a trading technique that fit me, like assembling a puzzle. Everything you need has already been invented — you just have to put it together into a well-working whole.

I'd "seen" it before and thought I got it in theory, but I wasn't yet the guy who could sit at the table with the sharks and take profits for myself.

If you dream of becoming a Trader and making a living from the markets, this book can help you survive, because it talks about human weaknesses and how to turn them into strengths.

If you're already earning consistently, most of what you'll find here will be familiar. Good principles are worth revisiting — there's always something you can improve.

Why am I writing this book?

Because I know what it's like to fight for every penny.

Because I know how valuable it feels to be able to support yourself and your family through your own knowledge and skills.

Because I know how much we sometimes need guidance, advice, support... hope.

I want to live knowing I wasn't here just to make money, blow it, and have a good time. I want the satisfaction of knowing I shared my experience and made other people's lives better because of it.

I don't sell courses. I don't have magic solutions.

All I can do is show you my path and point out the traps.

I make my living from the market — and that makes me happy.

If you want the same... take this book seriously.

2.4 Resilience...

Persistence and intelligence – still not enough to succeed in trading.
Few professions trigger such extreme emotions in a person.
When you start, you often carry a huge hope that trading will change your fate, because you're not happy with how life looks right now.
You picture yourself as the king of your own life, free from mundane worries.
You don't want to wonder if you'll have money for bread at month's end, or stress over the lights being cut off because the bill was a week late.

Trading stirs up extreme emotions far more than most professions.

The word **EXTREME** here is no exaggeration.
One day, you feel like the master of the universe, as if you had a magic wand multiplying the money in your account. The chart is so clear and obvious that every entry means profits, profits, and more profits.

Another day, you wonder if it was all just a streak of luck that's now over. Maybe it's better to quit trading and look for a "normal" job... or perhaps start running courses on trading techniques?
Ha... exactly.
Add to that the weight of your family's future, the pressure that failure would put you all in deep trouble – and it gets very real.

Sometimes in trading, you can feel like
John Rambo in the middle of the action. :)

If you're on your own and you blow everything, at worst you'll end up in your parents' place or a friend's garage, starting from scratch.

But if you lose your home and your family has to find somewhere to survive and rebuild from zero, the mental strain is extreme — and very few people are in a state to start a Trader career under that kind of pressure.

You have to be exceptionally resilient to operate under such stress.

I won't even count how many times I've had dark thoughts.

I've hit rock bottom more times than I can count, with that thought in my head: "I can't do this."

Yet every time, after those thoughts, an inner rebellion woke up in me.

I'm not stupid... If others can make it, so can I.

I just have to diagnose what I'm doing wrong — and tackle it again, this time smarter.

If I don't repeat the same mistakes that just took me out, maybe that was the last big obstacle... maybe my success is just beyond that dark forest.

Everyone has moments of weakness... What really matters is whether, when you fall, you get back up — and if you do, whether you've actually learned something from it.

Making mistakes is human.
Repeating them — that's just foolish.

In this profession, intelligence and persistence are essential, and setbacks and hard times are guaranteed. What matters is learning from them and moving effectively toward your goal.

2.5 Didn't That Scare You?

I'm telling you honestly about my struggles because you're stepping onto a difficult path, and I feel somewhat responsible for you.

I want you to be a happy person — because today the world is running a massive happiness deficit.

Do you realize that if one person helps two others, and each of them does the same, then after 32 repetitions, more than 8 billion people could have a better life?

32	8 589 934 591

I hope that with this book I'll manage to do more than just help two people.

I touch on my path to trading only briefly, because honestly, I don't think it's all that interesting.

I focus mainly on what goes on in the mind of someone becoming a Trader — because that's the most important part of this profession.

This isn't a job where you punch the clock, grind for eight hours thinking about your vacation, and then go home and forget it all.

Trading changes the way we see life...

If you feel this is for you, and you know you can handle it — an incredible experience awaits you.

Remember, you're doing this because you chose it — and you're doing it for yourself.

2.6 One More Thing — Please Forgive Me for This...

When you buy a book, you expect a professional product — written by a professional author or someone who did it on their behalf. Behind every book, there's usually a whole team of people: from editing and consultations to corrections and marketing.

In the case of this book, I'm handling all of those roles myself. I've never written a book before, so I'm sure I'll make plenty of mistakes. Maybe I'll forget something, or maybe I'll focus too much on a part that bores you. Each of us has, at some point, heard an important sentence from an ordinary person. That person probably wasn't a professional writer either, yet still had something valuable to share. I believe we all have something valuable inside us that we can give to others.

I also don't have the kind of setup most book authors have — like a large website, a blog, or other typical channels.
The website http://www.sherlocktrades.com is already in development — at first, it will probably be a simple business card page. I wondered how I could find out whether you enjoyed the book or if you have any critical feedback and... I came up with the idea of using YouTube comments.

I've recorded a short trailer for the book — under that video, you'll be able to leave your comment.

https://www.youtube.com/watch?v=qWleFoDfYmk

I'll be truly grateful for every comment.
I know exactly what goes on in a Trader's mind — that's why I'm confident in the quality of the information I'm sharing with you. What I don't know is whether the form is good enough and if I've managed to get across what's really in my head.
If you feel I didn't quite pull it off, please forgive me.
I plan to translate this book into several languages so it can reach readers beyond my country's borders. I don't have a publisher willing to invest in professional translators hoping for a profit from the book — I'll be using my own skills and AI.

If in some details the content isn't perfectly polished — I apologize in advance.
I'm trying to provide as much valuable content as possible, working on a minimal budget, and investing a huge amount of my own time and energy into this book.

This book will probably have its rough edges compared to titles polished by big publishing houses.
I hope that what matters most is the content itself, and that its value and authenticity will speak for themselves.

Yes... these few gray hairs of mine are the result of trading. :)
My desk and trading spot aren't some luxury office at the top of a skyscraper downtown.
I'm not going to tell you fairy tales about ruling the world from a golden throne atop Olympus, gazing down at Wall Street from my office window.
Juggling this many thoughts and pages is probably tougher than trading itself. :)
I know that many of the issues discussed here can change your life — if you truly want them to.
That's why it's worth buying and reading this book. There's even one chapter in it that might just save your life...
Chapter 52.2 — medical compression stockings.

3 Feeling Unsatisfied? Have You Seen the Series Dr. Death?

A friend asked me, "Send me a piece, show me what you've written so far..."
I sent him about the first 30 pages and got this reply:

"I want more!
In just a few pages, you've covered and discussed material equivalent to several hours of training.
A huge amount of knowledge.
I'm left wanting more."

It made me a bit sad, but I realized it's like looking at a chart...
I see this book through the lens of my own experience and knowledge. This is exactly what I'd want to hear from a mentor myself — minimum words, maximum content, or a precise tip on what to look for and where.
I thought a lot about Chris's opinion — he's a smart guy, and we've known each other for almost eighteen years. Am I making a mistake writing this way? Or does it only work for me?
I'm not writing this book for myself. It's meant to give value to the reader.
What I'm describing here is something I've already worked through a long time ago. Sure, there's always room for improvement — and that will be the case right up to the last grain of rice (I'll explain the rice thing to you later).
This is serious business. If Chris is right, I'll have to rework every chapter and pack in more content until each topic is covered in exhaustive detail. If I'm right — I'll keep going.

A Trader must be confident. At the same time, a Trader should also verify whether what they believe to be true really is.
After all, **the worst thing is being sure you're right — and being wrong.**

I'm going to do this… I'll reread all the chapters I considered finished and think about whether they're concrete enough for another reader.
Are they clear? Is it obvious what needs work and where to look for more details?

Probably not everything you read here will be necessary for you. If you notice that you've already mastered a topic, then good for you. Still, read that part anyway — even if it's just to see if there's some small detail you can improve.

I tried to write as **if I were teaching a young Trader from scratch**. I've touched on many topics multiple times from different angles to make sure nothing important slips through.
Did I revise a lot before reaching the final version? Absolutely.

Only a fool thinks they're infallible.

For a Trader, it's more important to have money than to be right.

3.1 If You're Still Feeling Unsatisfied…

That's very good.
It means my book has hit a specific spot in you that needs fine-tuning — or tearing out by the roots and rebuilding from scratch.

Becoming aware of a problem is the most important thing — it's the first step toward solving it. You've identified the problem, so now it's just a matter of finding a solution and turning what was once your weakness into your strength.

Even if this book doesn't solve a single problem but just makes you aware of them — I'll still count that as a big success.
The rest is your work and your responsibility.
You are 100% responsible for your life and achievements.
This may sound brutal, but the industry you're entering is like a psychopath with no empathy.

The market has no mercy for you. It doesn't even know you exist. You need to be aware of that...

No one on the market is going to handle you with kid gloves. No one cares that it's your last money, and that if you lose, you won't have anything to eat.

I could write this gently, pat you on the head, and tell you everything will be fine, that you just need to work on yourself a little...

Believe me — you'd rather get **the truth straight in the eye** here, in this book, than learn it from the market, which will, without sentiment, take everything you have in your pockets.

If a chapter hit on something important for you and you feel there wasn't enough detail — good...

What you need to do now is be glad this book helped you uncover that topic and go find help and an effective solution on your own.

You know what you need. You have the internet and an ocean of solutions at your fingertips.

Be self-reliant — go get what you truly need.

No excuses, no waiting for someone to hand you ready-made answers, no blaming others.

It's your life, your responsibility, your choices
— and the consequences, whether from what you do
or what you don't.

No one and nothing can stop you... except yourself.

3.2 What's This Dr. Death Thing About?

In a nutshell: the series tells the true story of a doctor who presented himself as an outstanding surgeon. In reality, he was a butcher who crippled and killed patients. Today, he's serving a life sentence.

I know many subjects well, and some — I'd say — very well.

If you were going to be operated on by a doctor who honestly told you he was good at it... wouldn't you prefer he recommended someone who could do it very well?

Exactly.

In this book, I often refer, for example, to NLP [7]. I've studied the subject, attended courses, and taken from it what I truly needed.

Am I an NLP master who could run courses and teach others? In theory, yes — but I've forgotten a lot, and there are far better experts you should learn from.

I specialize in trading, so I'm not going to operate on your heart just because I once saw how it's done in a YouTube video. :)

If a topic shows you there's something to fix in yourself, and what I've written isn't enough... and you still feel unsatisfied — go find the best expert in that field and use their knowledge.

I'm holding you to self-reliance.

I've committed myself to honesty and to sharing my knowledge and experiences.

I'll give you as much detail as I can on what matters to us Traders — and if you need more, you'll know what to look for and where to find it.

Let everyone do what's theirs to do — and do it well. :)

Do you feel hungry for knowledge? Good... :)

4 How to Work with This Book?

Life taught me trading and psychology — along with teachers at courses, books, and colleagues and friends who went through a similar process.
I've always had an analytical streak. I was curious about what goes on in our heads and why we make the decisions we make.

What you're reading is the result of over 50 years of life and self-development — shaped into a form that works for me today.
I'm not going to hand you academic formulas from psychology textbooks.
I'm sharing my practical approach to the problems you might face — because I, and many people like me, have been through them too.
I believe real-world experience can often be more valuable than theory detached from real struggles.

In this book, I often speak firmly, as if it were the only truth. Of course, such absolute truths don't exist — everything is relative and depends on perspective.
I want to show you an approach that I know works.
That's why I allow myself to take shortcuts and give clear judgments, without spelling out every possible alternative.

You don't need a catalog of every road. You need one that works. And that's exactly what I'm showing you.
At the same time, I keep emphasizing:

Question everything.

Questioning means consciously analyzing whether a given approach is good for you or not. If it's not, you reject it — or you modify and adapt it to your needs.
If you reject it, it means you've thought it through and made your own choice.

Along the way, you've examined other options and chosen what you believe is best.

In this way, even bad advice can lead to a good outcome.

A bad idea can spark a thought process that leads to a good idea — and something valuable is born.

When you start questioning everything, you'll discover how many programs are running in your head that aren't even yours.

Someone, at some point, simply installed them in your mind.

That's why **I'll be provoking you.**

And it's good if my opinion sometimes rubs you the wrong way — that's exactly when reflection begins.

I don't care about being right. I want you to adjust something in yourself for the better after reading this book — and start making money.

Treat this book like a conversation with a friend.

I'll tell stories, share thoughts — sometimes even philosophical ones.

Read. Reflect. **Question.**

Learn. Fill in the missing pieces. Shape yourself.

I'm not here to "shape" you. I can only be an inspiration.

I'm not God. I have no right to change anyone.

You can — and in fact, you have that responsibility.

Your life. Your responsibility. Your decisions.

My wish is that after this book you not only trade better — but also have a healthier approach to life.

I'm like you — a traveler through life. If my experiences become an impulse for you to reflect on your own path, then writing this all down was worth it. I'm rooting for you.

> *"What man is a man who does not make the world better?"* [8]

Make yourself a better version of both a person and a Trader — and then make sure the world around you becomes better too.

5 Where there's big money, there are also scammers......

As Dr. House said in my favorite TV series:
"Everybody lies."

Where there's money, there are always people eager to grab it for themselves.

When you start your journey in trading, you're making decisions that involve your own money. Think carefully before you transfer funds to anyone.

Personally, I have many contacts in the trading community, and that's exactly why — for your safety — it's worth raising a few points.

There's a saying that hits pretty close to the truth...

If someone can't make money as a Trader, they start teaching trading.

I'll tell you two stories I've personally experienced, both well known in my country.

I won't drop names — this isn't about shaming anyone.

I just want you to notice how important it is to check whether that flashy, polished course ad really hides anything worth your time and money.

The first situation took place in 2010.

The trainer of the course I attended invited one of his students from a previous edition. Since then, that student had earned — by our standards — a substantial amount of money...

About two years later, that same student was already running courses on how to become a highly profitable Trader. His ads were all over Facebook and other social media platforms.

I wrote to the trainer whose course I had attended, asking what was going on...

It turned out that after his first success, the student quickly lost everything and switched to teaching courses.

Someone who couldn't earn consistently was now teaching others how to do it.

And what can you learn from such a "teacher"?

Exactly what he knows himself — how to lose money in trading.

In reality, he was selling pricey courses that couldn't have been worth much, given that the guy himself couldn't make money in the market.

The second case was even more interesting.

In 2014, I met a young guy who — just like me — was attending a stock market training course. About a year later, together with a few friends, he started a company that trained Traders. They filmed commercials on expensive yachts, promising courses with outstanding results...

And then came a wave of backlash when students who had paid serious money couldn't manage to turn a profit.

These are just two cases I saw up close — and there are plenty more like them out there in the market. There's always someone trying to profit from people's naivety. It's sad.

There are two reasons why I won't be running courses.

First — I value peace. My ego doesn't need followers.

Writing a book in my free time is a pleasure for me.

Creating something from my own knowledge and experience is satisfying. Along the way, I've refreshed and deepened several topics — and that's what makes this work meaningful to me.

Preparing courses, working with people, and actively supporting them afterward would seriously disturb my peace. And ultimately, our actions should be about improving quality of life.

Second — where I live, almost every training course ad gets dismissed as just another "SCAM."

I wouldn't want to fight that perception or prove anything to strangers just because of what they write on Facebook.

I don't need that.

In the Bible, in the Gospel according to Matthew, there are two sentences I like and remember — wise, universal, and worth recalling.

"By their fruits you will know them."

"A good tree cannot bear bad fruit, and a bad tree cannot bear good fruit."

Buying this book for the price of a coffee and a piece of cake is hardly a risk. By the fruits this book yields, you'll judge whether it was a good deal.

I've poured so much heart, work, and coffee into it that I really hope you'll be satisfied.

The choice is simple...

You can chase easy, pleasant "solutions" promising quick success and big profits.

Or you can commit to effort, work on yourself, and — ultimately — earn the success you've built with your own hands.

There's plenty of literature with interviews of successful Traders.

Read them, and you'll see: not one of them reached success quickly, easily, or without hard work.

6 Have I scared you? Relax...

We'll start with small steps.

6.1 Every chapter, every sentence has a purpose

Everything I write here — every sentence and every chapter — has its purpose. Sometimes it's obvious, sometimes hidden.
Some things I give you in full — ready to use. Others I only hint at, so you can research and deepen the topic yourself.
Still others are meant to make you aware of something — to spark an idea or concept so you can draw your own conclusions.

Write that thought down, then revisit and develop it.
Once you've refined it — lock it into your subconscious and make it stick. Make it your new automatic program.
I'm not here to mold you like a clay figure.
You decide how to shape yourself — and you must do the work.

6.2 Have you learned how to learn?

It's hard to organize all the thoughts you want to convey. Sometimes, while talking about one topic, you unintentionally drift into another — and something important can slip away.
I've written countless emails, letters, posts, and comments in my life. Writing forces you to think through a subject and express it precisely.

If you come across an idea in this book that matters to you, write it down. I repeat this many times, hoping that if you don't follow the advice the first time, you eventually will. :)

Write it down — otherwise it'll slip away and be gone for good.
When you finish a chapter — or the entire book — go back to your notes and develop them as if you were writing a program for your own brain.
It should be an instruction that sinks from your conscious mind into your subconscious.

Write down the instructions for how you want to operate.
What topics do you still want to explore?
What skills do you need to master to become a complete Trader?
Step by step, you'll get further than you ever thought possible.

Most of us went to school. I remember various unnecessary subjects, but none that taught a child how to learn.
When our daughter reached the stage of conscious learning, my wife and I took her to special classes where she was taught how to remember and learn effectively.
I never had that chance as a kid. When I went to school, the country was under communism, and the Party decided what was "best" for everyone. :)
Only when I was 16 did the country begin to develop, and access to knowledge and the free market finally took off.
You have the internet and access to an ocean of valuable knowledge. Use it.

If you find a way of learning that really works for you, you'll move ahead much faster and hit goals I could only dream of back then. :)
The stock exchange in our country was created when I was 18, and I bought my first shares at 21. At that time, there was neither literature nor training on how to trade. Western books weren't yet available in Polish, and my English wasn't good enough to read and understand specialized content. There were no ebooks, translators, or other tools to make things easier.
Today, in many ways, things are easier, but every era has its pros and cons.
I believe it's always been just as tough to succeed.
The obstacles change, but the grind stays the same — sometimes almost more than you can take.

If a huge tree blocks your path to the goal, you can turn back and tell everyone how impossible it was to get through and how hard and unfair life is.
Or — if you're not a loser — you'll stop for a second, then crawl under it, jump over it, cut it in half, or walk around it.

Don't let any obstacle in your path stop you — let it make you stronger.

As for me, I'd call a friend and sell him that tree, since it's just lying there. :)

6.3 Have You Noticed How Much You've Already Learned?

I ask a lot of questions in this book and give answers...
Learning is like coding — if you don't know the language, it doesn't matter what you upload, the system won't run.
I've noticed that when I teach others, it helps organize my own knowledge, and as a result, I learn even better myself.
In my view, one of the most valuable skills is asking yourself the right questions — and answering them briefly, precisely, and to the point.

Pay special attention to making sure your answer logically follows from your arguments and leaves no room for doubt. It's like having a fact-based, logical discussion with someone.
If you're right and your reasoning has no gaps, your conversation partner can only agree with you... or get offended. :)
I checked online to see if my approach is backed by science. Turns out it is. Here are the conclusions that confirm this method works.

6.4 Asking Yourself Questions — Better Than Just Reading?

6.4.1 The Testing Effect

Research shows that actively recalling information — for example, by asking yourself questions — strengthens knowledge far more effectively than passively reviewing notes or a book.
Example?
A student who reads a chapter and then quizzes themselves will remember more than someone who just reads it twice.
With new material, I first get familiar with it, then challenge it by asking myself, "Does it really work like that?"
If I can convince myself it makes sense, I start explaining it to friends. In return, they sometimes teach me humility. :)

6.4.2 Learning Through Metacognition (a powerful method)

By asking yourself questions like:

- Do I understand this?
- How would I explain this to someone else?
- What would happen if...?

...the learner keeps track of their understanding and fills in the gaps.

6.4.3 Activation of Neural Pathways

Asking questions activates different areas of the brain – those related to logic, analysis, and working memory – strengthening memory traces.

When you learn something **new, connections between neurons form in your brain.**

These communication routes – called neural pathways – are responsible for memory, association, and adaptation to change.

The more often you use them, the stronger they become.

The brain has the ability to change its structure – this phenomenon is called **neuroplasticity**.

Thanks to this, you can learn, grow, and adapt at any age.

6.4.4 Better Encoding of Information

When you try to answer a question, your brain organizes knowledge, creates associations, and places it in context, making later recall much easier.

You create logical cause-and-effect links.

You don't just remember the fact itself – you remember where it comes from and what its consequences are.

6.5 "Make Haste Slowly" (Latin: festina lente)

The only thing you can do quickly in trading... is lose money. :) Learning takes work and time.
If you're ready for a long road filled with pain and setbacks... then you have a chance.
Learning, practicing, and gaining experience is a long process. How long it takes depends on you — months, or maybe longer.
Since this is a long-distance run, it's crucial to think carefully about the direction in which you're going to run.

There's no prize for speed. The prize is for reaching the goal.
If you focus on starting fast and running as quickly as possible, you may find out you've gone in the wrong direction.
In the markets, think first — then act.

At the start, figure out what you need to learn, where the best sources are, and only then — once you know it's the right direction — begin learning.
In my view, the best way to learn how to achieve a goal is to learn from those who have already achieved it.
One core principle I always keep in mind is:

Be careful who you choose as your mentor.

----

7 Be Careful Who You Choose as Your Mentor

Because it's possible that "everyone lies," it's up to you to discover where the real value lies for you.
Whatever someone offers you — be smart, stay alert, and question everything.
Always give yourself time to think.
If something costs you a day's wage, think about it for a day.
If it costs more — take longer to decide.

Time is money.

To make money, you have to invest time.
When you buy a book, a course, or anything else, you're spending your time twice: first to earn the money you'll spend, and then to absorb what you bought.
In pursuing your goal, you're constantly investing your time.
The question is: is the goal worth your time?

When choosing learning materials and a teacher to follow, the key is to verify **that it really works**.
Your time and money are too valuable to waste heading in the wrong direction.

7.1 Questions Worth Asking a Trading Teacher

1. Do you teach absolute beginners, or do you focus on more advanced Traders?
2. What technique do you teach? Is it backed by statistical results? Is it based on loose guidelines or on specific, repeatable procedures and scenarios?
3. Are you currently, or have you ever been, engaged in professional trading on your own account?
4. What type of trading was it? Were you a Day Trader or a long-term investor?
5. On which instruments and timeframes did you trade?

6. What results did you achieve? How much did you earn in percentage terms daily, monthly, and annually?
7. Can you show a live statement [9] and an equity growth chart over time?
8. What was the maximum percentage drawdown you experienced in the past?
9. What are your rules for risk management (Money Management)?
10. What percentage of your capital do you risk on a single trade or position?
11. Do you use Stop Loss orders, and how do you set them?
12. How long does the learning process take? Are there stages beyond this training? What happens if, after completing the course, I'm not achieving the profits suggested in the advertisement?

These are fundamental questions, but you need to understand that you won't always have the chance to ask them, and not everyone will take them positively.

Some of these questions may be seen as intrusive. For example, when asking about a live statement, the person may refuse because they don't want strangers to know how much money they have. Such a question needs to be asked tactfully – it's not about demanding to see their account balance. I wouldn't agree to that myself.

You also need to adapt your questions to the context. If I were talking to someone older and well-known, I might consider being more formal – though knowing myself, I'd probably just ask if we could be on a first-name basis and then jump straight to direct questions.

Use your own judgment here.

If you're dealing with someone respected in the trading community, whose credibility is already established, it's usually not appropriate to demand proof they can make money.

If, for example, Larry Williams were to run a training session, I wouldn't dare ask him whether he makes money or to prove it.

I'll share later what a legend Larry is in our industry.

Questions on other matters are perfectly legitimate. Any teacher who respects their students shouldn't have a problem with questions.

7.2 How to Evaluate the Answers?

Each of us can, to a greater or lesser extent, intuitively sense whether someone is lying or telling the truth.

The desire to attend a course that promises to turn you into a great Trader is an emotion... Choosing a mentor is better done rationally — emotions are a poor measure of real value.

1. **Do you teach from scratch...**

This question matters because if you want to learn from scratch but the course is for advanced Traders, it makes no sense to try "running before you can walk."

On the other hand, if the course is aimed at advanced Traders and the teacher accepts you without knowing your skill level, it raises the question: is he only interested in selling the course, or in actually teaching you?

If someone wants to teach at an advanced level, they must first define exactly what they teach and set requirements for their students. If you're a long-term investor using Ichimoku Kinko Hyo, but the course is for Day Traders based on Price Action [10], it's like signing up for Spanish when you really want to learn English.

2. **What Technique Do You Teach?**

If the technique is well known and described in many sources — for example, VSA (Volume Spread Analysis) [11] — you can easily check online whether this approach suits you.

You can also see who else teaches this method and what results their students achieve.
If the teacher struggles to answer or explains in a way you barely understand, chances are you won't gain much from their course.

The key point here is whether the instructor's trading is based on clear, repeatable procedures. Only trades that follow clearly defined rules give you the chance to achieve stable, consistent results.

Consistent results are the foundation for adjusting your Money Management and increasing the profitability of your trading – important, because a single change could, for example, double your profits.
Without consistency, it's hard to know if a year from now you'll have solid profits or almost nothing left.
I'll talk more about this later.

3. Have you traded on your own account?

This is a fundamental question. If someone is a practitioner with solid results, they know what they're talking about – and that's someone worth listening to. If they teach trading but have never been a profitable Trader themselves, that's a bit weak...

4. What kind of trading was it?

The answer I'd like to hear is: "profitable." :)
You have your own strengths, abilities, and expectations. If what the trainer offers matches them, that's fine.
If you plan to trade, for example, twice a week, for three hours on weekends, ask whether what they teach aligns with that.

Perhaps the trainer focuses on the crypto market, and your expectations can realistically be met. But if they work exclusively on classic markets that aren't active on weekends, you'd be better off finding someone in crypto. (I don't touch the crypto market myself... maybe I'll tell you why later if I have the energy.)

5. On Which Instruments?

If someone is a real practitioner, this question is a walk in the park. Every Trader knows exactly what they trade and how they trade it. You could wake me up in the middle of the night, ask about the contracts I work with, and I'd be able to tell you everything about them.

If someone dodges the question and can't give you a clear answer, you know what that means.

At that point, you can also ask how many monitors they use to track their instruments and what timeframes they keep open on each one. If they truly trade, these are no-brainers.

Later on, I'll show you exactly how I have my own screens set up. :)

6. How Many Percent Per Day, Per Month...

A long-term Trader usually doesn't care about daily results — their focus is on weeks, months, sometimes even years.

A Day Trader, on the other hand, knows their average daily, weekly, and monthly returns — and the percentage range they typically operate in.

If a Day Trader can't tell you their daily profit numbers, their trading is probably unstable. They might take big hits and try to recover with one-off "big shots," but that road ends in bankruptcy. Better steer clear of a teacher like that.

Asking about percentage returns matters because it shows you whether that person's results are realistic and satisfying for you. Remember — if you hear promises of absurdly high returns, that's a red flag right away.

I'll explain later what I mean by "too optimistic" profit numbers.

7. Can You Show a Live Statement?

This is a sensitive question, but if someone agrees to show you the equity curve [12], you'll immediately see whether their results are stable or just a series of losses interrupted by occasional "golden shots." Pay close attention to the size of their drawdowns.

Look for someone who can keep losses under control and achieve a relatively steady account growth over time.

8. What's the Biggest Drawdown You've Had?

Asking about the largest percentage drop in portfolio value is more important than asking about profits — it shows you whether the teacher trades like a gambler or operates like a professional Trader who keeps losses short.

If someone says their drawdowns [13] hit 30%, I'd be concerned. At 50%, I wouldn't ask another question — I'd just walk away and find a real mentor.

When you enter a position with a properly set SL (Stop Loss) in line with sound MM (Money Management) rules, there's only one thing you can be sure of — the maximum loss you can take on that trade. Losses are the only thing you can almost fully control.

There are no long-term profitable Traders who don't control their losses.

There's a wise saying:

"Cut losses quickly, let profits run."

I fully agree with that.

Only by following MM rules can you make money.

Ignore this, and you'll lose not only your money but also your nerves.

9. Money Management

Questions about MM — Money Management — are like a Trader's litmus test. If someone is a professional, they know their MM and can explain it clearly.
MM has to be tailored to the Trader's style and skill level.
This is a crucial topic — I'll cover it in a separate chapter because this knowledge is essential for every Trader.

10. What Percentage of Capital Did You Risk on a Single Trade?

Imagine every market entry as buying a ticket in a "special stock market lottery."
A ticket costs $10. Some tickets mean a $10 loss, some break even, and some bring a profit: $20, $30, $50, $100, or even $200.
You know the ticket price, and you know that most of the time you can win between $0 and $50. Occasionally, you'll hit around $100, and $200 might come up once a month at best.
If you have $1,000 in your pocket, you can buy 100 tickets and, with high probability, recover your money with a decent profit.

In the same lottery, you could instead choose tickets costing $500 each. Then you'd get only two tickets, with possible outcomes of ZERO or $10,000. The $10k ticket shows up rarely — maybe once a quarter.
When you buy 100 tickets, your result depends on the quality of your trading.
When you buy 2 tickets, your result depends on luck — and in lotteries, luck always favors the house. :)

If a teacher says they risk, say, 1–3% of their capital on a single trade, I'd listen closely.
If they push higher stakes, they're probably selling you a dream — and when you buy it, you'll lose twice: first on the course, then on your broker account.

11. Do You Use Stop Loss and Take Profit Orders [14]?

Questions about risk and Stop Loss go hand in hand. If a teacher doesn't use a Stop Loss, it's worth asking why and how they protect themselves from taking too large a loss on a trade.

Just because someone doesn't place protective orders doesn't mean they don't use a Stop Loss.

For example: someone might keep only 10% of their trading capital in their broker account, while holding the other 90% safely in a bank. This way, they automatically limit their maximum loss to 10% of their total capital. This is called SLK – Stop Loss on capital. Your broker account might hold, say, 10–20% of your total trading capital, with the rest kept safely outside the account.

This approach has another benefit – if the broker goes bankrupt, you won't lose everything, only what you had deposited with them. Of course, it's worth choosing a broker based in a country with strong legal protections for client funds and solid financial oversight. Still, no matter how good the safeguards, recovering funds can take time. And you don't want to be stuck without access to your capital.

It's worth asking for details, because not placing Stop Loss orders doesn't automatically disqualify someone as a mentor.

When you enter a position, you must know the maximum loss you can take – in other words, the exact risk you're accepting.

Here's how I calculate it...

Let's say you have $1,000 in your account. You enter a position and set your Stop Loss at $10. If the market moves against you, you'll lose 1% of your capital.

A 1% SL is reasonable, but not small. Generally, 1–2% is seen as safe, while 3% is already high risk – something only experienced Traders, who know their stats and enjoy a bit of adrenaline, might go for. :)

I personally – depending on the day and my confidence in the trade – prefer an SL in the 0.5–1% range.

If someone selling you a course talks about higher SL levels, it's worth asking for details. I wouldn't take that offer.
You can promise anything, but numbers don't lie.
Do the math yourself...

To lose half your capital with a 1% SL, you'd have to lose 50 trades in a row.
With a 0.5% SL — it would take 100 consecutive losing trades.
With a 3% SL, after just 17 losing trades you'd be down more than half your capital.
Now imagine a roulette wheel. The documented record for red coming up was 32 times in a row — in 1943 in the USA.
In 1913 in Monte Carlo, black hit 26 times in a row.

If the stats aren't on your side, sooner or later you'll see your account balance hit ZERO.

Trust me, you don't want to experience a bad streak with a high SL — it will wipe out your account.
Remember — if you lose 50% of your capital, you'll need to make 100% just to break even.
It's better not to lose that much, because the more you lose, the harder it gets to recover.
In the markets, a "Black Swan" [15] shows up from time to time. If your strategy doesn't cover such events, you'd better hope for luck.

12. How Long Does Learning Take?

This might seem like a light question, but it's worth asking whether the training is complete — from A to Z — or just a fragment of the full material. You might discover it's only the beginning of your expenses. If the course lasts only one day, it's unlikely you'll walk away a professional Trader — which also raises doubts about the teacher's credibility.
If you ask what happens if you're not profitable after the training, the teacher's answer will be just as important. Will you be left on your own, or will you get further support?
Learning is a long-term process, and it's a waste of time to head in the wrong direction.

And no, the above is not my ad. :) Mine would look like this:

8 Be Honest — Is Being a Trader Really for You?

I've told you about the long journey I had to take to reach my goal. Others, without running their own businesses, can achieve decent and stable results in about a year. It all depends on how much time you dedicate, what materials you study, and what your personal strengths are.

Almost anyone can learn trading — it's a matter of determination and hard work.

The key question is:
is trading truly for you?

Better answer that honestly, or you'll waste time and money only to abandon this path later.

I've already given you a taste of the risks, uncertainty, and traps...

If you decide to quit at this stage — I'll understand.

Everyone should assess whether a field is right for them or if, for some reason, they won't feel comfortable in it.

I always respect people who make conscious, well-thought-out decisions and take action to change their lives.

Happiness can be achieved in many ways — the most important thing is to find your own and truly be happy.

Most Traders I know say that to trade professionally, you really have to love it.

It's far too demanding a profession to dislike and still do well.

It's worth giving this some serious thought...

8.1 Is It Worth Devoting Your Life to Becoming a Trader?

Have you already asked yourself the most important life questions?

1. What is the meaning and purpose of my life?
2. What principles form its foundation, and how can I build on them a meaningful path I'll be proud of?
3. How do I want to go through life, what do I want to experience, and what do I want to create?
4. What matters to me, and what is a waste of my time?
5. Should the work that provides me with a living also create something?
6. In my work, do I want to be surrounded by people, or am I fine working alone with charts?
7. Many people want their work to create something, serve others, and be socially useful and meaningful. Is that important to me too?
8. What are we really doing when we trade the markets? Does it give anything to anyone beyond some winning and others losing? What's the true purpose of the stock market?
9. Is it worth choosing a profession that can be so mentally demanding?
10. When I close my eyes and picture the best version of myself — who am I, what do I do, and how do I make a living?
11. What will my loved ones say when I start trading?
12. Do I care what others think of me?
13. Do I want them to know what I do?
14. Do I want them to admire me for trading and winning big money?
15. Do I have an ego problem?
16. Am I choosing trading because it's my passion, or because I want to satisfy unhealthy desires — the need for admiration, greed, and the dream of stacks of cash in the closet?

17. Do I want to prove something to someone?
18. Is trading "healthy" for me — good both for myself and for my environment?
19. How can I live so that I can leave this world with a smile on my face?
20. Come up with as many additional questions as you can and answer them honestly. If you lie to yourself, you'll be the one to face the consequences.

Is It Worth Devoting a Big Part of Your Life to Being a Trader?

Yes... — No... — It depends...

This is a serious decision, and there's no single, simple answer. I can only tell you why I believe it's **the best** profession in the world.

8.2 Something You Can't Buy Back

One day I realized that somewhere in the future there's a specific date — a day, an hour, a minute, and a second — when I will die. From this moment until then, I have a fixed number of days, hours, and minutes left in my life.

Picture a huge — hopefully — bowl filled with grains of rice, where each grain represents one minute of your life.

Every minute, one grain falls from that bowl. Eventually, the last grain will fall, and our adventure here will come to an end.

Why am I writing about this?
Think about it... Your time is slipping away. One day, the last grains of rice will fall from your bowl. When you close your eyes then, will you think: "It was a good ride"?

Don't waste time. Don't postpone your dreams.
You don't know if "later" will ever come.

I can promise you I'll do my best not to waste your time. I'll make sure the advice I share is as short and precise as possible, while fully covering the topic at hand. Along the way, I also want to give you a bit of reflection and food for thought about life.

Philosophy — from the Greek — means
"love of wisdom."

So, is it worth becoming a Trader? In a way, that's a philosophical question.
On one hand, the job is challenging; on the other, it's exciting and deeply rewarding.
I'll tell you plenty about the challenges in this book, and you can probably already imagine the satisfaction of making money in the markets — because that's likely what drove you to buy this book.
If you discover the true face of trading and still want to become a Trader, I'll tell you why, for me, it's been the best path.
Later on, you'll find my answer to why trading — in the context of my parable about the bowl and grains of rice — is a worthwhile choice.

8.3 How Much Can I Sell an Hour of My Life For?

If you weren't born a millionaire — like most people — and you have to work to support your life, it's worth doing a simple economic calculation.

What are my fixed living costs, what do I want beyond the bare minimum, and how much does all of that cost? You'll end up with the amount you need to earn each month.

Let's say you need a frugal $500 for food, and for housing, a car, and various extras — another $2,500.

In total, you need roughly $3,000 a month.

You want to work 8 hours a day, 5 days a week, which comes out to about $18 per hour (I rounded up a bit).

This plan keeps you working, because new bills show up every month.

To earn more, you either have to work longer hours or negotiate a better hourly rate.

With your current skills, your market earning potential per hour has a ceiling you can't break.

I've always worked a lot, but I've also always dreamed of doing nothing and living well. After all, work is not the purpose of my life.

I wondered if my business could make twice as much as it does now — or even ten times more — and what it would take to get there.

If you currently earn exactly what you spend, you already know what your future looks like.

You can either accept it and wait for a miracle, or you can make a plan and take action so you won't feel regret in old age.

I'm not a materialist. But I always follow one principle: cut costs, increase income, and improve quality of life.

9 The Difference Between a Trader and a Day Trader

It's like the difference between a marathon runner and a 100-meter sprinter. A long-term investor might buy, for example, shares of companies or an ETF tracking the U.S. stock market index and hold them for months or even years.

If I recall correctly, Warren Buffett bought Coca-Cola shares and has been holding them for 35 years.

A Day Trader, like me, opens a position today and closes it the same day. A trade might last a few minutes or a few hours, but by the end of the day — when I shut down my computer — all my positions are closed. When I sleep, I don't have to worry about what's happening in the markets overnight. My mind gets to rest.

The downsides are real... It's hard work that takes hours at the charts, focus, calm, and emotional control. I use the word "work" because it's like a full-time job. Monday — markets open, so the Day Trader gets to work. Friday — markets close, the Day Trader wraps up the week and enjoys a weekend without charts.

Almost a normal job. :)

Almost — because you decide what hours you work, which days you trade, and whether to take a day off. If you're feeling unwell because of the flu or something has thrown you off balance, you take the day off — because trading requires good physical and mental condition.

It's a very specific, full-time job where you're your own boss.

The returns of an average, solid long-term investor might be around 10–15% annually. If someone beats the index average, they're considered an excellent player — we're talking about maybe 20% a year.

For a Day Trader, record-breaking fund results of 20–30% a year are acceptable... except for us, that's a monthly figure, not yearly.

It may sound strange, but that's the reality.

Keep in mind that the 10 largest investment funds in the world manage capital ranging from almost 3 trillion USD (the smallest in the ranking) to over 10 trillion USD (the largest, BlackRock). These numbers may change — that's how they stand as I write this. And when I say 10 trillion USD, I mean:

10,000,000,000,000 USD.

In Europe, a billion has 12 zeros, while in the U.S. that same number is called a "trillion." In the U.S., everything is bigger. :)

Large sums create limitations that a small Trader with a modest account will never face. We operate in highly liquid markets — our orders don't move the market or affect the price.

A large fund operating with massive capital can't just jump into the market for a few minutes and then exit just as quickly. Liquidity is limited — that's a natural barrier for the big players.

Another limitation: clients give money to a fund through a specific financial instrument. The fund can only turn that cash into a portfolio of assets — there's no room for creativity. The client buys units, the fund buys assets. When the client sells their units, the fund sells the assets and returns the money.

This is a simplification, but that's exactly how every ETF works — and ETFs are currently one of the most popular forms of investing among retail investors. Low costs, good diversification, and straightforward rules.

A Day Trader is like a sniper — watching the chart and taking the shot when the opportunity presents itself.

Even though both worlds revolve around the markets and charts, they're completely different universes.

10 Trading Hourly Rates and Earnings

10.1 Is the Sky the Limit?

There's a saying here that an Excel spreadsheet will accept anything you type into it...
I like spreadsheets because they let me see where I am, where I can get to, and how long it might take me.
Remember, these are the calculations of a Day Trader — a completely different reality from that of investors like Warren Buffett.

Account balance ($)	Daily profit ($)	Monthly profit ($)
	1%/day	15d/mo
1 000	10	150
5 000	50	750
10 000	100	1 500
20 000	200	3 000
50 000	500	7 500
100 000	1 000	15 000
150 000	1 500	22 500
200 000	2 000	30 000
500 000	5 000	75 000
1 000 000	10 000	150 000

If you need $3,000 a month to live, you'll either need over $20,000 in your account or returns of more than 1% per day.

And remember, in most countries profits are taxed.
With such small sums, you're unlikely to afford moving to a tax haven.

At this point, some will say that 1% a day is nothing special, while others will quickly point out that banks offer only a few percent a year — so 1% daily is an absolutely astronomical return.

10.2 I Won't Argue with Your Beliefs

I don't have to — I know the numbers from my own account, and they're nothing special. I know Traders better than me who make even more.

Obviously, there are good days and bad days.

Sometimes the markets behave as if they want to shower us with gold, and sometimes they throw the chart around like they're trying to rob us.

If you have solid technique, are mentally prepared, and manage risk wisely, I assure you that in day trading, a consistent average of 2–3% per day is absolutely possible. The question is: how many days a month can you sustain that intensity — because sooner or later everyone wants a calmer life.

To stay realistic, let's assume an average daily gain of 1.5%. That's no small feat — it takes full-time commitment to trading. And remember, we're talking about results maintained over many years, not once in a while.

Account balance ($)	Daily profit ($)	Monthly profit ($)
	1,5%/day	15d/mo
1 000	15	225
5 000	75	1 125
10 000	150	2 250
20 000	300	4 500
50 000	750	11 250
100 000	1 500	22 500
150 000	2 250	33 750
200 000	3 000	45 000
500 000	7 500	112 500
1 000 000	15 000	225 000

That would leave you with an average of $1,500 more than your monthly living needs.

Keep in mind, you'll probably have to pay tax on your profits in your annual return. And yes — I also think taxes are a scandal. So what happens if each month you earn just enough to live and reinvest the surplus to trade with a bigger stake?

10.3 This Is a Realistic Perspective

	Balance + profit ($)	Monthly profit ($)	Profit – expenses ($)
1	20 000	4 500	1 500
2	21 500	4 838	1 838
3	23 338	5 251	2 251
4	25 588	5 757	2 757
5	28 346	6 378	3 378
6	31 724	7 138	4 138
7	35 861	8 069	5 069
8	40 930	9 209	6 209
9	47 140	10 606	7 606
10	54 746	12 318	9 318
11	64 064	14 414	11 414
12	75 478	16 983	13 983
	89 461		

The calculations are largely simplified — for example, I'm not assuming an increase in trade size during the month proportional to the growth of the account.

It's better to assume less optimistic scenarios than to have inflated expectations and end up disappointed. To be clear — this isn't for a beginner Trader who just discovered trading and thinks they'll make millions in a year.

This breakdown is for a Trader who has mastered the rules, isn't greedy, doesn't take excessive risks, and values steady capital growth over quick cash.

Here's what the breakdown shows...

After the first month, you've made $4,500, paid $3,000 in living expenses, and left $1,500 in your account.

In the next month, you start with $21,500, earn a bit more, and also leave more in the account, since you're not increasing your living costs.

After 12 months of intensive, consistent work at the charts, you have over $89,000 in your account. Over the year, you've withdrawn $36,000 for living expenses and earned a total of more than $105,000.

Let's assume you paid a high tax rate of 25%, like in Germany.

After taxes, about $63,000 remains in your account. You've covered your living costs and tripled your capital.

Discipline, consistency, and restraint.

What happens next... In a few years, you might struggle to count the zeros in your account, and after a dozen years, you could pay off your country's foreign debt. :)

When running Excel simulations, it's easy to calculate capital growth to huge, abstract figures.

What will actually happen?

You'll start spending more on living and pleasures — after all, most people think the point of earning is not to live frugally.

You'll begin trading with larger amounts, which will bring more stress — a stage most Traders go through.

We all have a kind of "thermostat" in our minds that sets the limit of acceptable loss in a single trade. If your Stop Loss — the order that closes a losing position — is set at a reasonable 0.5% of capital, then with $20,000 in your account, the maximum SL in one trade is $100.

That's your risk when you enter a position — and what you can lose if the market moves against you.

Of course, this is a simplification, because sudden price spikes can happen – in that case, the broker will close your position at the first available price, and the loss could be bigger. Such situations, however, are rare.

A year later, with $80,000 in your account, your SL will be higher. You've gained experience, and your confidence and trust in your own skills have grown.

Now you're trading with a 1% SL – meaning $800 per trade.

See what optimistic Excel simulations miss?

If you put $1,000,000 in that spreadsheet and assume a 1% SL, you're risking $10,000 in a single trade. That's the amount you once earned in three months – and here, you could lose it in a minute.

If you had a billion dollars, your broker might not even want you to trade with them – for them, it's a huge risk. They might set additional conditions that would make things harder for you.

I don't have those sums, so I don't have to worry about it. Beyond loss tolerance and skill, there's another limitation: the market won't let you increase your winnings endlessly, because every trade needs a counterparty.

It's not hard to buy well – the real skill is selling well.

Oversized positions in contracts or shares move the market. That's why you can't trade huge amounts without triggering a reaction.

This is purely theoretical – in practice, none of us will likely face this problem.

Though I'll admit – I'd love to have it. :)

I'd buy a beautiful island, a helicopter, and enjoy every sunrise and sunset.

You create your own dreams.
No one should tell you what your goal — let alone your dream — should be.
Just consider the cost of making them a reality.
If my goal were to own a private island with all the luxuries, I'd first have to make really big money.
And to make big money, I'd have to invest a lot of time.

It might turn out I'd reach that goal at an age when I no longer want to sit on an island — simply because I'm too old.
Wouldn't it be better to be happy sooner?
I set smaller, simpler goals for myself and achieve them quickly. That way, I'm happy now, and my list of small, fun dreams is still long.
Every so often, I check another one off. Step by step.

11 What Goal Should You Set and How to Make It Work?

A big, lofty goal sounds great... but rarely works in practice. Most people set goals the wrong way, and they see the consequences of that.

Let's agree from the start on our working definitions of two concepts: goal and illusion.

11.1 Goal:

A goal is something you want to achieve.

It's something — material or not — that your mind perceives as realistically attainable. You might not yet know how to do it, but you must feel it, and your reasoning must give the green light: "Yes, this is achievable — I can do it."

A goal should be conscious and clearly defined.

It has to be specific enough that when you reach it, you can say with certainty: "Yes, it happened."

If you set sail in a boat toward "the exact center of the ocean" and your only navigation tools are the stars, you'll never know whether you've reached your goal or are just drifting somewhere out at sea.

Achieving a goal should be like reaching the summit of Mount Everest — when you stand at the top, you see there's nothing higher. That's when you have 100% certainty that the goal has been achieved.

If your goal is, for example, "to quickly lose weight," that's pretty vague but theoretically possible. The universe might even grant it quickly: you buy a beautiful glass scale for $200, unpack it, and drop it — it shatters into tiny pieces. You wanted to quickly lose weight, and you quickly lost $200. :)

A goal should have a time frame.

If you tell yourself, "Someday I'll finish medical school," you can forget about it.

A well-formulated goal might be: “In October this year, I’ll start my studies and within five years finish them with an engineering degree. In June 2030, I’ll pick up my diploma and drink an original champagne, which I’m putting in the fridge today for the occasion.”

11.2 Illusion:

People often set goals that are unrealistic or so distant that they never even try to achieve them. I call these “illusions” – a form of self-deception that offers a brief sense of relief. It works a bit like therapy.

To me, this image carries a powerful message on many levels. You can take a painkiller and stop feeling pain for a while, but you’re still sick, and the pain will eventually return.

People are masters at creating their own illusions.

You can buy a lottery ticket and imagine winning millions of dollars, buying a beautiful house and car, and having your neighbors envy you as you move out.

That’s not a goal. Simply going to buy the ticket is not working toward a goal – it’s buying an illusion.

Typical Lottery Odds – Main Jackpot		
Lottery	**Win Condition**	**Odds**
Polish Lotto (6/49)	Match 6 out of 49	1 in 13,983,816
Eurojackpot	Match 5/50 + 2/12	1 in 139,838,160
EuroMillions	Match 5/50 + 2/12	1 in 139,838,160
Powerball (USA)	Match 5/69 + 1/26	1 in 292,201,338
Mega Millions (USA)	Match 5/70 + 1/25	1 in 302,575,350

The odds of winning Mega Millions are more than 1 in 302 million.

If you played every day, you'd "theoretically" win once every 828,973 years – about once every 8,000 centuries. That's not a realistic chance. :)
That cannot be your goal.

Illusions are bad. Of course, that's not an absolute truth – sometimes illusions can work wonders.
Imagine a building collapses on you. You're badly injured, with virtually no chance of survival, but a rescuer gives you morphine and tells you everything will be fine. You believe them because you desperately need to. Your mind creates a positive scenario: firefighters lift the debris, pull you out, you end up in the hospital, and after a few months, you walk out on your own two feet.

You plan that as soon as you recover, you'll become a Trader – because you've always dreamed of it and will finally read that book you once bought from SherlockTrades.com. :)

And that's a good illusion, because it keeps your mind busy with something positive. You don't have to confront what you feel is inevitable and what you're not ready to accept yet.
Most illusions are simply an escape from an unpleasant reality into an imaginary world that will never happen in your life.
It's a waste of time on momentary, low-quality pleasures.

If you're struggling and can't come up with or believe in a goal that would truly serve you – I understand perfectly.

Life has its ups and downs. Sometimes, it's really hard.
Don't escape into illusions. It's like turning to drugs or alcohol just to feel better for a short while. Instead, **do something else**.

11.3 Kaizen: Set yourself one small goal

Let it be something as simple as cleaning one shelf in the kitchen tomorrow. **Just one.**
The next day, if you win this small battle with the shelf, plan to spend 5–10 minutes each day for the next week tidying a small part of your room or apartment.

After a week, sit down, look at what has changed in your surroundings, and plan the next week. If you feel up to it, make it two shelves a day or 15 minutes of cleaning anything.
Put your achievement plan on the wall and start making small changes for the better in your life.
Who knows — maybe you'll like it, maybe you'll feel better at home, maybe you'll start to believe that small steps can lead to big changes.

Small successes bring great satisfaction.

Small steps give you the confidence that you can achieve much more.

Only those who give up lose. If you don't give up, you will never feel defeated.

Lisbon in Portugal is almost the end of Europe. To a European, Beijing seems to be at the other end of the world.
Walking from Lisbon to Beijing seems impossible for an ordinary person.
Exactly...

If you believe something is impossible, you're right — for you, it will be 100% impossible.
But if you check the route on Google Maps, it turns out to be 16,412 km and about 3,767 hours of walking.

That's still a lot, but now it's a concrete number — not a distance in light-years.
If you can walk for one hour a day, you'll cover the distance in about 10 years.
And if you walk 10 hours a day, you'll finish in a year.
According to Google Maps, it's doable:

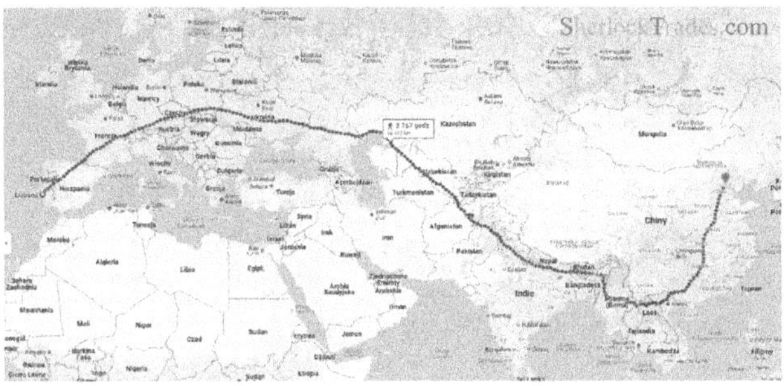

When I think about the 800,000 km I've driven, it means I've covered that distance almost 50 times. It's shocking how much of life can be spent on the road...
We really can go very far if we set ourselves realistic goals and plan the route well — so that every next step is achievable.

11.4 What to Do to Make a Goal Really Work?

You need to choose it well.

11.4.1 The Big Why Rule

A goal with true pulling power must be emotionally important to us — it must promise something exciting, something we genuinely desire.
You need a strong reason why you want to achieve it.

Simply saying, "I want to make a million dollars" has no real power.
But if you ask yourself "**What for?**", you may find out it's about ensuring your family's financial security if you were no longer around.
That's a powerful reason — and that's **why** such a goal works.

11.4.2 The Goal Must Be Realistic and Achievable

If you don't see the point in pursuing it, you won't take action. The more realistic and achievable a goal, the stronger the motivation.

A goal that's too far away won't work.
For example, if you plan to retire in 5 years from trading, it's worth having that plan — but break it down into smaller stages.
Focus on the first steps. The distant goal can remain in the background.
It's important that each smaller goal also comes with a reward — something you really enjoy, but only get after achieving it.

11.4.3 Formulate Your Goal Positively

"I want to be healthy" works.

"I don't want to be sick" — doesn't.
Well, technically it works, but not in the way we'd like. I'll explain this in detail later in the book.

11.4.4 The Goal Must Depend on You

"I will walk for an hour a day" is a good goal.
"My neighbors will clap when I walk" — doesn't work, because you can't control your neighbors.

11.4.5 A goal should trigger emotions and be easy to visualise

If you can't see it, feel it, or if it means nothing to you — it's not your goal.
You might stumble upon something by accident, but that's not a conscious achievement, and I wouldn't count on such chances.

11.4.6 A goal must truly be yours

You know that feeling when someone says: "This year you must get an A in math"? You have a goal — but it's not yours. It's someone else's ambition. **That doesn't work.**
A goal has to come from within — from your own needs, desires, and dreams.

Only then will it truly drive you.
A bad example would be: "I want to earn $20,000 a month because my mother-in-law expects it, and the neighbors will admire me."
That would spark rebellion in me.
I wouldn't agree to that. I'm not lowering my income to $20,000 just to please my mother-in-law. :)
Of course, I'm joking — you get the point. :)

11.4.7 A goal must align with who you are

It may sound trivial, but each of us has an inner set of principles, and breaking them causes psychological discomfort.
Call it a guilty conscience. No matter how "old-fashioned" that sounds — that's how the mind works.

It's about honesty and the ethical principles we all have hardwired. A goal must align with them; otherwise, it will become destructive for us.

If a goal goes against your principles and identity, you'll start subconsciously sabotaging it.

For many people, the goal is money. They want to be Traders because they saw in a movie that Traders make loads of cash.
That won't work if money is the only goal.
Trading is a full-time profession — a passion, a hobby, a lifestyle, and a philosophy of life.
If you see trading as a fascinating market game, part of the global financial system, aligned with ethics and economics — then you have the right approach and a real shot at success.

11.4.8 A goal must be specific

When ordering something from life, don't say "I want to be happy" or "I want something nice for my birthday."
The universe has no idea what you mean and might send you anything.

It's like calling a restaurant and saying: "Send me something." Instead, you choose a specific dish, sides, and the delivery time. It's exactly the same with goals.

If you can picture it so vividly it makes your mouth water — you're on the right track.

11.4.9 Let your subconscious do the work

Calm yourself for a moment, close your eyes, and let yourself be guided by your inner image of happiness.

- What are you doing in that image?
- Where are you?
- Who is next to you?
- What do you own?
- How do you feel?
- Do you see yourself as a Trader there?

This image can be a hint and an answer. If it fills you with peace and joy — it may be a good goal.

11.5 But why...

I really like this old, well-known story...

A young boy is sitting on a pier, happily fishing.
A luxury yacht pulls up. A businessman in a suit steps off, looking at the boy with a hint of condescension.
What are you doing, son?
— Fishing. They're biting well today.
— Why don't you catch more? You could sell them at the market.
— But why...?
— You'd earn money. You could buy better gear, then a boat. Over time, a bigger boat, then a fishing trawler. You'd hire people. After years, you'd have an entire fleet. You'd be making millions!
The boy looked at him calmly.
— And then?
— Well... then you could retire, move to the seaside, and spend your days sitting on a pier, happily fishing...
The boy just smiled.
— But that's exactly what I'm doing.

It's always better when we set our own goals — rather than letting some random businessman set them for us.

12 Why Do I Praise Being a Trader So Much?

Because as a Trader, I truly feel I'm the master of my own fate.
A Trader has no cap on how much they can earn per hour of work.
Even with modest capital, you can reach an hourly rate comparable to a full-time salary.
The bigger your capital, the more you earn per hour on average.

What other job lets you make in one day what others earn in a month?
This profession — demanding, yet without a boss over your shoulder — can get you to serious money in a relatively short time.

And there's that amazing feeling of being sharp.
You enter the market, observe, catch the moves of the big players, and ride the wave like a surfer — making money along the way.

You're like a compulsive gambler who's learned how to beat the casino.

It's like a healthy addiction that makes you profit. :)
Your self-esteem rises because you're the person who keeps landing on the podium in one of the toughest professions.
Once you've gone through the learning phase and made your mistakes, I assure you there's a lot of satisfaction ahead.

And then?
Your brain keeps working at full speed — which is very beneficial, especially as you get older.
It keeps you sharp for longer.
My final step is gradually building fully passive income — based on real estate, ETFs, and other tools within a diversified approach.
That's a pretty comfortable early retirement — provided markets and health cooperate.

13 Reminiscences of a Stock Operator

This book is a must-read.

It tells the story of legendary speculator Jesse Livermore, who made — and lost — several fortunes, notably in 1907 and 1929. Interestingly, some may know his great-granddaughter from the media.

I've read this book three times and listened to the audiobook twice.

I'll definitely return to it again.

I like revisiting Livermore's story because the way it ended serves as a valuable lesson and warning for me.

I won't reveal more...

I wish you an insightful read and plenty of meaningful reflections.

This example should make you aware of the deep respect and humility the stock market demands.

It's a place of great opportunity but also of huge risk.

Stories of million-dollar gains ending in bankruptcy are abundant.

Let your story be different.

Achieve calm, steady success — and enjoy a good life.

14 For Balance... 11,376% in a Year

I know — I'd love to repeat that year after year myself.

In 1987, Larry Williams won the World Cup Championship of Futures Trading.

He turned $10,000 into over $1.1 million in just one year, achieving a return of 11,376%.

Ten years later, his daughter Michelle Williams, at just 17 years old, also won the contest with a 1,000% gain.

If in Chapter 8 my calculations of roughly a 500% return seemed unbelievable, Michelle proved it's possible — at just 17.

Now you're probably thinking:

"If only I had a Larry in the family..."

Can that be arranged? :) Keep reading — you might be surprised.

Also, check what results other Traders achieve:

https://www.worldcupchampionships.com/world-cup-trading-championship-standings

Top Futures Trading Performances (1984–1988)			
Year	**Name**	**Return**	**Category**
1988	David Kline	148%	Futures
1987	Larry Williams	11,376%	Futures
1986	Henry Thayer	231%	Futures
1985	Ralph Casazzone	1,283%	Futures
1984	Ralph Casazzone	264%	Futures

Many Traders post outstanding results without ever competing.

Entering a contest adds extra pressure, which can push you into unnecessary risk.

Maybe one day, when I retire and get bored, I'll take part too. :)

15 A Few Percent of Traders Earn Consistently

Type into a search engine: what percentage of Traders make money, and how many lose in the Forex market.
It's another warning.
The profession I've chosen — and strongly recommend — is neither easy nor comfortable. I'm not telling you fairy tales that you can become a millionaire without effort, with little knowledge, minimal commitment, and starting from just a few dollars.

Reaching the goal of earning consistently on the market is absolutely possible. But don't kid yourself — it won't happen without hard work.
Spend the time to thoroughly study each chapter of this book, because every single one contains a piece of the foundation you must build to become a Trader ready for the daily battle with the market.
You'll also learn some interesting things from the statistics on Trader "survival" in the market.
You can skip ahead to the next chapter — or at least read my summary after these stats. :)

15.1 Trader Survival Statistics

Based on data from brokers, regulators, and other sources, the picture looks like this:

15.1.1 After 1 year:

- 80–90% of Traders lose money and leave the market.
- The remaining 10–20% still mostly fail to achieve consistent profits.

15.1.2 After 2 years:

- Only 5–10% of active Traders remain in the market.
- Just 3–5% of them earn stable profits — meaning returns that exceed both costs and the time invested in trading.

15.1.3 After 5 years:

- Only 1–3% of beginners reach consistent profitability.
- Some of them are former bank and fund employees; others are self-taught Traders with iron discipline and a well-functioning system.

These figures come from various sources.
Some studies found that in the United States, only 1–2% of Day Traders make more than minimum wage after 12 months.
In reality, that's good news — most players jump into the market unprepared, thinking they're genius kids who can outplay seasoned veterans. :)
Such players are needed too — we gladly welcome their money into the market.
Sorry, that's a bit of sarcasm from old hands who've been in the game for years. But it's probably worth knowing how new participants are really perceived.

15.2 Statistics and Causes of Failure

What do the numbers say about why beginner Traders fail?

- Lack of strategy and a clear action plan
- No risk and capital management
- Overtrading — excessive activity and addiction to action
- FOMO (Fear of Missing Out) — the fear of missing an opportunity
- Using excessive leverage
- Emotions: greed, fear, revenge
- Lack of patience — chasing the "golden system"
- Ignoring the psychological aspect

What can I tell you about this?

15.2.1 Lack of Strategy and Plan

It's obvious — if you sit down at the charts without a plan for when to enter, when to exit, and on what basis, your chances of success are slim to none.

If you haven't defined what and how you measure (e.g., Fibonacci levels), what signals you wait for, and what stats back your trades — I don't see how you can win long term.
I've never met such lucky ones.

15.2.2 No Risk and Capital Management

I'll be blunt: if you don't have a plan for risk and capital management, your chances of success are exactly ZERO.
I'll go into detail on this later in the book.

15.2.3 Overtrading (Excessive Activity)

Picture two characters: the first is a focused, patient sniper, waiting for the perfect opportunity to take a single, precise shot. The second is a frantic guy with a Kalashnikov, spraying bullets everywhere.
The first is a professional Trader. The second is a player the market will soon "take out."
Effective trading is built on focus and a small number of precise trades — executed strictly according to your strategy.

I know it's a strong comparison. In reality, nobody is shooting at anyone in the market. Traders compete using their minds, strategies, statistics, and capital.

It's a game for money — based on clear, known, and accepted rules. It's like roulette, except in a casino the house has the edge, while in trading you can have the statistical advantage.
If you lose because you broke your own rules — you have only yourself to blame.
When you trade according to your strategy and still take losses — you're acting professionally. Keep going. If your strategy is statistically sound, you'll make money in the long run.

15.2.4 FOMO (Fear of Missing Out)

The fear of missing out on an opportunity, a profit, or a big move. Markets were here yesterday, they are here today, and they will be here tomorrow. So will opportunities.
Real opportunities are rare. If you constantly feel "this is it" — that's classic FOMO. Look at a one-minute chart — you'll see bull and bear moves happening many times a day. There are plenty of opportunities; you don't need to catch every single one. Watch the market, wait for confirmation that the current move has ended, and only then plan your entry.
I'm not going to teach you exactly how to enter positions in this book — that's a broad topic, perfect for the second part.
Here's one hint: chasing the exact bottom or top rarely pays off.

You don't want to be catching fleas when the pros are hunting big fish.

15.2.5 Excessive Leverage

"Excessive leverage" itself is not the real problem.
The real problem is the lack of proper risk and capital management, which results in taking on too much loss in a single trade.

Leverage is just a tool. It can be used well or poorly.
For an experienced Trader, leverage is a useful tool that allows you to keep less of your own capital in the broker's account.
For an inexperienced Trader, it's a tool that makes it easier to cross the boundaries of acceptable risk. That's why people say leverage is bad. It's not the leverage itself that's bad — it's the way it's used, which in most cases is irresponsible and dangerous.

15.2.6 Emotions: Greed, Fear, Revenge

This is the root of the problems in this profession.
Where there's money, emotions run wild. You'll find more about this later — because it's a key challenge for every Trader. Completely eliminating emotions is not the solution.

The goal is to control them enough to make logical, rational decisions and consistently stick to your strategy.
Greed pushes a Trader to increase risk. Fear stops them from taking trades even when analysis and strategy clearly signal to enter. Revenge — trying to win back money you lost through your own mistakes — is absurd. The market doesn't know we exist, so it won't notice our revenge or crusade. Those are just illusions in our head. :)

15.2.7 Lack of Patience (Searching for the "Golden System")

It's a bit like chasing the Holy Grail. Instead of focusing on the real essence of the problem, beginner Traders look for easy, magical solutions marketed as "sure trades" or "super-effective systems." Of course, when you're starting out, you need to explore what the market offers and what methods other people use.
But how do you choose wisely among so many options?

That's a good question – and a big challenge for someone just entering this world. I believe that if you read this book carefully, you'll find real value in it and answers to the questions raised here.

15.2.8 Neglecting the Psychological Aspect

Without working on your mindset, you won't survive in the market. Mastering emotions is the foundation. After a few losses, a Trader without psychological preparation falls into panic, stops thinking logically, and the mind switches to the "fight or flight" mode, in which rational analysis disappears.

Many Traders have achieved this before you, and their success was no accident. The path is already paved. All it takes is hard work on yourself, personal growth, and consistent self-development.
Looking back, everything seems straightforward.
At the beginning of the journey, we feel like we need magic spells, secrets guarded by dragons, and some kind of forbidden knowledge. But in reality, there are no magic solutions. It's all straightforward. Price movement is a mechanism known for thousands of years. You just need to understand it, learn to observe it on the chart, master a few concepts like Elliott Wave Theory and Fibonacci levels, and you can start building the foundations of your own trading technique based on proven methods.

16 “I don’t want to be poor” — that’s a bad goal!

16.1 We say “No” to “No”!

Let’s take a moment to examine what’s happening in your mind — both in the conscious part you can control and in the unconscious part that belongs to you but plays by its own rules.

Did you know that if you set a goal like “I do NOT want to be POOR, I’ll try to become wealthy,” your chances of avoiding poverty just plummeted?

Why? Because this sentence contains three fundamental mistakes when it comes to goal setting.

Your subconscious doesn’t understand the word “NOT”.

On the conscious level, your brain understands the logic perfectly. A goal is something you strive toward in the future — and it’s primarily your subconscious that’s responsible for making it happen.

Here’s the problem: your subconscious doesn’t register the word “NOT”. This is not a metaphor — it’s how your brain actually works.

Let’s say you have a habit: movie + candy. While watching, you repeat to yourself: “I’m not eating candy... I won’t take one... I won’t eat...” If you’re focused and consciously in control, it might work. But once the movie pulls you in and your attention drifts, your hand will automatically reach for the candy.

Why? Because what your subconscious recorded was: “eat candy, eat candy, eat candy.” That’s exactly what you unintentionally programmed it to do.

Don’t think of a pink elephant... Well? You just thought of it.

It works the same way every time — the subconscious ignores “not” and focuses on the image behind it.

"Don't do this" sounds like "do this" to your subconscious.
"I don't want to work a regular job..." — Oops, you've just started programming exactly that.
As long as these words stay in the conscious mind, it all makes sense. But once they slip into the subconscious... oops.
If you want to be wealthy, create images of wealth in your mind. Instead of talking about poverty, bring up what you desire, not what you want to avoid.

Watch The Secret and read Joe Vitale on the law of attraction. Your mind works in images — when you say "poverty," you see poverty, and that's not your goal.

Be careful with "I'll try to..." What happens when you say: "I'll try to open the door"? You start trying, not opening.
Don't say: "I'll try to become a Trader" or "I'll try to get rich."

I am a Trader. I am becoming a wealthy Trader.

Isn't that a stronger, more powerful message for your subconscious? If you feel this is your path, act with full commitment. Don't try. Just do it.

16.2 Faith and Belief

For programming your subconscious mind to work, you must truly believe in what you say — and your emotional state must confirm it.

When you say: "I don't want to" or "I'll try," you're sending a signal that you don't fully believe it's possible. And if you don't believe it, you can't convince others — and, most importantly — you can't convince yourself.
Start by finding proof that your goal is realistic. Once you convince your conscious mind, your subconscious will look for ways to make it happen. Speak confidently, clearly, and positively about what you want to achieve.

If you object to a declaration because it doesn't feel true — for example, you say "I am rich" but you only have enough in your pocket for one instant noodle soup — replace it with a positive and truthful statement like: "I am becoming rich."
You're not there yet, but you're working on it, so you are gradually becoming a wealthy person.

Imagine holding a winning lottery ticket, the prize already waiting for you to claim. The cash isn't in your wallet yet, but you feel it's already yours — it's a done deal.
Because you won't give up.

16.3 Picture It and Feel It

Have you ever had a moment when music, a smell, or a taste brought back a vivid memory?
That's exactly how the subconscious works. It doesn't store long descriptions, but it perfectly records sensory impressions: the image of your dream house, the color of the car, the smell of new leather upholstery.
These details are what stick in your mind.

That's why in the evening, in silence, sit down and imagine exactly what you desire. Feel it with all your senses, as if you already had it and were truly enjoying it.

Visualization that triggers real emotions is one of the most effective ways to strengthen your goal.

16.4 Ecology

Make sure your goal is "ecological" — good not only for you, but also for your loved ones, friends, and the people around you: neighbors, shopkeepers, colleagues. Why is this so important?

Because every normal person wants to experience good and do good. If you feel that your goal is good, you won't have any inner resistance to wanting it and striving for it.

That's why, in one of the chapters, I answered the question:
Is trading an honest profession?
Of course — yes, absolutely yes.

16.5 I Want to Be Rich — and Fast

That's like giving your subconscious autopilot the command:

"I want to get somewhere, sometime."

Does your subconscious even have a chance to lead you to your dream goal with such an instruction?
A sentence like that is just a wish — like placing an online order without saying what you want, where to deliver it, or when to expect it.

16.6 Optimization and Action

If you notice that your mind and thoughts haven't been working optimally for you until now, you already know what you need to work on. Programming the subconscious is like talking to a computer. Your subconscious needs specifics, precise data, and clear commands.
Speak about the future as if it's already happening — you have a plan, you're working, you're making progress. It's only a matter of time.

Enough thinking. Time to act. **Do it.**
You can visualize, affirm, and think positively as much as you like — but if you don't move, nothing will change.

16.7 You Have Traders in the Family — or... Imagine Them

Sounds a bit like a referral for a psych evaluation?
Maybe, but if it works...
Robert Kiyosaki wrote a great book, Rich Dad Poor Dad.

I remember reading it over 20 years ago — it made a big impression on me and was a pleasure to read. The main character didn't have a mentor in his family, but he found one.

You can do the same... even if that person exists only in your mind.

Most of us don't have professional Traders in the family to learn from. It would be great to have that support — many things would be easier. Imagine your grandparents or great-grandparents were brilliant financiers who passed down their money skills through their genes. Wouldn't it be amazing to feel you have it in your blood?

What if you had someone close to you who was a wealthy Trader and wanted to teach you the ropes... wouldn't that make things easier?

Now picture this: It's night. You're alone, watching a terrifying horror movie. Do you feel fear and tension? If yes — it means sound waves from the speakers and pixels on the screen were enough for your brain to believe in something that doesn't actually exist.

That movie was made in a studio, played by actors, fully directed. Yet your brain fell for it.

Why? Because for thousands of years, humans perceived as reality only what they could see and hear here and now. That's why the brain automatically treats what it sees and hears as true.

In December 1895 in Paris, the Lumière brothers showed people their first film. Soon after, they presented their legendary scene — a train pulling into the station...

After hundreds of thousands of years, our brain suddenly started receiving false images and sounds — and evolution hasn't yet had time to teach the subconscious how to distinguish fiction from reality.

Have you ever flinched during a movie because something looked dangerous? It's just a film, not reality — and yet your "reptilian brain" recognized a life-threatening situation and triggered an automatic flight reaction. Your body experiences emotions as if what's happening on the screen were happening for real.

You do the same when playing intense video games. Now think about children spending long hours fighting zombies on the streets of virtual cities. What images are being imprinted in their minds? What consequences could that have for their perception of reality and everyday life?

This proves one practical thing: our brain is easy to fool.

If you feel it would be easier for you if you had different ancestors, better advisers, mentors, or loving parents — take a look at NLP.

Want to have an advisor in your head like Larry? You can.

There are people who believe they are Napoleon or Elvis.

If an imaginary advisor can help you — create one. **Why not?**

Since our brain has such power, believe that you can make small adjustments to your memories — if you truly need it.

Are you wondering if there's a chapter later about modifying memories?

I've never tried rewriting my own memory, but during trading I imagined my teacher standing behind me, calmly observing what I was doing on the chart.

It was a strange feeling — I felt more confident and also the pressure of his judgment. I tried harder than I would have if I'd been "alone."

At that moment, I felt more or less like this:

Our mind can truly surprise us. :)

Among Traders, there are not only men, so I went a little wild here — we've got two visualizations. :)

In the second image, that's probably how my wife feels when she comes to remind me I've once again skipped vacuuming — despite my promise. :)

16.8 Where to Look for Solutions...

For me, a truly groundbreaking discovery over 20 years ago was NLP — Neuro-Linguistic Programming. In practice, NLP allows you to work effectively on your beliefs and replace them with ones that serve you better.

It also helps you define your goals precisely and program your mind to effectively attract and achieve what you truly want.

What ultimately convinced me about NLP were recordings of therapy sessions conducted by Richard Bandler, the co-creator of this method. If, like me, you enjoy good psychological thrillers, you might like these sessions. It was like a journey into the depths of the human mind — discovering where destructive mechanisms were installed and removing them instantly, without years of therapy.

For me, it was incredible. In a single session, Richard would remove phobias from patients who had been struggling with them unsuccessfully for years. With NLP, breakthroughs sometimes came after just one conversation.

When I find something this simple, brilliant, and effective, I feel like a pig that's just sniffed out a truffle. :)

You can struggle for years with your limiting beliefs — or get rid of them like Bruce Lee, kicking them straight out of your head.

These techniques work like a magic wand — allowing you to change and improve the programs in your head so that they support you instead of holding you back.

I won't bore you with this topic any longer. If you feel it's important for you — you'll study and apply this knowledge.

And if not, come back to this chapter one day and ask yourself what program in your head made you skip something that could've sped up your path to success...

You can lead a horse to water, but you can't make it drink.

I'm writing about this proverb because most people read something, think it's great, and then put it off for "later." That "later" often turns into "never.

Don't allow yourself to make such costly mistakes.

Lost time cannot be bought back. If you use the internet, you will certainly find exactly what you need.

Check out the names of these authors (on NLP, beliefs, law of attraction):

Richard Bandler — co-creator of NLP, a classic authority in the field of belief work and changing internal representations. I've read many of his books. What Richard developed I consider groundbreaking for anyone who truly works on themselves.

Joe Vitale – a key figure in popularizing the law of attraction. Presents a practical approach to changing beliefs and manifesting. I once downloaded a pirated recording of his lectures online. It gave me enormous value, so I immediately sought out a legal version of the material and bought it. To give back, I also purchased all available books he had written – I wanted to feel I was returning something in exchange for the value I had received.
That feeling is worth far more to me than the money spent.

Mark Joyner – a simple, logical system for setting and achieving goals, elements of NLP, and "deprogramming chaos."
Rhonda Byrne – author of The Secret, which combined NLP, visualization, affirmations, and spirituality into a simple, accessible message. I've watched her film many times – it always lifts my mood and motivates me to act.

Tad James – NLP, future pacing, goal visualization, timeline work.

Esther & Jerry Hicks – the source of the Abraham-Hicks philosophy; a systematic approach to vibrational attraction, affirmations, and shifting your point of attraction.

John Assaraf & Murray Smith – practical application of the law of attraction in business; a combination of NLP and neuropsychology.

William Arntz, Betsy Chasse, Mark Vicente – creators of the film and book What the Bleep Do We Know!?, exploring the connection between consciousness, quantum physics, and creating reality.

Ihaleakala Hew Len (in cooperation with Vitale) – Ho'oponopono, or spiritual cleansing of beliefs that block the attraction process.
I personally attended NLP trainings in Poland with two of the most renowned trainers in the field. I'll mention one of them – his book is also available as an audiobook.

For Polish readers, those could be a very valuable two hours filled with practical knowledge.
Unfortunately, Andrzej is no longer with us.

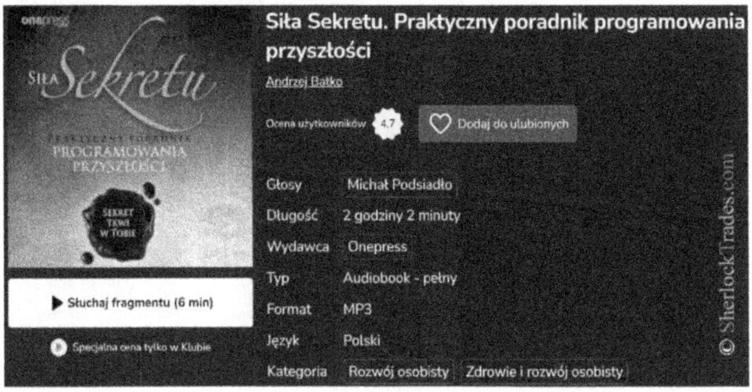

16.9 Did you know that most people will do nothing about it?

People often say they don't like their life and that they need to change something. And what do they do after such a statement? Nothing!
If you truly want to make changes in your life, you must understand the opponent you're facing — and it's inside your own head.

In simple terms: our brain evolved gradually over time — from basic survival functions to more "ambitious" capabilities. Forgive me if my descriptions of biology aren't always scientifically perfect, but in trading, what matters is the effect, not strict biological accuracy. Everything I write about the brain is true in practice — let's leave the theories to neurosurgeons.

There are a few versions of how our brain came to be.
One says it was created in a single day — the sixth day of creation. Another speaks of an evolution lasting millions of years. We'll go with the second one.

Remember — build good habits. Stay on a direct course to your goal.

Don't let emotions lead you astray.

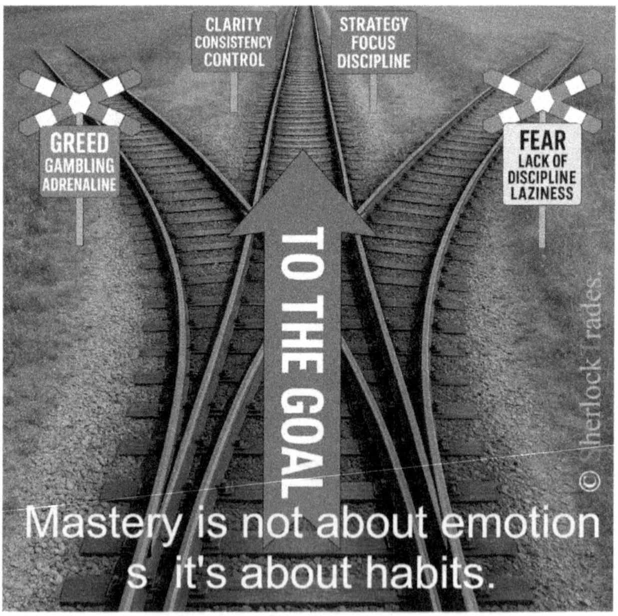

17 How many brains do we really have?

17.1 The reptilian brain — how does it get in our way?

Around 500 million years ago, our ancestors developed the brainstem, also known as the so-called reptilian brain.

This part is responsible for basic life functions and survival instincts. The fact that our heart keeps beating even when we're unconscious, that we breathe, cough, and react to sound and visual stimuli — all of that is thanks to this oldest part of the brain.
From an evolutionary perspective, the most important elements here are survival instincts.
The reptilian brain doesn't analyze or weigh options — it acts quickly and automatically.

17.1.1 Fight or flight!

When the brain perceives a threat, the reptilian brain triggers a simple mechanism: fight or flight.
It doesn't ask our conscious mind whether what it perceives as a threat really requires a reaction. It acts without warning — and that's why it often sabotages our actions.

Have you ever seen people so stressed before an exam that they turned around and didn't even try to take it? Or a dog cornered, lunging at a person because it has no other choice?
That dog also has a reptilian brain — the same survival instincts we do.

Primitive mechanisms make everything unknown trigger fear in us.

Change makes us feel fear as if it were a life-threatening danger.

17.1.2 Fear of change

A new school, job, apartment, relationship — every change triggers some degree of anxiety. The more changes you've gone through, the less you fear them — because your brain has "learned" they're not deadly, not necessarily painful, and sometimes even pleasant.

Fear of change hinders growth. If you don't like your life, you have two options: accept it or overcome the fear and take the risk of changing it. Evolution shows change is good — it helps us adapt and survive.

Change is natural and built into our existence: we are born, we grow, we change. It's inevitable. There's no point fearing change just because your reptilian brain kicks in on autopilot.

Change will come whether we want it or not.

We can't fully control change, but we can control how we react to it.

The smart move is to analyze the change.

Key questions worth asking yourself when analyzing a change:

- Can this change kill me?
- Could it lower my quality of life, and if so, by how much?
- Is it reversible or final?
- What exactly could the consequences be?
- Can it be undone and at what cost?
- If it turns out to be the wrong decision, do I have a plan B or C?
- What will I do then?
- Create a step-by-step plan. Decide when you'll conclude the change isn't delivering the desired results and what you'll do then to replace it with a better solution. :)

I'm sure you can add a few more smart questions to this list.

Once you answer them, you'll have a main plan, a backup plan, and an exit plan — and change will stop being something unknown and uncertain. Instead, it becomes a logical, well-understood path in the evolution of your life.

If change won't kill you, you don't need to fear it or run from it. You might even grow to like it.

The reptilian brain is also responsible for many of our habits. Some of them are harmful to us.

Actions we repeat over and over become behavioral patterns — like automatic programs that activate in response to a trigger. When the conscious mind no longer has to deal with them, they turn into instinctive reflexes. I sometimes catch myself wondering whether I locked the door — because I do it automatically and don't register it consciously. Sometimes I deliberately "mark" the moment in memory so I won't doubt it later.

How many times have you thought after leaving home: "Did I turn off the iron?" or "Did I shut off the gas?" We often act unconsciously, as if we're living and operating on "autopilot."

Since we can encode habits deep in the unconscious areas of the brain, it's worth asking: how can we change them?

We don't want to be slaves to our own bad habits. We programmed most of them ourselves — over a long time.

If we managed to "install" something in our primitive brain once, **we can install something new.**

It's not as simple as swapping a file on a hard drive, but if it matters, we need to put in the work.

How do we change habits?

This is where it pays to look for solutions yourself — so you're not dependent on whether this book covers the topic. :)

What other tricks can our reptilian brain play on us?

In psychology, there is a phenomenon called tunnel vision.

The term comes from an eye condition in which the patient can see clearly only what is directly in front of them, while their field of vision is greatly narrowed — they don't notice anything outside the point they are focused on.

Psychologically, tunnel vision is when over-focusing on one problem narrows your perception. In such a state, we fail to notice what is happening around us — neither opportunities nor solutions.

So what does our reptilian brain do under intense stress?

This primal system takes control. In such a state, we stop thinking logically, our perception narrows, and the body directs all its energy toward one goal: survival.

Notice how much simpler everything gets once you understand how our "onboard computer" works.

A Trader staring at a chart feels strong emotions — stress and a rush of adrenaline. The brain's defense mechanisms activate in response. When the reptilian brain takes over, we stop thinking logically.

We can't think clearly because survival mode kicks in: fight or flight.

That's why trading psychology is fundamental.

Without it, there's no chance of success, because our brain — in trying to protect us — will lead us to bankruptcy.

What's the solution?

The reptilian brain takes the wheel in moments of extreme emotion. The fix is simple: structure your trading so extreme emotions don't arise in the first place.

Sounds simple, right?

We haven't yet covered risk management, Stop Loss levels, and other key elements. Later in the book, everything will gradually come together into a complete picture and provide answers to the issues raised here.

Trading isn't about the Trader playing the hero — enduring huge pressure and still analyzing the market clearly and making good decisions.
There's no point in working against nature.
It's better to understand it and act in a way that makes it your ally.

Imagine you're driving in winter conditions. Snow is falling, the road is slippery. You drive slowly because the road is treacherous. Nothing serious threatens you — you remain cautious, your brain feels no stress, and the reptilian brain doesn't take control. Everything is under your control. You calmly head toward your destination.

Now picture a young driver in the same conditions. He thinks his old car is a WRC rally machine — and that he's Tommi Mäkinen [16]. Emotions run high, adrenaline surges, and his brain stops thinking clearly.
This scenario too often ends tragically. On the road it can mean death — in trading, bankruptcy.
Do you see the analogy with the young, overly eager Trader?

The stats are clear: drivers under 24 are far more likely to die in crashes. Their risk of a fatal crash is roughly twice that of older drivers.

I remember getting my driver's license over 30 years ago.

My father told me that in the first year young drivers have minor fender-benders — they're still learning the basics and making mistakes. By the second, third, and fourth year, they start having serious accidents.

Why? Because they've gained confidence and think they're masters behind the wheel.

Why do drivers go faster than common sense — or the law — would allow? Because they're chasing the adrenaline rush.

A Trader must ask themselves one important question:

Why am I trading?

If it's for the thrill — I wish you luck.

If it's for profit — then trading should be boring.

Making money in the market should be like visiting an ATM — calmly and systematically withdrawing stacks of bills. No rush, no greed — but with certainty and regularity.

Understanding this rule took me a while because — as I like to say — "I'm not a slow driver." I have always loved driving. I visualized taking corners fast and imagined passing where others would back off. My imagination never failed me, and despite the crazy driving, I never had an accident. I was lucky. Once I had a family, risking my life on the road would've been plain stupidity.

It was the same in trading — at some point it hit me:

I had to choose: money or excitement.

The market doesn't give you both. I chose money.

Believe me — changing my approach wasn't easy at all.

17.2 What Does Our Mammalian Brain Do?

About 200–300 million years ago, when we were primitive mammals, the mammalian brain began to take shape.

The mammalian brain — the limbic system (amygdala, hippocampus, and other structures) — is newer than the reptilian part of our brain).
Emotions appeared — and they are responsible for a large portion of a Trader's problems.
In addition to emotions came the ability to remember and form bonds. Bonds mean herd behavior, caring for offspring, learning, and growth.
Territorial fights and social hierarchies also emerged.
I think that's when the first "politicians" appeared. :)
The world was no longer simple.

The mammalian brain — that is, the limbic system — is primarily responsible for emotions, motivation, and emotional memory.
It governs our emotional reactions, which often precede logical thinking and have a huge impact on our behavior and decisions.

From a Trader's perspective, the problem is that the two oldest parts of the brain cause ... "nothing but trouble."

We'd like to act based on analysis and rules, but one part of the brain behaves like a circus monkey, while another — once awakened — either bolts or wrecks the house.
I'm not turning this into a brain-programming manual, so I'll just flag what this layer of our "onboard computer" can actually give you.

Here's what can actually be useful to you:

17.2.1 Anchoring Emotions [17]

Do you have any simple behaviors that can change your emotional state?
For me, one thing that works is this: when I feel tension building, I sit up straight in my chair, take a deep breath, then slowly exhale while straightening my arms as if pushing something away from me.
It calms me down and helps me gain perspective.

When I get tired, I stand up, grab the two dumbbells by my desk, pretend I'm sparring with Mike Tyson — my circulation picks up instantly and the fatigue fades for a bit.

17.2.2 Changing Submodalities

Do you have a mental image of a situation that was stressful for you?
Are there people in it? Are they big, loud, and dominant?
Submodalities are the properties of mental images that shape how intensely you experience them. Find a good NLP book and learn to change your images yourself.
In your imagination, you can:

- push those people farther away,
- make the image black-and-white,
- shrink them,
- make them look a bit silly.

Put clown hats on them in your mind. :)
Finally, slowly push the image away until you can barely see it. You'll notice the emotions tied to it fade — just like the image.

Here's an example:
Imagine you're afraid of spiders and you're looking at one of those fly-hunting monsters. :) Your imagination paints it as a beast.
So what should you do about it?

I don't know — that's your fantasy. :)
Here's what I'd do: I tilt my head — and the spider tilts his head.
I tilt it the other way — he does too.
Then I straighten up and... he smiles at me.
He's missing two front teeth and looks ridiculous.
The little spider waves at me with one leg, then with a few more.
He starts dancing, spins around, and it turns out he's wearing polka-dot underwear.
At that point, would you still be afraid of him? :)

Of course, this is an oversimplification — but it's exactly how you can deal with what's already programmed in your head.

17.2.3 Reframing (Changing the Frame of Meaning)

What is it, exactly? You enter a trade and, shortly after, your Stop Loss (SL) gets hit.
You think: "I'm so stupid... how could I lose again?"
Instead, change the frame of meaning. Think: "OK, I bought a ticket, and this time, instead of a profit, I got a lesson."
Check if the trade was technically justified, and look for the next entry.

Instead of dwelling on the loss, **think constructively**: the SL worked, the entry was technically sound — which means the strategy works. The SL cut the loss, and you can keep going.

When I lose something (not only in trading), I tell myself: "OK — I bought myself a lesson. I'm alive, I'm healthy, nothing bad happened. It's fine." Since I've already paid for it, I might as well get value from it.

Or I put my head in my hands, smile, and think: "That was so stupid of me." On the other hand, "stupid mistakes" are typical of people aged 18–20. Which means that, despite being 52, my brain still fires like a young brain. I smile and turn it into positive internal dialogue.

Remember: **if something has already happened — it's not worth wallowing in it**. It does nothing except waste time and increase emotional costs. Breathe. Think about how to turn it into something valuable, and keep moving toward your goal.

A story from my life:
Once, my wife took our new car (it was only two weeks old) and called me an hour later, worried:
– I wrecked the car.
I asked:
– Are you hurt?
– No.
– Great. Forget the car.

Think about it this way: if you hadn't hit that guy, maybe a truck might've hit you at the next intersection. Maybe what happened actually saved you from something much worse.

You don't know what would've happened next — but since it already happened, don't dwell on it. Move on to the plan: call the insurance company. Tow truck. Coffee. Relax.

Once the accident had happened, there was no point in overanalyzing it. The only conversation worth having at that moment was about what to do next.

And don't think we had a bunch of cars and I didn't care. It was our first car, bought brand new from the dealership — on credit. Wrecking it was upsetting, but in the end, it's just a car.

My wife was unharmed — and that alone was a huge relief. A car is just a pile of metal — there are millions of them.

But my wife is one of a kind.

When she sees I'm feeling down, she usually asks:

– So? Are you done wallowing in the mud, or do you need a little longer?

17.2.4 Time Line Therapy

It's an interesting technique, but to be honest — I never mastered it. I never felt the need, so I won't go into detail on methods I don't personally use.

For context: it's an NLP method for releasing old emotions and limiting beliefs.
It helps locate the root of a difficult emotion (fear, anger, grief, guilt), release it without having to relive the trauma, and then transform the belief or decision associated with it.

How do I handle it? I prefer to grab the bull by the horns, experience the trauma until I get bored of it, and reach the point where I feel no emotions about it at all.
It's a bit like EST therapy [18] — it's not about avoiding pain, but about living through it until it loses all meaning.
The first time you face it, it's intense.
By the fifth time — less so. By the twenty-fifth time, you're bored, not scared.
I prefer this slightly more brutal way of changing past emotions.

17.2.5 Swish Pattern

The Swish Pattern replaces an unwanted reaction to a specific trigger with a desired one.
It's one of my favorite NLP tools — it works brilliantly in practice, so I'll spend a bit more time on it. That doesn't mean other NLP techniques are less important or won't be more useful for you.
It's just that this particular technique has helped me many times, and I think it's worth knowing.

The Swish Pattern is an NLP technique used for:

- changing an unwanted emotional reaction,
- breaking an unhelpful habit,
- redirecting an automatic response (fear, anger, procrastination) into a desired state.

It's like switching tracks in your brain: instead of going down the same harmful path, your mind starts forming a new automatic route.

Example:

Every time you go to enter a position, you feel fear.

You postpone the decision, even though the signal from your chart analysis is clear and unambiguous.

Instead of acting according to plan, you just sit there watching the market move without you.

You know you were right, but you did nothing.

Instead of profit — frustration, wasted time, and a missed opportunity.

How do you handle it using the Swish Pattern?

STEP 1

Identify the image that triggers your mental block.

Close your eyes and think back to the moment right before you click "buy" or "sell." [19]

What do you see? Maybe your facial expression, the chart on the screen, a feeling of tension in your body, or the thought: "What if I lose again?"

Back then, I saw only one thing: the balance in my account shrinking by the second.

I was afraid I would lose again. And then again. And again.

In my head, a dark scenario would unfold — torpedoing my dreams.

This is my “old” image (trigger [20]).
What does yours look like?

STEP 2

Create the desired image. Imagine yourself in the same situation as a calm, focused person — confident in yourself and your analysis.

You see a clear signal on the chart, fully aligned with your strategy. You have calculated the exact position size. You wait patiently, and when all conditions align — you enter.

The market moves immediately in the direction you predicted.
Your account balance grows. You secure the position.
On the pullback, you spot another opportunity — you enter again.
Your profit grows twice as fast.
After a few hours, you have so many open winning positions that you could easily take a vacation until the end of the month.
You feel like the king of the world.

You see the end-of-trend signal — you close everything.
Your speakers play the sound of coins and crowd applause.
You’ve won.
Perfect analysis, flawless entry, and position management.
You’ve earned complete satisfaction and a moment of relaxation.

STEP 3

Overlay the images.

In the center of your mental screen, display the fear-triggering image — your old picture.

In the corner — let's say the bottom right — place a tiny thumbnail of the new image: the calm, confident, successful you.

The thumbnail should be very small, about the size of a postage stamp.

STEP 4

In a split second, the new positive image expands and fills the entire screen, replacing the negative image. Hear in your mind the sound: "SWISH!" — that's the moment of change.

The old, negative image shrinks rapidly.
In your mind or out loud, say “SWISH!” — like flipping a mental switch. At that moment, the new positive image expands to fill the entire screen.

The old image disappears, as if pulled into a tunnel or swallowed by darkness. It flies off your mental screen, shrinks to a microscopic dot, and vanishes completely.

STEP 5

Repeat the entire process 5–7 times.

Do it as quickly as possible each time. Always start with the old image — SWISH — then let the new one appear.

Your brain learns: old trigger = new response.

STEP 6 — Test

Visualize the original situation — the moment that used to trigger your old image. Does the new state now appear automatically?

If yes — congratulations, the reaction has been overwritten.

If not — has it at least weakened?

Repeat the exercise as many times as needed.

Remember — you've been programming your mind for years.

Don't be surprised if the change doesn't happen at the snap of your fingers.

Result:

You — a Trader — with a new, better program in your head.

Instead of fear — calm. Instead of paralysis — positive focus.

You're ready to keep trading — focused, alert, and on the hunt for real opportunities.

17.3 What Does Our "Einstein" Do?

The neocortex — also called the isocortex — is the outer layer of the mammalian brain responsible for higher cognitive functions.

It's your analyst and the architect of success.

It can map the path to your goal, yet often loses out to emotion and instinct if it isn't active enough.

It's the most recently evolved part of the brain.

It's the one you know best, because you use it almost nonstop — from waking up to falling asleep.

What is our "Einstein" responsible for?

- Conscious thinking and logic
- Planning and decision-making
- Analysis, reasoning, forecasting outcomes
- Learning, language, understanding symbols
- Emotional self-control (when engaged)

Want to quiet reptilian impulses and mammalian emotions? Switch on Einstein: ask questions, breathe consciously, plan, analyze — use your new brain to teach the old ones new tricks.

Your instinctive, subconscious impulses push you to act the way you've always acted. It's your conscious mind that can stop you and say: "This isn't the best for you. Do it differently — smarter." It's your "new brain" that, thanks to the clever tricks described in this book, can rewrite old programs, reflexes, and habits.
You just need to think a little, work a little — and then you'll be surprised at the level of success you can achieve.

Write a smart plan, execute it, and... there you have it: a new, better life. Unfortunately, the plan might be new, but you're still the same you. The one you're not entirely satisfied with.
That's exactly why you're reading this book.

Cause drives effect.
Recognize the negative effect — and you'll find its cause. Root out the cause — and the effects will disappear.

18 You Are Not the Result of Your Choices

It may not sound flattering to realize that most of what you do comes from unconscious, automatic choices.
But it doesn't matter how it sounds — what matters is the truth, and what knowing it can do for us.

18.1 Changes in Our Brain

When you repeat a certain behavior, you strengthen specific neural connections. The brain physically changes its structure, creating permanent "pathways."

This applies to:

- motor habits (e.g., driving a car)
- emotional habits (e.g., responding with fear)
- cognitive habits (e.g., thinking "this will never work")

Over time, these pathways start to dominate.
You become a product of your own behavioral loops.

18.2 "You Are the Result of Your Habits"

This isn't just a wise saying — it's a neurobiological fact.
Your brain, your decisions, your life — all run on repeated behavior patterns that eventually become automatic.
Do you think you are who you are because you consciously made those choices? That your mind, after careful analysis, rationally decided?

No.

Most people don't become who they want to be, but rather who their habits, fears, environment, and unconscious patterns allow them to be.
What we call "choices" is often just a justification for something we already did — driven by emotions, childhood beliefs, the need to belong, or the desire to avoid pain.

Consciousness is often just the spokesperson for decisions already made deeper down.
Psychologists and neuroscientists agree: the overwhelming majority of a person's life decisions are not made consciously.

Approximate breakdown:

- Conscious, analytical decisions: ~5%
- Automatic, habitual, intuitive decisions: ~95%

Sources of that 95%:

- habits (learned behaviors)
- heuristics (mental shortcuts)
- values and beliefs imprinted in childhood
- emotions that trigger action patterns
- subconscious reactions to environmental stimuli

Most "choices" are in fact reactions to specific conditions — automatic and instantaneous. Conscious decisions that weigh options, analysis, and logic are rare and energy-intensive.

Now that you know this, ask yourself: within that 5% of conscious control, wouldn't it be smart to start reprogramming the machine that's been rolling the dice for you?
If you start working on the subconscious programs that make decisions on your behalf, you stand a real chance of steering your life toward where you truly want to go.
And if you're not satisfied with where you are today — maybe this is your last chance to change the ending of your own story.

18.3 "You Will Be the Result of Your Previous Choices"

Do you have a favorite team you've supported since childhood, sticking with them even if they finish last, season after season? Or maybe you've got a phone with a bitten apple on the back, and your next one will be from the same company simply because you're used to it: the phone with the bitten-apple logo?

You buy shoes from the same brand because they're "the best," even though you've never tried others?

Consistency — supposedly your choice, but often a trap.

If you once made a bad choice, chances are you'll keep making them. If you once broke your own rules, it's easier to break the next ones. That's not bad luck — it's your brain's mechanism.
It works like a habit, an automatic reaction — a belief accepted without question.

Start questioning it. You can stop, think, and choose what you — after rational analysis — decide is best.
If you're buying another expensive phone just because you bought your first one from that brand ten years ago, then — out of respect for your own intelligence — ask yourself:
"Why this one, and not another?"

I know — I can already hear your brain bombarding me with reasons why it's the best choice.
But shouldn't it be the other way around? First the reasons, then the decision? Wasn't your decision emotional and automatic?
Just because you chose something once, you keep choosing it today — to avoid the effort of analysis.

And how do you know that first choice was even the right one? Maybe think it through again — before dropping another $900 on a new phone when the old one still works fine and you mostly just swipe and scroll.

I know I'm drifting away from trading here — and this is a book about trading. But...
The exact same mechanism applies when placing trades.
That's why you need predefined scenarios, checklists, and preselected setups — ones with a statistically proven edge.
Your brain doesn't like to analyze — it likes to save energy.

It will keep suggesting shortcuts and oversimplifications.
Your job is to take control of that process and turn improvisation into rule-based execution.
After hundreds of repetitions, the new habit will become automatic.
But before that happens, you have to do the work: run the checklists, analyze, compare.
Only then do your stats have real meaning.

If you trade according to a specific scenario (e.g., X, Y, Z) and have 100 such trades, you can see the average risk–reward ratio (R:R) and check whether that scenario gives you an edge.
If your trading is chaotic and you don't stick to your rules — you have no way to measure it.
If you've built your strategy honestly and diligently, you can trust your stats.
And then you can grow your account, scale your positions, and... make more money — without emotions, stress, or adrenaline.
Because you have certainty.

But if you skip the checklists and ignore your stats — all you're left with is belief, not knowledge.
Your subconscious knows that.
It will start warning you — with stress, tension, and adrenaline.
Do you think trading for money has to come with emotion?
In that state, you end up fighting the market, relying more and more on "intuition" — until a single candle wipes you out.

You have to choose how you want to live and make money.

I prefer knowing tomorrow will be a calm, predictable day.
That there will be no traps, just the same work as always.
I like the boring, steady routine that brings in more than I spend.
And I can keep doing it for 10 or even 20 years.
And you? How do you want to spend the next 10–20 years?

18.4 The Bottleneck of Your Potential

Think about what you know, what you can do, what resources and potential you have, and what you'd like to achieve. Between your potential and the realization of your dreams lies a road you have to travel.

Along that road, there's usually a bottleneck.

It might be a lack of knowledge, skills, or resources.

Maybe you don't have the necessary means.

Maybe you simply don't know what's holding you back.

The first step is to become fully aware of the whole picture.

Define precisely:

- What is limiting you?
- What is slowing you down?
- What is stopping you from reaching your desired goal?

Do you know what the most common bottleneck is?

18.4.1 Rules

You have certain rules, and in theory your conduct should align with them.

You might have a rule: "I don't smoke."

But execution varies — which is why simply setting good rules is not enough.

You also have to successfully implement them in your daily life.

18.4.2 Monitoring

You observe your own actions and catch the moments when they are inconsistent with your rules.

What we write in our "Rules" is usually the result of rational thought — and often doesn't sound particularly exciting.

In practice, we often choose what's pleasant over what we wisely decided earlier.

That's why we need to set up a control desk.

18.4.3 Control

Your control desk will weigh what you feel like doing in the moment against your rules and everything you've built in your mind over the years:
the influencing factors that will determine whether you break the rules or stick to them.
Which side will tip the scale? What will you choose?

18.4.4 Self-Discipline

This probably needs no explanation. :)
You know those states — laziness, lack of motivation, inconsistency, the thought "I can't do it," procrastination, and abandoning goals?

So why is it that, even if you have a dream — for example, to become a Trader and live freely without a job, without restrictions — you still haven't made it happen?
Self-discipline isn't magic; it's the result of many interconnected factors — both short-term impulses and long-term foundations of your effectiveness.
Understanding this network of influencing factors allows you to better manage your own reactions and habits.
The right, lasting set of such factors ensures that changes and new habits stick for good. Until you build that, you have to use temporary solutions — short-term influencing factors that help you follow through with your plan.

18.4.5 Short-Term Influencing Factors

These are factors that affect us "here and now," often outside our awareness:

- Influence of other people and environment — support, but also social pressure, group norms, the atmosphere of a place, emotions triggered by others.
- Psychological factors — emotions, moods, beliefs, cognitive biases.

- Current level of willpower — a limited reserve of mental energy.
- Ways of resisting temptation — strategies to avoid, ignore, or delay gratification.
- Desire for the outcome — how much we want it and how that impacts our motivation and actions.
- Momentary sense of self-efficacy — the subjective feeling that we can pull it off.

All of this affects our self-discipline — the ability to take action and execute the plan to reach our goal.

18.4.6 Long-Term Influencing Factors

These are the foundations of our lasting ability to maintain self-discipline:

- Standards and monitoring — internal rules and the ability to keep track of your own actions.
- General sense of self-efficacy — belief in your own agency.
- Habits — automatic behavior patterns.
- Level of willpower — your individual ability to resist temptation. How much can you handle? How do you strengthen it? For example: get a good night's sleep before trading.
- Reward system sensitivity — how strongly rewarding stimuli affect you. How do you set up a reward system that keeps you motivated to act.
- Mental self-image — who you think you are and how that influences your decisions. If you see yourself as an effective, disciplined Trader — that's a huge advantage.

These deeper factors create an internal environment that either supports or hinders disciplined action.

18.4.7 Focus on the Process

Change in life is usually a long process.
Even if you make a decision in a split second, maintaining that change over the long term can be a challenge.
You can throw a pack of cigarettes in the trash — but the nicotine cravings will stay with you for a while.

So how do you start well?
Every morning, while drinking your coffee or tea, do a quick review of your goals, rules, and commitments.
Make a checklist.
Remind yourself what matters — and why you got up today.

Find 15–30 minutes each day for something that helps you grow — a book, a lecture, a webinar, anything tied to your goal.
Ideally, target the bottleneck you've identified in yourself.
Introduce small changes, new habits: 5–10 minutes of meditation, a morning walk — anything that gets your mind and body moving.
The more of these small actions you implement, the easier it becomes to build bigger, more demanding habits.

Also, build the habit of seeking quality literature on psychology and personal development.
What you've just read points to what's truly worth exploring further.

18.5 Introduce One Easy Habit into Your Life

Introduce one new habit. It doesn't have to be important. It can be something minor — as long as it's easy to implement.
This seemingly insignificant action can do far more than you might think.

Why? Because adopting it requires little effort, doesn't trigger strong resistance, and helps create new neural pathways in the brain.
Once a new behavioral pattern is established in your brain, further changes come more easily — because you already have the "tracks" for the next habit to run on.

Don't start with a huge change.
Start with one small thing. Even something trivial.
Do it once, then twice, then a third time... until it becomes the norm. Then add something more challenging.

Small things don't trigger resistance, but they build your capacity for bigger changes.
It works.

18.6 Information Overload

The amount of data your brain has to process is far too massive for you to consciously analyze every situation and make decisions based on that.
Look out the window. How many details are in the scene you see? How many gigabytes would it take to store every detail of that image on a hard drive?

Inside your brain are structures called the basal ganglia – they're responsible for automating behavior. That's where habits are stored, and that's where the key to success lies.
All you have to do is program them correctly.
The brain simplifies everything and only picks out what it considers important. But... that's not entirely true. :)

If you spot an angry dog in that image running straight toward you, your brain will lock onto it – because you have a stored pattern: IMMEDIATE THREAT ALERT.
Suddenly you no longer see the whole world – you see the dog. You analyze its direction, assess whether it's charging at you or at the cat hiding under the fence.

You don't do this because you're guided by wisdom. Your life is run by reflexes and habits.
Since childhood – entirely unconsciously – someone or something has installed small "programs" in you for every possible situation. A stimulus appears – a familiar trigger – the database activates, matches it, and runs reaction program No. 11,305.
A moment later, you're doing exactly what you always do.

Those programs are you. They lead you through life – exactly the way they have so far.

Unless you realize your brain doesn't detect what's truly important – only what it has already tagged as important.

You may encounter something valuable – but you pass it by because it isn't in your database and you aren't focused or open enough to see it.

Don't like who you are or how you live?

Once you realize it and understand where it comes from, you can start looking for ways to change it – to reprogram yourself into a better person.

The world is full of people whose bad habits and mental programs have led them to the point where they finally say, "I don't want to live like this anymore."

That moment of awareness is the start of change.

It means consciously catching your automatic reactions and replacing them with new ones.

If something was once recorded in your mind – it can be overwritten. Install the new program once, twice, three times... and eventually the old one disappears.

You'll become a new version of yourself.

You are the result – but you're not a closed book; you can still write new chapters.

It's up to you how your story ends.

How legendary the ending will be – and whether it will inspire others – depends on how much work you put into writing "your book."

Otherwise, it might end up as a mediocre story – one among billions – headed for the recycling bin because no one will want to read it.

If you're not satisfied with your life – start thinking about which programs in your head are worth changing.

Your brain is like a lottery machine. A trigger appears — the machine spits out a number — and you have a reaction.
Your job is to figure out which reactions map to which numbers — and swap them for ones that work in your favor, so that no matter which number comes up, it's still a step forward.

18.7 Want Some Good News?

Read books by Daniel Kahneman, Joe Dispenza, and other researchers who study human behavior.
It's not personality that determines actions.
It's actions that shape personality.

If every day you make decisions that are:

- lazy — you become lazy,
- responsible — you become responsible,
- aggressive — you become combative.

You don't just have habits. You are your habits.
And that's the good news:
If you put in the work and truly think it through, you can change them. You can become a better person, a better Trader, and ultimately have a better life.
One small change can disrupt your entire system of habits. One seemingly trivial thing — like taking a morning shower and making your bed — can trigger a domino effect and force a reorganization of your entire "software."

Change one small thing every day — and in a year,
you'll be a completely different person.

You'll be surprised how far you can go by taking only small steps.

19 Start Taking Action...

If you want to see the greatest movie of your life — it's not enough to write a brilliant script and leave it in a drawer.

Imagine standing at the beginning of a long corridor.

At first glance, the corridor looks empty.
But as you move forward, you'll see that every few steps doors appear — and behind each one are new opportunities.
If you stand still and wait for someone to bring you something valuable, you might wait forever.

Move, go, take action — do anything; just don't stand around hoping for a miracle to fall from the sky.
Even if you make mistakes — that's good (as long as they're not the kind that cost you your shirt).
Many times, I've done things that seemed unremarkable at first, but they led me to meet people, discover inspiration, and find new paths.That's what life is about — we stumble in the dark until we finally find what's meant for us.
I'm reminded of an old Jewish story:
An old shopkeeper prays to God every day:
— Yahweh, let me win the lottery!
— Yahweh, please, I beg you, let me win!
— Yahweh, I've served you my whole life — make it so I finally win!

Many years pass until one day a voice from heaven say:
— Moshe, **give me a chance** — at least buy a ticket!!!

A Trader who spends hours analyzing charts, waiting for a sign from heaven, won't win anything if they don't "buy the ticket" — meaning make a decision, accept risk, and see what happens.
I think, I analyze, and if what I see matches my strategy — I act.
At the start of the corridor, you stand there with a **desire**.
A specific **vision** forms in your mind.
You make a **plan** to achieve it.
You take **action** — without that, nothing will happen.
And as you move forward, opening door after door, you'll get **results** — the payoff for effort and stepping out of your comfort zone.

The most famous shark — the great white — must keep moving to breathe. If it stops, it dies from lack of oxygen.
Humans are similar. If all you do is stand still and dream about change, nothing will happen. Will you stand there until you run out of oxygen?

20 Where to Start? Have You Thought It Through?

Writing a short book that truly changes lives is anything but easy. There are so many topics I'd like to touch on, explore, and expand on — but I'm aware that too much content can discourage you.
If you get lost in a jungle of digressions right at the start, no real change will happen.
I wrote "start taking action...," but then I felt a sense of responsibility — a bit like a parent. Will you head in the right direction after reading that sentence?
Or will my words lead you into a dead end, wasting your time before you realize it wasn't the right path?
That's why my suggestion is simple:

Before you start, read this book through to the end.

If you feel the need — read it again.
Take notes, think them through, and only then create your action plan.

Your actions can go in several directions at once:

- grow as a Trader,
- for balance, read something inspiring from psychology,
- analyze your habits and change them — one by one.

Since your habits will determine who you become, they should always be at the top of your list. Identify them and adjust them.
Program your autopilot so it takes you exactly where you truly want to be.
If you neglect this, it's like allowing a hostile guerrilla force to operate in the background of your life — sabotaging your path, blowing up bridges, and making every step harder.
Make life easier for yourself. Do the "hard" work on yourself — because it's the simplest real path to your goal.

21 What Should Your Trading Look Like?

21.1 Like This?

You know. You already know how your brain works and what it's doing right now.

It's certainly not analyzing options or considering alternative scenarios. In that state, your thinking is blocked, and making good decisions becomes impossible.

Never let yourself be in that state when looking at a chart.

Never!

It's really simple.

Think about why people run from a bear and fight for their lives: **because they entered the forest unprepared** – with no plan, no awareness of the risks, no weapon, no protection.

It's exactly the same with Traders who open positions without analysis, timing, a clear plan, or a solid Stop Loss (SL).

Then the inevitable happens. No trading psychology book will help you at that point – your fate is already in the bear's paws.

In trading, you have an advantage:

You can always close the position, turn off the computer, and ask yourself:

"What on earth did I just do?"

21.2 Or Maybe Like This...

The small fish Labroides dimidiatus has learned to survive among ocean predators.

It's a perfect example of symbiosis – mutualism, where both sides benefit without harming each other.

Retail Traders are like these little fish.

We don't fight sharks. We don't hunt for the big fish.

We swim alongside them and take advantage of the waves they create.

How?

- We observe where the biggest players are heading.
- We join in and swim in the same direction.
- When something gets in their way, they do the fighting – not us.
- And if they lose, we look for a new leader and swim with them.

The little fish shouldn't think it's a shark.

We swim with sharks, not against them.

22 Trading and Life — Does It Make Sense?

In very simple terms:
A Trader must stand firmly on two legs — on one, they'll eventually topple over.

We — our personal and professional lives — are like a picture made up of a million puzzle pieces.
If a few background pieces are missing, the world won't fall apart.

But the most important pieces must be there
— without them, we're not complete.

22.1 Psychology, Puzzles, and Speedboats

That's exactly what this whole book is about. It's the most important thing you need to develop and nurture — an effective Trader's mindset.

Your mind doesn't operate in a vacuum — tied only to the chart. You have a private life too — and plenty happens there as well. Everything has to work together.

Trading is a complex and demanding profession. It requires taking care of many aspects — technical and psychological, professional and personal.

> ------------------------------
>
> *If you've got a great speedboat built for speed,*
> *you need calm waters to enjoy it.*
>
> ------------------------------

If you head out in a storm and hit 20-meter waves, you'll sink — that boat was built for racing, not for battling the elements.

Your life is a puzzle. To operate effectively, you need all the key pieces in place. If something is missing — in trading or in your personal life — fill in those gaps. It's one of the simplest ways to make your path to success easier.

22.2 Trader's Work and Life — Yin and Yang

At 22, while studying at a polytechnic in Poznań, I decided not to waste time on boring lectures and switched from full-time to weekend classes. On weekends I had lectures, and the rest of the week I devoted to running my small business.

Since then — for over 30 years — I've run various companies, always looking for something that would make me say, "I'm happy."

Separating life into personal and professional spheres?

For me — Nonsense!

It's an artificial construct — everyone knows private life affects professional life, and professional life affects private life.

A day has 24 hours.
Let's assume you sleep for 7 hours. Add an hour before bed, and another after waking up for a shower, coffee, and getting into gear.
That leaves 15 hours.
A typical person in our region works 8 hours to earn their salary. Add the commute, and it's 9–10 hours.
That leaves 5–6 hours of life.
Groceries, meals, doomscrolling the "important" news about celebrities and politicians, maybe a series or a movie... and endless swiping on your smartphone...
There's not much left, and usually, all we want is to rest.
Those few remaining hours we have for real life are often wasted — and the next day, the same routine awaits us.

Why — in my view — it's worth being a Trader: for me, true happiness comes from balance and fulfillment in personal life. What it means, though, is different for everyone.

For me, it's a happy family: a life partner who's also my best friend, and a child who grows into a good human being..

Family is the foundation of my happiness — it's what I build my professional success on. Without it, I'm not sure I'd have the strength to overcome obstacles. Without peace and stability at home, trading can be exceptionally hard on the mind.

I'm not saying it's impossible — but it definitely requires extra effort.

It all depends on perspective.

For one person, it's support; for another, an obstacle. What feels hard today may be easy tomorrow — once you've worked on yourself.

There's a saying:

"Because they didn't know it was impossible — they just did it."

If you have a clear goal, nothing will stop you.

There will always be a solution. Of course, that statement isn't 100% true.

And so what? :)

If you assume you can do anything — maybe you actually can.

And if you believe it won't work — then it definitely won't.

Faith moves mountains.

It doesn't matter where you are in life. If your path is tougher than others' — you'll simply have to push harder. And maybe it's exactly because of that effort that you'll succeed. :)

Maybe if it were easy, you wouldn't put in the work — and you'd never achieve something extraordinary.

Life surprises us.

I dedicate this passage to my friend Chris "Yossel."

We've had each other's back for years in different businesses. Now we're both Traders, and we still keep each other strong.
The changes Chris has made — and keeps making — in his life could fill a book.
If you think your path is tougher than his, I really doubt it.
Chris and I are living proof that life can get brutally hard.
But if someone's got strength and stubbornness inside, they can fight for their life and win.

I'm not talking about just surviving — I mean a full-on collapse, hitting rock bottom, and rebuilding from scratch in circumstances that would make most people break, give up, and take any job, tossing their dreams aside.

Never settle for a life without dreams.
Always get back on your feet and keep moving forward — see what fate has waiting behind the next door.
Only death can stop us. I know it sounds dramatic — but how else do you talk about stuff like this? Maybe if I were a writer with real talent, I'd phrase it more elegantly. :)

22.3 So, Is It Worth Being a Trader or Not?

From where I stand: **definitely YES**.
Everything I write here is MY truth, MY beliefs, MY perspective. You can hear me out — but your goal and the path to it are yours to decide.
And you alone are responsible for that. Responsibility gets its own chapter — because it's fundamental.

And what does life look like for a Trader who has reached the level where trading becomes a real profession?

- You don't have a boss above you.
- You don't have to go anywhere or commute.
- You can rent an office as a trading room — or, like me, dedicate one room in your house as your "command center" (I'll post a picture later, just don't get scared :)

- You don't have to listen to anyone.
- You're a free human being, and you alone decide about your life.
- You live where you want — all you need is your setup and an internet connection.
- You want to trade — you trade. You don't want to — you don't. You do this for yourself. (For example, I'm writing this book right now just because I felt like it.)
- You need time off — you take it. If you don't have to hit a specific monthly target, you can afford it.
- You set your own working hours. You can start at 8 a.m. CET if you want to catch the DAX and London move. You can keep your mornings free and start around noon when the U.S. opens. Or you can skip the whole day and start in the evening when the market slows down but the U.S. session is still rolling. Between 6 p.m. and 10 p.m., you can pull some really nice profits. The only thing I never tried was staying up all night watching the Japanese battle it out with their candles. :) Check a night chart and you'll see why I prefer to sleep.
- You're doing something most people don't get. You click — and money shows up. It's an elite job that brings a ton of satisfaction. Just be careful not to fall into the God syndrome — that always ends badly. :)
- Trading changes the way you look at life — in my opinion, for the better. I'll expand on that in another chapter.
- You've got opportunities...
- You've got money — so you can help someone whose problem can be solved with it.

I once memorized a wise saying:
"If you have a problem that can be solved with money — you don't have a problem, you have an expense."

„If you have a problem that can be solved with money, but you don't have the money — then you've got a problem."
That's why it's worth putting in the effort and making sure you always have money in life.

- You have time — so you can be there for someone who needs you. Sometimes your presence is the greatest help.
- You have time and money, so you can do whatever you want. :)
- As you get older, you realize there are priceless things that still come with a price — like health.

With money, you can take better care of your health and happiness — yours and your loved ones'. And that's the true value of money.

Money by itself has no value.
The value comes only from what you can buy with it.

It's up to you whether you turn it into something meaningful — or waste it on nonsense.
You could keep stacking up arguments in favor...
But are there also downsides?

22.4 The Downsides of Being a Trader

When you read about freedom, money, and indulging in whatever you want, you might wonder:
„If it's so great, why isn't everyone a Trader?"

Exactly... Wherever there are huge advantages, there must also be some serious downsides.

As I mentioned earlier — this is one of the toughest professions in the world.

At first, I wanted to just list the downsides and come back to them later, but...

I won't hit you with a list that would just scare you off.

We'll deal with these disadvantages right here, right now.

22.5 Serious Downsides, Mostly for Beginners

22.5.1 Stress

You put your own money on the table and never know whether you'll win or lose. That uncertainty is what creates stress.

When one losing trade is followed by another... and another — it stops being fun very quickly. Statistically, nothing unusual is happening, but emotions don't work like cold math.

Remember when red came up 30 times in a row at roulette? There's always someone who thinks that after so many reds, betting on black is a sure thing. That's when emotions shut down logical analysis.

Greed pushes us into stupid decisions.

It doesn't matter how many times black or red came up before — the probability stays the same.
Why? Because on the roulette wheel there are 18 red fields, 18 black fields, and one green "0".
That single field gives the casino its mathematical edge.
In the European version (with one zero), the chance of winning on a color bet is 48.65%. In the American version (with zero and double zero), it's only 47.37%.
Since the casino has the edge... **what's the point of playing?**

The conclusion is simple:

We only play when we have a statistical edge.
If we don't — we're just donating capital.

How to Tame Stress?

Stress is just an emotion — and every emotion carries information. Since it's information, you need to treat it like a signal: when you feel stress, stop and analyze the situation. Most often, stress shows up when you're risking too much.

22.5.2 **Stress** — the Classic Move of a Capital Donor

According to your money management (MM), you should risk no more than 0.5–1% of your capital per Stop Loss (SL). But... you see the perfect setup. The chart looks way too good to ignore.
Only a fool would pass on such an opportunity, right? :)

So you throw 10% of your deposit on the SL — because, after all, "no risk, no champagne."

Broken Strategy? Oh yes.

Your strategy might not have been exciting, but it gave you an edge. And yet you gave in to temptation, convinced this was a sure thing.
Blinded by the vision of quick, easy money.

The market didn't go where you wanted. **Stress kicks in**.
They're dropping, and they were supposed to rise...
At first, a slight discomfort...
Then your stomach tightens, sweat in your palms.
You tell yourself: "Relax, it's about to bounce."
You look — price dangerously close to your Stop Loss (SL).
You think (or rather pretend you're thinking):
"I'll move it a bit, because if I get stopped out, they'll 100% turn around..."

You move your SL. Now **you're risking 15% of your capital**. Price doesn't turn. **The pain is physical** — burning palms, pounding heart, heat rising. One thought left: "Just break even..." It's no longer about profit. You're begging to get out flat, shut down the computer, and escape the market.
Just dreaming for the suffering to end.

One last "logical" move:
You push the SL to 20% and **add a second position**.
If it bounces, maybe you'll claw back to zero and be done with it...
The market actually turns — for a moment.
You're almost at break-even and... **boom. Red candle.**
Heat again.
You should've closed. Maybe still... just a bit more...
They keep dropping.
You're down **over 30%.**

The room is dead silent.
You hear your own heartbeat.
In your head — pure hell: lightning, hurricanes, chaos.

You switch off your Stop Loss (SL) because you're afraid a shakeout will take you out. [21]

Better to decide yourself than get kicked out by a candle's shadow.
Sound familiar?
You feel like throwing cups, swearing, yelling at the whole market.
Your account is **down 50%.** And that's... well, exactly.
You've had enough.

The Einstein in your head checked out long ago.
The monkey's going wild. The T-Rex is ready to bite.

And suddenly you remember a wise piece of advice: "When you feel stress — think."
How? :)
When you're sitting on a 60% loss, feeling like praying and cursing at the same time...
You promise yourself: "As soon as I get back to break-even, I'll quit this damn thing..."

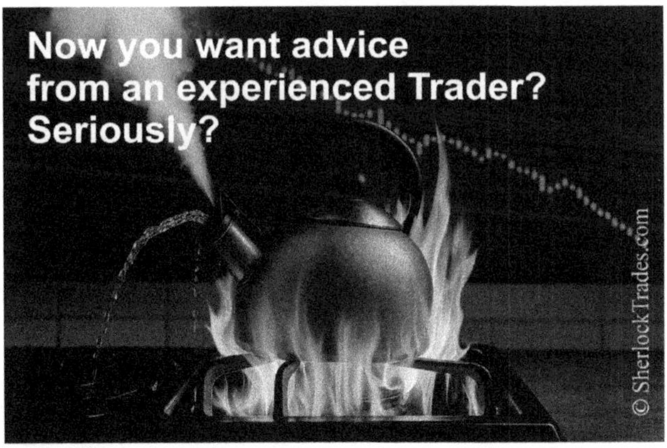

You've had enough.
Your account has shrunk to just 33% of its original capital.

You close everything, shut down the computer. You don't feel anything anymore — maybe just helplessness.

And one sentence keeps looping in your head:

"How could I be THAT STUPID?!"

Losing almost 70% of your capital in a single day...

Do you feel it now, reading this?
Stress. Pain. Regret. Loss of hope. Doubt in yourself.
You start asking: does any of this even make sense?
Feel it.
Because if you ever let this happen on your own account — trust me, **you'll regret** not taking that advice.

I've been there.
And the version where you close at –70% — that's the optimistic one.
Usually, you're already so drained you truly don't care anymore: whether it bounces, whether you get a "Margin Call" [22], whether the broker quietly closes your worst positions and leaves you with a handful of crumbs and a ton of regret.
Believe me — you DO NOT want to live through this.

Be smart. Learn from other people's mistakes — on their money, not yours.

It was supposed to be about managing stress, but it turned into a burned-out kettle. :) So how do you really tame stress?

22.5.3 **No Stress —** The Move of a Professional Day Trader

Imagine you're no longer that young, overhyped Trader craving adrenaline, emotions, and quick profits.
You've got experience. Calm. Perspective.
You look at the chart, spot a familiar signal. Decision: **you're in**.

----

*You set your **Stop Loss (SL) at 1%***
*— because hey, **it looks like a sure thing. :)***

Just like the hundreds of other "sure things" you've seen before. The market, instead of bouncing, hits your SL.
You lose 1%.

To blow 70%, you'd have to mess up like this 69 times in a row. OK, that's a simplification — since with each loss your position size shrinks, it would actually take way more than 69 in a row. Even at the roulette table, black doesn't hit that many times straight.

You're out of the trade. No big deal. That's part of the strategy. You look at the chart:
"Alright boys, show me what you're painting there..."
You analyze: did you read it right? Misinterpreted the candle structure?
From this angle, you see — it wasn't that solid of a setup after all.

Decision:
I'll wait. Until it clears up. Until it's obvious we've got a new direction.
No more looking for longs. Time to play the shorts.

You see increasing selling pressure. A pullback on low volume. That looks promising.
The pullback reaches Fibonacci geometry — at the top, a clean, textbook "two bar reversal" shows up.
Price dips a bit, then starts climbing again. Volume is light, but on the top a shooting star forms — this time with a kicker: a bit more volume.
That's exactly the kind of post-pullback test and strong signal I was waiting for.

I go in.

----

*You set your **SL at 1%***
*— because, as usual, **it looks like a sure thing. :)***

Let's go, boys — down we drop...
They didn't disappoint. Price slides down smoothly.
At some point it stops falling and starts climbing in a way that looks worrying. Volume is low on the way up — it's just a pullback.
I wait.
At the top of the pullback — another great signal. Price reaches the level of the previous low.
What do I do?
I throw more fuel on the fire.

The first trade is already nicely in profit — I secure it with a Take Profit (TP) at +1%.
I open the second trade with double the size, Stop Loss (SL) at – 2%, because the selling pressure is huge.

If the market turns, I'll lose 2% on the new position but gain 1% on the first one — so overall risk still stays at 1% according to my Money Management (MM).
I could also set the new trade at -1%, or move the first TP higher, say +2%, but... you can really feel the strength in these drops.
Shortly after the second entry — BOOM — long, aggressive red candle.
Perfect.
I lock the first position at R:R 1:3 (Risk:Reward).
If they reverse — I've already banked 3%. The move runs far, so I'm calm.
On the second position I'm already above 1:2 — secure it at breakeven, just in case.

Price keeps falling.
Another pullback shows up, but with no clear signal or level — so **I don't add more.**
On the first position I'm already at R:R 1:10 — I move **TP to +5%.** On the second, I move **TP to 1:1.**

I wait.
Let's see what they paint next.

Damn... I feel sorry for those still holding longs.
That long red candle must have hurt.

The market keeps sliding, though somewhat sluggishly...
The bearish impulse is clearly losing steam.
First signs of demand are showing up.
Alright, **I pull up TP** on both positions — the profit is solid now, **no point giving it back**. Supply is clearly weakening, and heavy volume is appearing on those "hammers."

Time to pack up with the cash.
I'm not waiting for a pullback — I close manually.
First trade: R:R 1:12 — +12%, beautiful.
Second: "only" 1:8, but I doubled the size there, so +16%.
Total +28% with just 1% overall risk.

Executed flawlessly. A good day.
This single trade gave me 28% profit, which means I can now afford 28 full SLs in the next trades — all on the market's tab.
Now I can hunt stress-free — I'm playing with their money.

Beautiful. :)
How can you not love this game? :)

That was a brilliant entry.
Yesterday was tough: two losing trades, three barely breakeven, one mediocre...
But today the market rewarded my patience.
Time for a reward: a walk, then a good movie. Phew.

Do you feel it? Do you see the difference?
If you've got a plan, strict rules, and a proven method — stress stays minimal.
Crossing a busy street is probably more stressful...
Managing stress isn't about turning into some meditation guru sitting in full zen while losing 70% of your account.

That state can be reached faster, but I wouldn't recommend it — I don't drink alcohol myself, and I don't encourage others either.
If you're a professional and don't play greedily — meaning you keep risk very limited — your stress level will be low.

The only truly effective way I know to deal with stress: have a proven method and adjust your SL (Stop Loss) to the quality of your trading and your stats.

The better your stats, the more risk you can allow per trade.
By "more," I mean maybe 1.5–2%.
And if you're truly a master and tough enough — maybe 3%.
I don't feel like stressing myself, so I stick to 1%. That relaxes me.
I'm not saving for a Lambo, so I don't need to. :)
Tomorrow is another day — maybe again with good volatility and a clear trend.
Today's shift is over. Time to put the shovel down and relax.
How long can you keep working that hard, anyway? :)

22.5.4 Learning from Others' Mistakes

There are things worth experiencing — and others that are better left to the imagination.
Not everything has to be lived through firsthand.
Some experiences build you up — others can destroy you.

Smart people learn from the mistakes of others.
They can imagine, feel, understand... and decide:
"Thanks, but I don't want to go through that."
It's enough that someone else already made that mistake.
Some lessons you only need to read, reflect on... and avoid completely.
Experience what develops you. What brings you happiness — today and in the future.
You don't have to jump into the fire to know it burns.
Let others go through the costly mistakes for you.
That's very expensive tuition, and a diploma in failure is not a ticket to a career.

Why do something that doesn't pay off and makes no sense?

Not every path leads to a place worth going.

22.5.5 Want the Recipe — a Million in a Month?

I almost forgot the most important thing!
No need to write so much about effort, stress, and hard work... pointless.

I could've started right away with a simpler, "guaranteed" solution: for the price of a good coffee — let's say $20 (so you don't think I don't value you) — I'll reveal The Secret that guarantees anyone who follows my strategy:

„No luck. No hype. Just 1 month. 1 million".

A million dollars in a live account within a month — not some demo.
Did I say "a million"?
Sorry, I meant: at least a million.

Buy Me a Coffee

https://buymeacoffee.com/sherlocktrades.com

I'll tell you a secret: once you've sorted out that coffee, at the very end — in the chapter "Top Secret" — I've hidden the detailed blueprint of this method.
But hey... that's just between us. :)
And one more thing... **for the first billion people** who buy me that coffee, there's a surprise — exclusive trade-management cards. Don't wait too long — the number of PDF cards is limited, and I can't guarantee they'll still be available by the time you read this. :)

And don't take shortcuts, because it's solid work that brings real results and true satisfaction.

22.5.6 Pressure

If you have a regular job and trade only with spare money, your trading results won't change your life.
You pay your rent and groceries from your salary.
But if you live solely off trading, the thought creeps into your head: I must make money.
Of course — if you've got billions, you don't care about paying your electricity or gas bills.
I don't have billions, and probably never will — simply because I don't need them.
I mentioned earlier the resilience you need to withstand pressure.
Let's think about how we actually generate this pressure ourselves.
As kids, we played outside (okay, today it's more on smartphones) without feeling much pressure.

Life was carefree — at least in the beginning, when parents took the weight on themselves and shielded us from the "bad" world. Then came school: competition, fighting for status in the group, dominance, and a ton of other nonsense.
We finish school and enter another race: for a better job, more money, social prestige, a house in a nicer neighborhood, a better car... just better something.

People never run out of ideas for what they want next. The list of goals that give only the illusion of happiness feels endless.

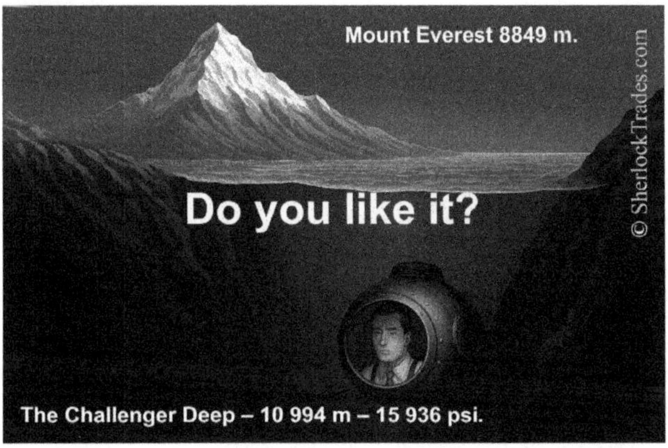

Imagine the last grains of rice slipping out of your bowl — your final minutes of life.
Stop for a moment and feel what you feel right now.
What do you regret? Which memories and images bring a smile to your face?
What was truly important and valuable — did you achieve it, or did you run out of time chasing illusions?
What did you once give enormous weight to, only to realize now, at the end, that it had no value and only wasted your life?
What did you neglect, only to realize now it was priceless?

Think carefully about what really matters to you.
And focus on exactly that.

The rest isn't worth your time — you only have a limited amount of it. When you strip away everything unnecessary and focus solely on what counts, **the ballast falls off**, and your submarine rises to the surface.

The pressure disappears — because you chose how deep you dove...Many sources of pressure can be removed with a literal snap of your fingers. Others need only small adjustments, easy to implement. And yes, some will demand more effort.

Start with the simplest — cut it out without sentiment.

Since we're talking about making a living, begin by reviewing your expenses. Maybe you're paying off an expensive loan, leasing a luxury car, or carrying other costs you could easily live without? Which expenses cover your real needs, and which just feed your EGO?

Tackle the harder ones next: analyze, plan changes, and implement them consistently.

I know — it sounds simple, but life rarely is. Sometimes, though, what seems difficult is nothing but an illusion.

The things we think we can't live without
often turn out to be unnecessary.

I'm 52 years old, and I've really lived through a lot.

Sometimes I feel like this accumulation of experiences — good and bad — would be enough for three lifetimes.

When you're around 20, you think you'll stay young forever, and that people in their 40s or 50s are already old — basically ready to pack it in. Here's a little secret: if you're 20 now, in 30 years you'll be 50. And then you'll realize age is just a number.

What really matters is what's in your head.

Some are born mentally old, others die at a late age still feeling young. I won't bore you with the cliché that older people are always worth listening to. Some of them are — but only those who have truly achieved something meaningful.

22.5.7 XXL Pressure

Let me briefly tell you about a Pole,
Władysław Bartoszewski (1922–2015).

During World War II, he was a prisoner in the German concentration camp Auschwitz-Birkenau.
Around 1.3 million people ended up there — barely about 200,000 survived. Imagine 20 people you know — out of those 20, only 3 would have made it.

After leaving the camp, he fought for his country's freedom as a soldier of the Home Army (AK) and a member of Żegota.
After the war, he was arrested and tortured by the communist authorities of Poland, branded as an "enemy of the people."

For those unfamiliar with Polish history, here's the short version. In 1939, Poland was invaded by Germany and Russia. After Germany's defeat, Poland was "liberated" by the Russians but in practice stayed under their occupation until 1993, when the last Soviet troops finally left. That's why some Poles fighting for Poland were at the same time branded enemies of Poland — the one run by its occupier, Russia. Strange times indeed, and their consequences are still felt today.

Despite these dramatic experiences, Bartoszewski became a professor, journalist, historian, diplomat, senator, advisor to the president of Poland, and lecturer.
He was often called "**the voice of the nation's conscience**."
He played a key role in the Polish-German reconciliation process — even though he himself had been imprisoned by the Germans in a death camp.

Just imagine the enormous stress, suffering, and pressure this man endured over the years. And yet — he managed to rise above it.

He managed to forgive.

Why am I bringing him up?

There are two reasons:

- Bartoszewski once said a legendary sentence:

"It's worth being honest, even if it doesn't always pay off. Being dishonest may pay off, but it's not worth it."

What does this mean in the context of life and pressure?

It's worth enduring pressure if the goal is truly worth it.

Pressure is sometimes the price you have to pay.

Sometimes it's temporary — and then we can say that by enduring it, we've paid for reaching our goal.

But often the pressure is constant, while we're not moving forward at all.

We sit at the bottom of the Mariana Trench and feel the crushing weight, yet it brings us nothing of value.

We keep paying more and more, and get nothing in return.

If a goal is only seemingly valuable — discard it without regret.

It's not worth wasting your life and enduring pressure for something meaningless.

It pays to pursue what truly matters — even if it's hard and costly.

- In his 1532 treatise Il Principe, Machiavelli formulated an idea that still serves as the motto of dishonest politicians:

"The end justifies the means."

Władysław Bartoszewski answered simply:

"...it's not worth it."

Unfortunately, far too many people are willing to do "whatever it takes" just to get money... That's sad.
Let's get back on track — enough running around the train. :)
Pressure and emotions are part of life — you won't eliminate them completely.
Your job is to think and make smart choices.
Not automatic ones, but truly thought-out and conscious decisions.
Sometimes it's worth enduring pressure if it leads to a meaningful goal.
Other times we stay under pressure pointlessly, blindly following a path that gives us nothing.
Often, we create that pressure ourselves — building illusions and living in a fiction we don't even need.

Pressure carries information — and our task is to check what that information means for us.
It's a good moment to re-evaluate the goal and the path.
Is the goal really worth the pressure?
Is the path we're on the right one?
Can we do something to reduce that pressure — or make it disappear entirely?

22.5.8 Pressure — Example 1

Our goal is to make 5% profit this week.
We raise the SL (stop loss) to 2% and start feeling the pressure.
The goal may be fine — but maybe the path is wrong, and that's what generates stress. Maybe a 1% SL is more than enough. Instead of playing with higher risk, we could spend an extra hour or two at the charts, make a few more trades, but with lower risk — and without unnecessary stress.

Why do I mention Bartoszewski here?
Because he was able to forgive and let go.
Despite horrific wrongs, he chose reconciliation.
Many people never let go. They nurture negative feelings, clinging to hurt as if it were something precious.

But that never pays off — not even “coldly,” from a business perspective. Is it worth paying costs when we gain nothing?
It’s better to cut losses, release pressure and stress, than wallow in the mud without any benefit.

22.5.9 Pressure — Example 2

You’re in a tough financial situation. You don’t want to worry your wife or family, so you take a lousy, harmful job — because it pays better.

You think: “It’s only temporary.” Six months go by, then a year... You don’t tell your loved ones what’s going on. You want to protect them, keep up the image of the one who “always manages.”
You shut yourself in, suppress your emotions. Your family senses it but doesn’t understand — because you say nothing.

You fear reactions you’ve imagined yourself. Under the pressure of those fictional scenarios, you do something that ends up hurting everyone.
You wanted to protect them, but the result is the opposite — more harm than good.

What if you laid your cards on the table instead?
Said directly what the situation was. Maybe even took that tough job — but in an atmosphere of honesty.
Then the pressure is different — shared among all of you.
You have a common goal, a common problem to solve.
And maybe your partner will come up with an idea that changes everything.

In hard times, I bet on honesty.
Even when I have to act alone, I feel supported — because we’re in it together. That builds a relationship, one based on real partnership.
As we say: we pull this cart together.

Do a little simulation:

Scenario 1.

You say what problem you're facing, and together you work on a solution. Everyone knows what's going on, so there are no silly arguments:
"Why can't I buy those shoes if everyone at school has them?"
You get through it together — stronger and happier.

Scenario 2.

You struggle with it alone. The story plays out just like in the example above...
Overall — a failure.

Scenario 3.

You talk about the problems; your partner dumps you because "your problem is your problem."
You've won... because why would you want a partner only for the good days? :)

Remember:

Pressure is a symptom.
Find the cause, analyze it, and do whatever you can to get rid of the pressure as fast as possible — or at least reduce it.

22.5.10 Pressure — Example 3

You've got financial problems.
Maybe it's your own mistakes, maybe bad luck — medical bills, dishonest people at the company... It doesn't matter anymore. What matters is this: you're in a tough spot.

Approach it like a Trader — cool and analytical.
Analyze: what happened, why, what scenarios are possible, how long they might last, what they'll cost, which ones make sense. Once you've mapped out the scenarios, think about who to discuss them with.
Emotions can distort your judgment — a different perspective can reveal new options.

Ask for help.

Don't treat it like a life tragedy — it's a technical problem to be broken down and solved point by point.

Since you've already lived through all the stress in your head, the emotional costs are "booked." Everything that could go wrong has already happened and belongs to the past.

You have a plan, but emotions paralyze you? You don't know how to get moving? If that's the case, deep down you haven't really decided to get up after the fall.

The question is simple:

Do you stay where you're lying — or is this not yet the last page of your book?

If it's not the end yet, don't waste time.

Get off your butt and get to work — now.

22.5.11 EST

About 50 years ago in the U.S., EST (Erhard Seminars Training) was popular.

You won't find it on training menus today — it's a controversial method and has long been retired. I once came across a book describing EST sessions. And while many criticize it, I took something valuable from it — something I've used ever since.

The takeaway? I'm responsible for everything that happens in my life. Even if a meteor hits me and takes my leg off — that's still my responsibility.

Sounds absurd? Think about it: if I take responsibility, I hold the power, and I'm the one who can do something about it.

What else did that old book give me?

I no longer build illusions in my head about my life.

I'm ready for any brutal truth — because even the worst truth beats a comfortable lie.

If a problem is lurking somewhere, I say:
"Come here, you little punk — I'm about to deal with you," and I take it apart, because I'm sick and tired of complications. Any problem that steps in my way, I'll crush. I don't have the time or the desire to baby problems.

For that to happen, I have to take full responsibility, confront difficulties right away, and make no excuses. It is what it is, it'll be what it'll be — and my job is to do everything I can to make it right.

22.5.12 Pressure — Example 4

If a meteor hits me and rips off my leg, I'll still call it my responsibility. I know, it sounds absurd — but think...
If I take responsibility, it means I decide and I can change something.
I don't waste time blaming the world or feeling sorry for myself.
I take it on the chin and look for a solution.

If I didn't survive — fine, I've got no worries anymore.
If I survived — also fine. I've become a legend: the first person whose leg was ripped off by a meteor. :) TV invites, lectures, a new chapter of life... :)

See what I did there? I took responsibility not for what happened, but for my reaction — and I started planning what to do next: life without a leg, but with a comet in my CV.
I'm the one who chooses how I respond.
I can sit, cry, and feel sorry for myself — or make a plan and build a great future on top of that catastrophe.
That's my decision.

22.5.13 Do You Know Why I'm Writing This Book?

Because I've been through a lot. I've had moments that were truly hard to carry. And yet it's precisely those disasters — and the fact that I managed to get up, stand on my feet, and build a good life for myself and my loved ones — that are my greatest treasure.

Yes... it wasn't the good days that shaped me, but the bad ones. If not for them, I wouldn't have become a Trader and I wouldn't have written this book. I wouldn't have the inner conviction that I have something valuable to share with people who, like me, fall — but want to rise.

If you decide to get back up, a beautiful life may lie ahead of you. Remember:
An easy life creates weak people.
A hard life builds strong people — as long as they don't give up.

And you? Who do you want to be?
The one who won — or the one who gave up?

22.5.14 Pressure — Example 5

Do you know the story of twin brothers?
One became a lawyer, the other ended up in prison.
Both were raised in the same harsh conditions.
When asked how their lives turned out, both answered the same:
"I had no choice — I grew up in hell."
One decided there was no way out except the gang.
The other — that he had to break free, no matter what.
Same start. Different decisions. Different ending.

22.5.15 Enough talk about pressure, I guess. :)

Pressure is a signal. Information from the body: something has to change.
When the topic is tough, I reach for the EST approach.
I don't run — I break the issue down into parts.
I let myself feel the emotions that come with it.
And then I start cleaning up.

It's like an anti-personnel mine.
You can stand there and fear it for the rest of your life.
Or you understand the threat, fire up a YouTube video :) and, despite the pressure, you defuse it, toss it into the bushes — maybe even sell it — and then move on.

22.5.16 Uncertainty

People like stability. The certainty that tomorrow will be just as good — or just as bad — as yesterday.

The markets and trading are constant uncertainty — you have to learn to live with it. Uncertainty means risk and change. Change fires up our lizard brain, and suddenly the onboard computer panics because the T-Rex woke up and doesn't know whether to eat the opponent or run.

The funny thing is, nothing in life is ever truly certain anyway. Today you've got a stable job — say at Enron Corporation — and tomorrow it turns out that was an illusion. You've got neither a job nor a pension, because the company did creative accounting and the "stability" around your job was fiction.

Today you own a house. Tomorrow a tornado scatters it into rubble across the neighborhood.

Our whole life is one big uncertainty.

I once watched a program about people who "conquered the Wild West" in the U.S. between 1800–1890. Think about the risk they took — and compare it to the uncertainty trading brings. **Everything is relative**.

Our risk, stress, and uncertainty on the charts are a serious challenge — but humans have faced tougher tests.

So if you truly want it — you can handle it.

Uncertainty is the lack of certainty about the outcome — doubting yourself and your method. The less prepared you are for trading, the greater your doubts.

Doubts generate emotions — stress, fear, hope, loss of faith.

That leads to compulsive reactions, changing plans, and jumping from method to method.

Instead of focusing on technique, you start hunting for confirmations and miracle fixes — the next Holy Grail that will solve everything. Uncertainty makes you slip: bad entries, bad exits, no trades because nothing feels certain.

Then come the next mistakes: revenge trading, abandoning a method you haven't even learned yet, and chasing a new one you also won't learn — because you're looking for shortcuts.

Maybe I'm exaggerating a bit, but you get the point.
Uncertainty is a constant — accept it and draw conclusions.
Which ones? In a world of uncertainty, you need proven solutions. The more consistently you stick to them, the more stability you have. Of course — without fanaticism.
Check whether your method is complete and gives you a statistical edge. Stick to the rules you chose and tested.
Keep a Trader's journal, analyze your stats, and prove to yourself that your method works.
Make only small tweaks and test their impact on results.

Statistics are the only thing that gives you certainty.

No stats — no data.

And without data? Only uncertainty remains.

22.5.17 Do You Want the Holy Grail of Trading?

Life gives you no guarantees. Math is different.
If your stats clearly show that your capital is growing without major drawdowns, you can plot a chart of how much money you'll have in 5 years.

That chart has one serious flaw — you. :)
The human factor is the biggest constraint.
We don't really need to worry about market liquidity unless someone insists on trading niche, illiquid instruments.
I don't recommend that.

Understand one thing:
Analyzing your statistics is the only thing that can give you real "certainty" — and certainty is your ticket to profits.
Want to size up and raise your SL (Stop Loss)?
You must have Certainty.

Without it, you have Uncertainty. And that means stress, emotions, and chaos.
Emotions switch off your inner Einstein, and then the whole careful plan... is worthless.
Math. Trader's journal. Statistics.
I don't like it either, but **it's a vaccine against emotions.**
I know — I'm repeating myself, but I'd rather bore you than let you ignore this.

This is the Holy Grail of trading:

Statistics build certainty.

Certainty dampens emotions.

Lack of emotion lets you think analytically.

Analysis, an effective strategy, and consistency create quality.

Quality guarantees results.

You've got a machine you put money into — and take it out multiplied. Either you use that machine, or you keep struggling and improvising.
Your choice.

22.5.18 Constant Failures and Setbacks

If you see yourself as wise, infallible, and an authority :) — the market will quickly bring you back down to earth.
When you enter a position, you usually have a higher chance of losing than winning. For me, about 50% of trades end in a loss or close to breakeven.
From the remaining 50%, part of them are just average trades with a risk–reward ratio (R:R) of 1:3.
Most trades — despite knowledge and effort — don't deliver spectacular results.

Do you imagine it like this?
Eight hours a day in the ring with the market. Blow for blow.
Fighting bulls and bears just to make a living.
If that were daily reality, hardly anyone would ever become a Trader. :)
And yet — for those who fail — that's exactly how it feels.
They don't study, don't read, don't grow.
They step into the market unprepared and expect to take someone else's money.
That's naïve, but everyone has the right to their own mistakes.

In trading, the real failure is having access to valuable knowledge about psychology and technique... and still refusing to grow, breaking your own rules, and losing.

22.5.19 Constant Risk...

Trading is almost like gambling — every trade is like spinning the roulette wheel. You've got technique and a plan, but in the end you either win or lose.
Risk becomes as natural as breathing — you either get used to it or you won't last as a professional Trader.
You take risk, feel fear and uncertainty, yet still act — because that's the game. No bet, no win. The difference between gambling and trading? In trading, you can have a statistical edge.
In gambling, the house always wins.

Over time, you stop feeling the risk. After a thousand trades, the next one doesn't move the needle anymore.
You enter the market according to your plan, strategy, scenario. Your SL (Stop Loss) is set based on Money Management (MM).
You take the trade, the market does its thing, you log the outcome in your stats and look for the next setup.
The fear of loss that once paralyzed you eventually becomes irrelevant.
Someone might say that's not true — that trading without an SL or with a wide SL (3–5%) is still stressful. Sure. But here we're talking about professional Traders who stay in the game for decades, right into retirement. There are no gamblers in that crowd — they drop out earlier, because they end up with no capital.
What matters is statistics.
If you've got an edge and the numbers are on your side, there is no risk.
The only real risk is you — the human factor, the emotions that can mess everything up.

I could throw in a hundred more potential dangers, but why ruin such a nice "motivational message" with details. :)
And if you're a sharp analyst, you already know that line about "no risk" isn't completely true. :)
Looking at politics... who even cares about the truth these days? :)

There are countless factors outside your control — but should you really build your strategy around alien invasions or an EMP wiping out all electronics? If you want to focus on "Black Swans," go to Australia.
For teaching purposes, sometimes it's worth bending the truth a little — it's not about dogma, it's about shaping the student.

A parent who lets their kid ride a bike for the first time without training wheels and says: "Go on, nothing will happen to you!" might not be entirely right — especially when the kid ends up in the bushes. But that's how learning happens. :)
The kid just found out that adults sometimes bluff. :)

22.5.20 The Risk of a "Sure" Investment in Silver

Let me tell you an interesting story about the Hunt brothers. The Hunt brothers — billionaires from Texas whose family made a fortune in oil — decided that the dollar was nothing but paper (technically speaking, more like a rag made of cotton and linen). After the "Nixon Shock" in 1971, 35 dollars no longer had any backing in one ounce of gold. From that moment on, money could be printed "without limits" — a recipe for inflation.

Today, more than 50 years later, those same 35 dollars will buy you a coffee and a pastry.
An ounce of gold, at the time of writing this book, costs nearly 3,500 dollars. To simplify: one cent from 1971 has about the same purchasing power as one dollar today.
Back then, 35 dollars bought you one ounce. Today, for the same amount — just a fraction of a gram.

The Hunt brothers correctly predicted that the dollar would lose value. It's the perfect example that being right doesn't necessarily mean you'll make money.
Between 1973 and 1980 they accumulated massive amounts of silver — both physical bullion and futures contracts.
They accumulated around 200 million ounces.
The price climbed from about 6 to nearly 50 dollars per ounce.
For seven years they fueled the bull market themselves, creating demand and building their position.

Even if Comex and the regulators hadn't imposed position limits or the so-called "Silver Rule 7," their trade would still have been almost impossible to unwind. With large capital you can pump up the price of an asset, but the real problem is selling later without crashing the market.

Jesse Livermore described this problem well in his memoirs — how to sell large positions without dumping the price.

The Hunt brothers apparently never read that book — they went bankrupt, and silver collapsed from nearly 50 down to about 10 dollars per ounce. Risk is always there.

Especially when you think you've got everything under control.

22.5.21 A Digression on Adolf and Today's Financial Bubble

Since 1971, the U.S. has been living in an era of growth fueled by printing money without backing.

The "Nixon Shock" ended the Bretton Woods era and launched the "golden age of fiat money." [23]

For more than 50 years, the financial bubble has swelled to a size that — in my view — nobody really controls anymore.

Nobody knows how to defuse it or where it's heading.

Politicians prefer to maintain the illusion rather than search for real solutions. Inflation is rising, credit is still being handed out. That's a **serious risk for us** — both as people and as Traders.

The idea of building growth on "printing empty money" isn't new. For example: Adolf Hitler financed the expansion of the Third Reich in exactly this way, building military power in a country that had previously been mired in crisis.

If you're curious, look up the story of MEFO and Hjalmar Schacht — head of the Reichsbank and Minister of Economics in the Third Reich.

You'll see how, in a world much like ours, money printing without backing can be manipulated. It's enough that people keep believing that this paper means something, or that one day someone will repay the debt wrapped up in bonds, notes, and the like.

Adolf had a simple plan: cover his obligations with the spoils of war. Hard to believe such a man cared about bond maturity dates.
That's the past — horrifying, but instructive.
The real question today: what's the plan of our leaders? Who will they rob, what will they sell, to keep this paper economy alive?

Let's get back to trading — we won't solve the world's problems anyway.
Let's just make ourselves a bit of that worthless money.

22.5.22 Trading Is Not a Team Sport

It's you and the market.
Only you make the decisions, and only you bear the consequences.
No teammates, no fans. Just you, face-to-face with the chart.
If you're social and can't stand loneliness, you might struggle.
The trading floor has long been empty — today it's computers and a global network that do the trading.

22.5.23 No Applause for a Win

Only your account knows whether you've won or lost.
If your ego craves admiration, you might be better off on stage — lectures, seminars, the spotlight.
That's where you'll find an audience.

22.5.24 Silence...

Focus needs silence.
When I sit down at the charts, I want peace.
No music playing, no phone ringing, the door shut.
I don't want emotions coming from the radio, Bloomberg, or CNBC. In fact, with full focus, I wouldn't notice them anyway.
Maybe you work differently. Or maybe you only think you do.

22.5.25 Money Doesn't Buy Happiness

In our country, it's a kind of "folk wisdom."

Recently, I was watching a series with my wife about the 90s and VOGUE magazine.
It focused on fashion and its transformations.

Normally, I'm skeptical about fashion — I associate it with celebrities and absurd prices, like a "$20,000 handbag" that looks like something from a cheap market stall.

Money doesn't buy happiness, but shopping... :)
Whether someone turns money into real value or into illusion — that's their choice. We're free — each of us decides what something is worth.
A Trader can't buy happiness with money, but I don't know anyone who constantly lives in financial deficit and is truly happy.

Interestingly, that series changed my attitude toward fashion.
Even though I still think paying a fortune for a logo is questionable, I have to admit some designs were stunning — true works of art.
That shows how a person can change their mind even after years — it just takes the right impulse.

And if one belief can fall apart, maybe there are others we've never questioned?
You probably carry beliefs about money and earning that you treat as your own — even though you never came up with them yourself.
Often they're views planted by family, by your environment — the foundation of our worldview. And we stick with them... until some fashion series stirs things up. :)

In the next chapter, we'll talk about emotions.
Where do they come from? Are they really ours?
Or were they programmed into us?
Maybe all it takes is to question them — and think them through?

23 Which Emotions Are a Trader's Problem?

23.1 Greed – "Greed Is Good"

This somewhat provocative statement from a legendary movie has become anchored in our industry, but in my opinion, its message is usually misunderstood.
Gordon Gekko – the character from Wall Street (1987), played by Michael Douglas – said in a boardroom speech:
"Greed, for lack of a better word, is good. Greed is right. Greed works."
Greed is just a feeling. It's neither good nor bad. Only what we do under the influence of that feeling can turn out good or bad.
For a Trader, greed generates a few key problems:

23.1.1 Greed pushes us toward increased risk

We want to make more, faster – ideally one trade and the money train is already waiting for us.
That's not going to happen.

This desire can end with a zero balance on the account and a forced reflection on your Trader's mindset.
Pushing risk beyond reasonable, statistically proven levels is bound to end badly.

23.1.2 Greed Is a Creation of Our Ego

Have you ever asked yourself why you want to make more money?
I understand the part about covering basic needs. A better apartment, a good car — those are normal human desires.
But if you're buying a Bugatti without any plans to drive 300–400 km/h, then the question is: why do you want it?
Why would you want a huge, expensive house if, in reality, you only need three rooms, a kitchen, a bathroom, and a garage for three cars because you love classics and own a few?

If you don't process this topic within yourself, you might discover that you're forcing yourself into something you don't even truly want.
That would be rather sad.

23.1.3 On Greed — Movie Lessons

In Wall Street: Money Never Sleeps (2010), Bretton James is asked by Jacob what amount of money would make him finally walk away from the banking and investment business. His answer: "**More**."
There are levels of greed.
At first, we usually crave big money. Once we already have too much, the money itself stops being exciting. We start craving something else — power, control.
For many people, money and power are such important goals that they never even ask themselves what the meaning of their life really is. That's sad, because it's precisely the richest and most powerful who shape the world we see outside our window.

In the movie Gladiator (2000), Emperor Marcus Aurelius wanted to hand power over to General Maximus so he could turn the empire into a republic governed by the senate.
Maximus refused, and the Emperor said:
"Maximus, that is why it must be you."
I know it's just a film, but the ambitions, emotions, and desires it portrays are real. Maximus didn't long for power — he wanted to go home and enjoy a peaceful, simple life.

What do you want? What do you truly desire?
It's crucial to define a goal that aligns with our values and real desires. Once we know it, it becomes easier to see that many temptations are nothing but **false desires**, trying to steal something valuable from us and pull us off our path.

23.1.4 What Is Marketing?

Before I give you my definition, let me share two examples.

In the 1950s and 60s, **black pearls** appeared on the jewelry market. Until then, they were considered ugly, defective, and therefore very cheap.
Importer Jean-Claude Brouillet asked famous New York jeweler Harry Winston to help promote them.
Harry set a very high price and advertised black pearls alongside the most expensive white diamonds.
The market "bought it."

"**A diamond is forever**." At the beginning of the 20th century, De Beers practically had a monopoly on diamond mining.
At that time, diamonds were considered impractical and too expensive.
Only about 10% of engagement rings featured diamonds.
In 1947, facing falling demand, De Beers commissioned the agency N.W. Ayer to create an ad — and the slogan "A diamond is forever" was born. Fifty years later, over 80% of engagement rings featured diamonds.

The monopolists, with control over supply and demand, maintained diamond prices for decades.
A diamond is compressed carbon, yet countless people bought into that campaign and paid massive sums for “a piece of glass in a ring.”

Marketing is the art of creating a need in the customer that they didn’t have before — and then offering a product that supposedly satisfies that implanted need.

Be careful with advertising. Its goal is to take your money and push something you never actually needed.
You trade your time for a useless item — and in the process, you stir up a desire that feeds your greed.
The manipulation of dream-sellers can turn you into a “sucker” handing over your life in the form of earned money. Pardon the bluntness, but sometimes it’s pointless to sugarcoat the truth.

According to Wikipedia, natural diamond prices fell by about 26% from their 2022 peak to early 2025, while lab-grown diamond prices collapsed by about 74%.
Sometimes advertising alone just isn’t enough...

23.1.5 Rebel

I know the definition of marketing I presented here is different from the one they teach in schools.
I’m not writing this book to pass on common knowledge — my goal is to shake you out of fixed patterns of thinking.
If any extreme statement in this book triggered you — great.
That means you questioned something. And that’s a good thing.
Now you can reflect on it and check whether your automatic, subconscious system of values and judgments really serves you.

You don’t have to agree with me.

It's enough if you start thinking independently and verifying both what I write — and what's been programmed into your subconscious. If my point of view differs from yours, then one of us is probably wrong. But which one... :)

23.2 Fear

Fear, anxiety, stress... all of it stems from a lack of trust — either in the system or in yourself.
A lack of trust points to insufficient preparation. If you were 99% prepared, you wouldn't doubt that your system works and delivers profits.
Uncertainty leads to "stupid trades," those lead to losses and painful experiences, and the memory of them produces fear.
See where the problem lies?

Always in the same place:

- master your psychology,
- refine your technique,
- test your system,
- check if it's repeatable and statistically profitable.

Once you do that, the rest is just formality.
You enter the market, you exit with money. Most emotions (apart from greed) come simply from a lack of preparation.

This is the cure for most problems:
professional preparation for trading.

23.3 Revenge, Payback, Getting Even, Chasing Losses

If you read the previous point, you already know everything.
Losses you try to make back come from psychological mistakes, breaking strategy rules or not having them at all, and from terrible Money Management (MM).

Don't do stupid things — and you won't have to fight those demons.
If you make a mistake, admit it. Bow your head, accept what happened, then lift it up, analyze the situation, and do everything to prevent it from happening again.
Fixing one mistake with another stupid move... well, you get the point.

23.4 Hope

We have a saying: "Hope is the mother of fools."
That's not always true — in life, hope can be necessary and give strength.
But in trading?
In trading, hope usually **leads to bigger losses**.
There's no room for waiting until the chart turns around and the market answers your prayers.
No strategy has a chapter called "hope." Forget about it.
Belief in a proven system and your own skills — yes.
Hope — no. That's just self-deception.

23.5 Confidence

Confidence is an asset — as long as it's built on facts and data confirming the effectiveness of your strategy.
Confidence in executing your plan is essential.
But if it's based on gut feeling, beliefs, or ego, it can be very dangerous.
Misplaced confidence leads to ignoring rules and ramping up risk ("because I'm right, because I'll prove it").
That's a straight road to disaster. False confidence can destroy a Trader.
Confidence built on illusion can be deadly.

23.6 Fear of Loss

The extreme opposite of confidence is the lack of faith in your own knowledge, skills, and effectiveness.
That breeds fear of loss.
You feel that if you take a trade, you'll lose — and that fear holds you back.
Is that bad? If you don't believe in your knowledge and skills, fear is a natural warning signal sent by your brain.
First eliminate the cause — only then start trading.
Check your knowledge, test your system on demo, and once you have proof that it works — then trade.
Fear will turn into nothing more than an unjustified worry you'll need to tame.

23.7 Regret, Shame, Guilt

Lost money in the market?
OK — you're not the first and you won't be the last. Everyone who makes money today has lost before. It's part of the learning curve: at the beginning we make mistakes, we learn from them, over time we make fewer, and eventually we become pros.

Regret, shame, and guilt are toxic emotions in trading.

They bring nothing positive, though they are completely natural.
If you're not a psychopath, you know them just as well as I do.
They're signals you need to read and act on.
If you feel regret, it means you believe you did something wrong.
Draw conclusions, change your approach, and don't repeat the same mistake. Then regret has done its job — you can move on with your head held high.
Some, however, remain trapped in these emotions for too long.
They punish themselves instead of forgiving themselves. They wallow in the mud instead of getting up and moving forward.

If it's temporary — fine. But if it lasts for years, it becomes toxic. The key is the ability to forgive yourself. Make amends if you can. If not — forgive yourself, improve, and move on. You'll regain balance by doing something good in another area.

Staying stuck in regret is a form of self-punishment. It's also often the result of fear of change. As long as you sit in regret, you have a convenient excuse not to face the challenges ahead.
To get out, you need to act: admit the mistake, adjust, and move forward. Maybe it's hard, maybe you don't feel like it... but it's better to act than to pity yourself.

I also feel sorry for myself sometimes — for a minute. :)
Then I get back to work, because life's too short for sulking.
I mentioned the EST program earlier...
Facing your own demons is the only fast track forward I know and use.

23.7.1 Made-up excuses to avoid pain

Do you realize that while writing this book, I have no idea what exactly you're going through or to what extent your feelings are justified?
Maybe you stole money from your grandma, lost it, and now you have a reason to feel ashamed — only you can judge that.

Every piece of advice I write here is accurate
— until it isn't. That's the honest truth. :)

Life and emotions are complex matters. There are no simple, universal tips that can heal broken hearts and broken bones.
What I can guarantee you, though, is that this advice works.
Will it work in your case? That depends solely on you — on whether you allow it and whether this particular advice fits your situation.
Either way — congratulations for even starting to think about it.
That's undoubtedly the first good step toward change.

And now — my recipe for emotional pain, regret, shame, and everything else you can come up with:

Stop. Just stop.

Think: there's no cloud above you handing out punishment. There's no law that orders you to suffer.The fact that you feel this way right now — **that's your own idea**.
And since it's yours — you can just decide that it's over.
And move on to something useful. And one more thing...

Would you like to switch off those sick emotions the way I told you, but fear immediately kicks in? That's natural, because if you forgive yourself, you'd have to do something about it — check your strategy, make another attempt to become a good Trader.
Do you feel uneasy? Are you afraid it won't work out again? That you're not cut out for it? The fact is, you probably jumped into trading too soon — you were hyped up but unprepared.

Eureka. Since you now know the root of the problem, what should you do? Exactly — do your homework, test your readiness on demo. And when you see consistent profits in your stats, you'll return to the market — with small amounts, minimal risk.

Don't turn pain or failure into an excuse.
Pull yourself together and fight for your dreams.

23.8 Boredom

People rarely talk about it, but one of the most common problems for a professional Trader is simple, plain boredom.
If you're bored, ask yourself: what are you actually doing here?
A Trader should feel "bored," because trading isn't meant to be an emotional rollercoaster.

You don't come to the market for thrills — you come for money.
If your goal is different, stop wasting time reading this book.
Boredom can mean you're not analyzing the chart deeply enough.

If you feel like you were watching the chart, price took off, and you just stood there, ask yourself why.
The average human can fully concentrate for 30–60 minutes. You can't track charts in full focus for hours. Boredom is a sign that your concentration has slipped into standby mode.

That's a signal to take action — I'll describe exactly what later in this book. Boredom is also a signal that **you shouldn't be clicking** "Buy" or "Sell" right now. If you're bored, it means you're not analyzing. And without analysis, any trade will be weak by definition. Trading isn't a cure for boredom — and if someone treats it that way, they've picked a very expensive medicine.

In our profession, a lot of time is spent waiting, and during that time boredom is a frequent companion. Look at it differently: you're not bored — you're resting, waiting for the signal that the hunt is about to begin. Patience and the ability to wait for the right moment are traits of experienced, effective Traders. That's not boredom — it's prep time before the action.

23.9 Disappointment, Doubt

As you probably feel yourself, these emotions come from poor preparation and mistakes in execution.
A system that has statistically proven its effectiveness shouldn't disappoint or raise doubts — unless you're not following it consistently, which makes your results worse than expected. In that case, you simply need to fix it. There's no magic pill for this. Get back to basics, strengthen your foundation, and once you remove the cause, the effects will disappear.

23.10 Loneliness

I mentioned this before — trading is a one-on-one duel: you versus the market. The market won't solve the problem of loneliness. A Trader needs peace, so during the game you must isolate yourself from your surroundings.
And what your life looks like outside trading is entirely up to you.

23.11 Perfectionism

Extremes — even in positive traits — can be harmful.
Chasing perfection can be just another way of avoiding actually entering the market. If you're the analytical type who fears risk and losses, you could spend years fine-tuning every detail of your strategy... until you end up a retiree who never once clicked "Buy." You never tried, but at least everything is perfectly polished.
But what's the point... Striving for perfection? **Yes**.
The desire for perfection? **No.**
You'll never reach a 100% statistical edge. A 51% edge is enough — then work on pushing it to 52%, 53%... maybe up to 80%.
You'll sense where the line of reason lies — beyond that, the system becomes unnecessarily complex and effectiveness actually starts to drop. If something is too precise, too complex, and too detailed, you won't be able to apply it in practice — where a new candle forms every minute. On top of that, markets are constantly changing, and we have to adapt. On the one hand, you must stick to the rules. On the other — you need to know where to stay flexible.

23.12 Emotional Chaos

This hardly needs explanation — if your emotions are a mess, deal with them before you sit down to trade.

23.13 Indifference, Apathy...

This sounds like someone who fought, tried, and then gave up. That's a dangerous state in trading — you lack motivation, the drive to analyze the market, to trade. Maybe you don't even care anymore whether you win or lose.

Get your head straight first — only then even think about trading.

24 Emotions Don't Take You Over Without Warning

I don't need to explain to you how an emotion is born inside you — you've experienced it a billion times. The only question is: have you ever really observed how it happens to you?

Once, a well-known man named John wrote: "In the beginning was the Word..."

Think about the last emotion you felt and ask yourself: **what was there at the beginning?** It's always a process made of stages. You heard something, you saw something, you smelled something... One of your senses picked it up and triggered the launch sequence.

What state were you in at that moment? Maybe you'd just downed ten coffees, or hadn't slept all night and were dodging the light?

From now on, give yourself one simple exercise:

----

*The moment you feel an emotion — good, bad, whatever — **stop right there**.*

24.1 Pause Button

At this moment, you step outside yourself and observe what just happened. You're the professor analyzing the case — and the case is you.

Note down — in your head or on paper — what state you're in.

What was going on one second earlier, and before that... until you reach the very first impulse that triggered the reaction.

When you find it, file it under "impulses."

Now fast-forward your inner movie, step by step, watching how that emotion built up inside you.

When you reach the point where you hit Stop, ask yourself:

- Does this make sense?
- Is this reaction really what you want to feel?
- Is what you're about to do next the best choice?

The initial impulse was probably an external factor beyond your control. But every frame after that — that's your own directing. You're the screenwriter and — who knows — maybe in a second you'll even turn stuntman, throwing out a line to your mother-in-law: "This soup is too salty." :)

Seriously though... once you've stopped the film, traced it back to the source, and analyzed the impulse plus all the steps that led you into that emotional state — ask yourself: does this emotion still linger, or has it already vanished?

Build a simple procedure for yourself to study your own emotions. That will be your tool.

An emotion appears — **FREEZE FRAME!**
You step outside yourself as an analyst in a professor's lab coat, holding a large notebook and a pen. You start the case study.
You rewind your movie, scene by scene, until you reach the impulse that started it all. You stop at the beginning. You record the details of the impulse, its source, and its context.

You mark that moment as your **trigger** — an emotional switch. Next time it shows up, you'll recognize it instantly and understand what it's trying to ignite in you.
You watch the following frames — carefully analyzing how the emotion built up.
Return to the moment when you stopped the film.
Ask yourself: do you really want to stay in this state?
Does what you see serve you?
If you still hear the echo of that scene — **turn down the volume in your head.**
Blur the image: let it fade to black-and-white — dull and misty.
And now — slowly, calmly — **push that image further and further away.**

When the image is far away, switch to something good — something you enjoy. Forget about that silly emotion.
And when the same or a similar trigger shows up again, tell it:
I KNOW YOU! I SEE YOU! THIS TIME I'M IN CHARGE! NOW YOU – POLITELY LEAVE. :) BYE-BYE.

Emotions are great – when they bring pleasure and make life exciting.
In our business, emotions can also blow up our accounts.
In trading, emotions are dangerous... but you can use them.

24.2 How to Use the Fact You're Not a Psychopath?

You're in the middle of trading when you start feeling emotions – STOP. You freeze the movie, put on the lab coat with "PROFESSOR TRADER" written on it, and analyze: what exactly is happening here?

Are you following all the rules 100%, or did you just skip something and consciously do something stupid?
If you haven't entered a position yet, you can step away from the desk – it costs nothing – and think about what really happened. Analysis is what you're good at, Professor. :)
If, however, you've already clicked and done something stupid, you'd better hope you didn't break your position-sizing rules or breach your max SL.

If you followed that golden rule, calm down and think about what you can do now. You can always close the position and analyze what happened. Or leave it open — as long as your SL is in place — and wait to see what gets painted on the chart.

If the market hits your SL, thank it for the lesson — you just paid 1× SL in tuition. If the SL doesn't get hit, be clear with yourself: it was a dumb trade, and the fact it worked out was pure luck. **That's not how you trade.** Don't program your brain to think that breaking the rules gets rewarded. In fact, for your future, losing here would be better.

When you train a dog, you don't reward bad behavior.

Observing your emotions should become a habit.

Building the habit of recognizing emotional triggers is how you create a new version of yourself — a better one.

The version of a Professional Trader — someone in the top few percent of the market.

A tough one who comes to the market to take their money. :)

You buy and sell — you make money. You create the market, you create liquidity. You give those you buy from the chance to sell. You give those you buy from a chance to sell, and those you sell to a chance to buy. Isn't that both beautiful and useful? :)

24.3 How to Stop Emotions Stronger Than You — With Force!

If the emotion is still small, you can stop it with just a thought. The strength of the emotions you can stop — that's your individual superpower. :)

As a human being, you basically have two states:

- Emotional state: what's happening in your head.
- Physical state: what's happening in your body.

Your emotional state affects your physical state — you might feel heat, your hands might shake — and it also works the other way around.

Your physical state affects your emotions — and that's the beauty of it. :)
You can train your mind for years like a Tibetan monk... or simply get up and go for a run. Problem solved.

Imagine you're really down — what do you look like?
You sit slouched, shoulders dropped, wearing a sad face...
Maybe you're sprawled there like a dead fish washed up on the riverbank...
That's pretty much how you look...

Of course, you can try to chase the bad thoughts away and work on changing your mindset, dredging up every technique humanity ever invented...
Or...

All it takes is to stand up, do some squats, jump around, laugh, clap your hands... When your body starts acting as if you're happy, your mind will follow.
You'll change your emotional state by force — just get up from your chair and dance like someone who just hit the lottery.

Your mind is a fascinating mechanism. It's so easy to trick it. :)
Luckily, we can do it in ways that actually serve us. :)
The shift in emotion from jumping or running isn't very long-lasting, but it's a great starting point for building a better, more durable emotional state.

In many things, the hardest part is simply starting.
This method gives you a quick, effective launch — you can fire your rocket off the ground and start flying.
You've got enough fuel for a solid takeoff.
From there, to maintain the state you'll need a plan — but by then you already have positive thoughts in your head, so you've got a shot. :)

24.4 Build Your Own Rescue Mechanisms

Since you already know quite a lot — and thanks to this book you'll become The Professor of your own mind — design a rescue system that pulls you out of bad spots at the charts.
Treat it like a game — make it a mini-ritual: "Restart."
The key is that it's simple, repeatable, and kicks in automatically the moment you feel an emotional drop.

It could be:

A deep breath, a light tap on the desk :), and a firm word: STOP!

Over time, this new emotional state will anchor itself, and you'll be able to recall it instantly — unless you smash your desk. :)
The moment you feel at the charts that something in your mindset is off... STOP — switch to "Restart" mode and change direction.

Your train is back on track, heading straight for your destination — not into the weeds.

You're not an amateur. You don't come to the market to wallow in drama. You're a professional. You've got a clear plan to execute — make money. Either execute the plan like a pro, or take the day off.

The work you put into changing yourself can transform your whole life. You can apply the same technique in other areas, too. One small change, one small win can trigger an avalanche of change.

You can become a new, better version of yourself — the person you truly want to be.

25 Chemistry in Our Head

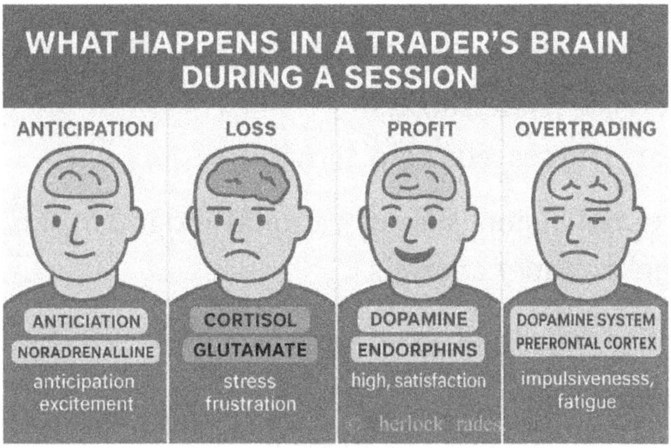

If you're aware of what's happening in your body. You can actively adjust your state. The version of you that appears when your system is flooded with chemicals — that's not really you. That's the "high" version of you — and that version shouldn't be making decisions about your money.

Been drinking? Don't drive.
Flooded with dopamine, adrenaline, or cortisol?
Don't trade. Don't make any financial decisions in that state.

25.1 What Happens in a Trader's Body

Let's break down what happens in your body chemistry depending on the situation — and the emotional state it triggers.

25.1.1 WAITING — "something's about to happen"

Neurochemistry:

- dopamine (reward anticipation, excitement)
- norepinephrine (heightened alertness, tension)

Effects: accelerated heartbeat, arousal, weakened logical thinking, excessive optimism, susceptibility to FOMO

25.1.2 OPENING a POSITION — "the action begins"

Neurochemistry:

- adrenaline (fight-or-flight response, emotional surge)
- cortisol (risk-related stress)
- glutamate (increased brain activity)

Effects: tunnel vision, loss of rational judgment, and impulsive action without proper analysis

25.1.3 LOSS — "the trade goes against you"

Neurochemistry:

- cortisol spike (heightened stress level)
- dopamine drop (feeling of failure, frustration)
- glutamate (cognitive overload)

Effects: muscle tension, stomach pain, and mental patterns such as "recover the loss," "I can't lose," and revenge trading

25.1.4 PROFIT / WIN — strong reward

Neurochemistry:

- dopamine (reward, high, satisfaction)
- endorphins (relief, bliss)
- testosterone (boost in self-confidence)

Effects: euphoria, a sense of brilliance, higher risk appetite, and reduced self-control

25.1.5 OVERTRADING — pushing on after a win/loss

Neurochemistry:

- dopamine overload (receptor desensitization)
- prefrontal cortex fatigue (loss of control, shutdown of situational analysis)

Effects: running on autopilot, impatience, a "gambling trance," and nervous system exhaustion

25.2 Long-Term Effects

After 5–10 years of trading, you'll probably want nothing more than to manage your capital calmly and enjoy life.
That's exactly my plan.
If every trading day left me emotionally overloaded, then after a decade of that "adventure" I'd be better suited for a psych ward than for an early, well-deserved retirement.
Think about it — you can handle a day, a month, maybe half a year, but eventually your body will rebel and shout: "ENOUGH!"
See what's at stake if you ignore this.

Here are the long-term consequences of emotional overload:

Brain

Dysregulation of the dopamine system, decline in logical thinking

Hormones

Excess cortisol — burnout, insomnia

Psyche

Nervousness, impulsiveness, irritability

Body

Chronic fatigue, muscle tension, digestive issues

25.3 How to Fight It — STRATEGIES

25.3.1 PHYSIOLOGICAL:

- Diaphragmatic breathing — instantly lowers cortisol
- Sleep and recovery — rebuild dopamine receptors
- Physical activity — balances serotonin and endorphin levels

25.3.2 PSYCHOLOGICAL:

- Emotion and decision journal — increases self-awareness
- Entry/exit rules and daily limits — protect against impulsiveness
- NLP techniques, meditation, and visualization — help reprogram reactions

25.3.3 SYSTEMIC:

- Pre-trading checklists — reduce chaos
- Trading plan with profit/loss limits — reduces the "greed vs. fear" effect
- Breaks every 1–2 hours — a chemical reset for your brain

Remember — the goal isn't to stubbornly suppress emotions and bottle them up. The goal is to make trading like any other job: you show up, assemble the Lambo, execute step by step — and in the end the car is ready, then you can take it to the track for some fun.

25.4 Caffeine, Taurine, and Other Stuff

Now that you know your body can produce "hard chemistry" on its own, think about how you "help it out" when you sit down at the charts with a cup of coffee, an energy drink, or a cocktail... I won't wade into drugs here — not my field.

25.4.1 What Does CAFFEINE Do in the Brain?

- Blocks adenosine — the neurotransmitter that signals fatigue
- Increases dopamine and norepinephrine — stimulation, sharper focus
- Raises cortisol and adrenaline — mobilizes the body as in a stress response

The effects can be pleasant, but the side effects come right along with them:

- excessive stimulation, shaky hands
- anxiety, panic, impulsiveness

A small coffee (50–100 mg of caffeine) works for me — placebo or pure biochemistry, it works. At around 200–400 mg, you may start to feel the negative side effects.
If you're tired, the solution isn't coffee — it's sleep and recovery.

25.4.2 What Does TAURINE Do in the Brain?

- Stabilizes the nervous system
- Supports concentration
- Regulates calcium and electrolytes
- Enhances caffeine's effect

Possible positive effects:

- slightly calming; reduces neuronal excitability
- suppresses overactivation (glutamate antagonist)
- improves intercellular communication
- helps you focus under heavy mental load
- supports heart, muscles, and circulation
- synergistic effect: longer alertness, but a higher risk of overstimulation

I've heard that caffeine, sugar, and taurine amplify one another — I avoid those mixes.
I'm no chemist. Check your sources before you try anything.
In my mixes, I rarely add caffeine — only if I'm really tired.
Taurine I use more often, but in small doses. I don't fully trust boosters: a little is fine, too much breaks something. So I stick to small amounts — body calm, head calm — and it works.

25.4.3 What Does SUGAR Do in the Body?

- Quickly raises blood glucose — instant energy boost
- The body releases insulin — glucose levels crash fast
- Effect: a roller coaster of energy and mood

The consequences aren't great:

- immediately after consumption: stimulation, a short burst of focus, a false sense of confidence
- after 30–60 minutes: energy crash, sleepiness, irritability, impulsiveness
- with long-term use: mood swings, brain fog, poor decisions, lack of patience

Sugar works like nitrous oxide in an engine — it gives you a kick, then cuts out and you reach for another dose.
In our house, there's no sugar at all. We've also cut out flour, bread, pasta — basically anything loaded with carbs.

If you like lemon water, like I do — here's a tip: I used to buy lemons all the time, and I always ended up with a mess of leftovers and food scraps. Then I discovered you can buy organic lemon juice in small glass bottles (200–250 ml) with no preservatives.
Since then, I haven't bought a single lemon. :)

25.4.4 WARNING — Sugar Acts Like a Drug!

Sugar affects the brain in a way similar to drugs — it activates the reward system (mainly dopamine), creating a quick feeling of pleasure.

Effects:

- Strong dopamine activation — similar to cocaine or nicotine, though weaker
- Tolerance — you need larger doses to get the same effect
- Withdrawal symptoms — irritability, fatigue, cravings
- Compulsive habits — reaching for sugar despite negative consequences
- Psychological addiction — "fixing your mood" with sweets

Research (mostly on rats) has shown that:

- sugar can trigger a stronger dopamine response than cocaine if consumed regularly
- it causes neurochemical changes typical of addiction

Conclusion: biologically, sugar acts like an addictive substance — not for everyone, and not as strongly as hard drugs.
How many times have you thought, "I could use something sweet"? That wasn't you — it was your inner sugar addict talking. :)

25.4.5 WARNING 2 — Sugar Again!

A Trader's job means hours in front of a screen — definitely not the healthiest lifestyle. Add sugary drinks, sweets, and carb-heavy meals on top, and soon you'll see the warning sign — on the scale. Prevention is better than a cure. Sugar, our "sweet drug," disrupts the natural regulation of hunger and satiety.

Effects:

- Increases appetite — especially for sweets and other high-energy foods.
- Blocks leptin (the satiety hormone) — fructose in sugar weakens its effect, so the brain doesn't get the signal that you're full.
- Raises insulin — triggers a rapid surge after the glucose spike, leading to a sharp drop in blood sugar — hunger, fatigue, cravings.
- Disrupts the gut microbiome — which affects hunger hormones (ghrelin) and appetite-control mechanisms.
- Promotes fat storage (especially visceral fat) — mainly via excess fructose — leading to fatty liver and insulin resistance.

In short: sugar increases cravings, disturbs satiety, and fuels weight gain — not just through calories, but by disrupting the hormonal and neural systems that regulate eating.

Simply put: **SUGAR IS KILLING US**.

Read up on it — it's a bit scary, and it's worth knowing, especially in our profession, where movement is limited, stress is high, and the fridge and snack cabinet are often just a few steps away.

25.4.6 What Does L-THEANINE Do?

- Calms without sedating — increasing alpha waves in the brain — a state of "relaxed alertness."
- Reduces stress and anxiety — lowers cortisol levels
- Improves focus — works synergistically with caffeine, giving "clean focus" without the jitters.

- Stabilizes mood — affects serotonin and dopamine
- Supports sleep (without daytime drowsiness) — helps you fall asleep and improves sleep quality

Sounds great, but it's not a magic "flip a switch and the problem's gone." It's more like gentle support. It's worth reading more about it so you can make an informed choice.

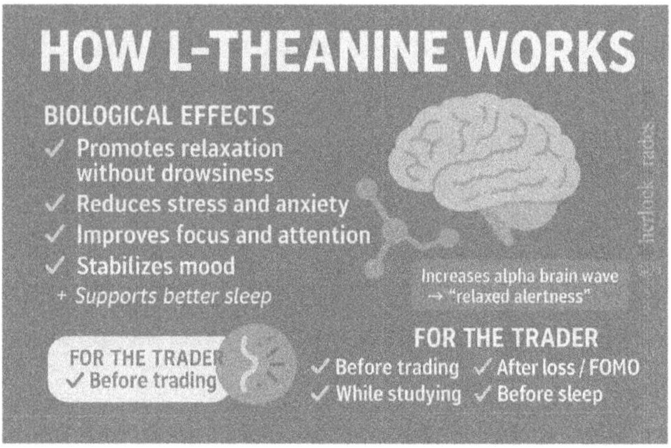

The natural source of L-theanine is green tea. I drink it often — I've got a "special" mug that holds a full liter. :)
And the strainer? It's huge, too. :) Remember to add lemon only after the tea has cooled down a bit. :)

And my mug? It's basically a small bucket. :)
The big strainer I use?
It's technically meant for soup spices — and it works perfectly!

25.4.7 What Does VITAMIN B6 Do?

In my vitamin mixes, a key element is the B-complex; I also add extra B6.

Why? Because it supports:

- Neurotransmitters — helps synthesize serotonin, dopamine, and GABA
- Mental energy — involved in glucose metabolism in the brain
- Mood — B6 deficiency can cause irritability and fatigue
- Stress response — supports the nervous system during tough moments (like trading)

I hope I got you thinking about what's worth drinking while trading. We've got plenty of options — combine them wisely, and they can really help.

Remember: this is a marathon. Support only makes sense if it's healthy. The wrong boosters are pure stupidity — and they always end badly.

Guess I'll have to ditch those energy drinks if that's what a smart book says. :)

26 Don't Wind Yourself Up Too Much...

...because eventually the spring will snap.

What's your first impulse when you read that something works? Buy a whole bucket of it and dump in as much as you can? NO!

Slow down. Easy. Step by step. Use common sense.

It doesn't work that way: today you start, tomorrow you succeed, and the day after you collect your rewards and buy yourself an island.

This is a longer journey — take it slow. Stay consistent, avoid procrastination, and don't try to force speed.

Seriously — if you approach it calmly, with a cool head, you'll reach success faster than those who jump in blind with fiery enthusiasm. I've seen it countless times.

That rush to get to the charts as fast as possible and start making money — I've seen it. I went through the same thing at the beginning, so I know exactly what I'm talking about.

The result? Sitting down at the charts, the Trader lacks basic preparation.

No developed Money Management (MM) rules or strategy; no structured workflows or playbooks. They dive into the market like a dolphin into the waves. The outcome? A painful lesson — and if they learn from it, they go back to the basics and make up for what they skipped.

27 Train Your Brain Like a Commando

Trading at a desk may look safe, yet many Traders get up from their chairs exhausted as if they'd just been through a battle.
What's striking is that some Traders, after putting themselves through extreme emotions, actually experience something similar to what soldiers experience — post-traumatic stress disorder (PTSD). A bit of overkill, isn't it, to make a living in a way that wrecks your psyche?

Look at a commando's training — he literally fights for survival. Even though his life is on the line, much of that preparation can be applied to your own battlefield.

What does a commando do? He trains to survive and complete the mission — despite chaos, pressure, exhaustion. He doesn't run from stress. He learns how to act in spite of it. He doesn't seek comfort — only habits that will take over when logic fails.
Now swap "commando" for Trader and read that again.
Commando training isn't just about muscles — it's mainly about the mind, built to function under the toughest conditions.
Here's what mental training for commandos looks like — a bit crazy):

27.1 Stress Inoculation

Exercises under pressure include noise, darkness, fatigue, explosions, and shouting.
The goal is to desensitize the brain — to stop panicking and start reacting automatically.
Example: simulating an operation after 48 hours without sleep.

27.2 Combat Simulations and Scenarios

- Rehearsed hundreds of times: entries, evacuations, and ambush responses.
- The brain doesn't decide — it acts from working memory automatically.

27.3 Focus and Perception Training

- Learning to pick up key signals in chaos: sounds, movement, changes.
- Training to recognize patterns and assess situations instantly.
- Staying alert despite fatigue and lack of sleep.

27.4 Emotion and Self-Control Training

- Mastering fear, anger, and impulses.
- Techniques: box breathing (4–4–4–4), heart rate regulation, muscle relaxation.
- Drills: for example, shooting practice straight out of ice-cold water.

27.5 Mental Rehearsal

- A commando visualizes every mission — before it happens.
- The brain doesn't see the situation as new and acts automatically.
- Body and decision-making become one.

27.6 Decision-Making Under Time Pressure

- Reactions in under 2 seconds.
- Decisions: "Attack or retreat?" "Shoot or hold fire?"
- Eliminate hesitation — because hesitation kills.

27.7 Building Mental Resilience

- Analyzing your own reactions — journaling, conversations, and reflection.
- Sense of purpose: "Why am I fighting?" "Who am I?"
- Tools: Stoicism, meditation, NLP — building mental strength.

Good thing we don't have to learn how to take a position after being thrown into ice-cold water. :)

28 DEFCON 1, 2, 3

If you like action movies, you've definitely come across this term. DEFCON (Defense Readiness Condition) is a five-level scale of U.S. military readiness. DEFCON 1 means hostilities have already started, or someone is about to press the button.

And in a moment, you're about to enter a position. :) We don't have briefcases with launch codes, but we absolutely need our own readiness levels. What could that scale look like in trading?

28.1 DEFCON 3

The market is drifting – no clear direction. No signals meet the requirements of my checklist – it's not time to trade.

I check other instruments – maybe something's happening there. For now, DEFCON 3 – observation.

I calmly wait for the chart to "speak," signaling that something is starting.

28.2 DEFCON 2

It's getting interesting. Dynamic moves show up and volume rises – money is circulating. I don't see an entry yet. I need to wait for clear setups.

I look for strong signs on the chart. I mark Fibonacci levels, check whether Elliott Wave Theory suggests anything interesting. I dial up the focus and keep watching the chart.

28.3 DEFCON 1

Game on! All signals point to a change in direction and a potential new move. Volume, patterns, waves, corrections – everything says: "Focus!". I grab my checklist and search for the optimal entry in line with Money Management (MM). Calmly, fully focused, I wait for the right candle in the right spot. I've got about a minute to decide, so the full context is already analyzed.

Watching the charts at full concentration, you'll last half an hour — maybe an hour at most. You need a signal system — Focus Triggers [24] — that snaps your attention back. Your plan and strategy must account for the human factor.

Your endurance is limited. Pick the best hunting hours for yourself and manage your energy. Operate on different concentration levels so that when all the signals scream DEFCON 1, your brain is rested and ready for maximum focus and analysis until you enter the position.

If your focus signals show up but you've already spent the last two hours staring at a chart where nothing has happened — good luck making a solid trade in that state.

Another key point — if you stare too long at the market without any clear opportunity, fatigue starts pushing you into action for action's sake. And eventually you'll find something — but it'll be a weak trade.

So plan your levels of focus wisely — relaxed but deliberate. Decide which signals will move you up to a higher DEFCON level. That way, your entries will be much sharper. Once the position is open, the rocket has launched. You can step down to DEFCON 2 and calmly watch the flight, adjusting your Take Profit (TP) from time to time.

29 Destructive Beliefs of a Trader

If you haven't read it yet, I recommend T. Harv Eker's book Secrets of the Millionaire Mind. It's an easy read that delivers a solid motivational boost. It also describes many mental blocks we've programmed into ourselves.

Below, I'll discuss similar themes inspired by his approach.

29.1 Money Is Evil

If you see yourself as a good person but believe that money is evil, your subconscious will do everything to make sure you don't have any. You'll be a "good person"... but poor.

Wouldn't it be better to be good and wealthy?

A good, wealthy person can do far more for the world than someone who has no resources. Money is just a tool – sometimes paper, metal, or a digital record. By itself, it's neither good nor evil.

It's people who decide what to do with it.

My father used to say: "You discover a man's true nature when you give him power and money."

My father was born just after World War II. I fully agree with what he said about revealing someone's true nature. In democratic countries, no one has absolute power. That kind of power existed in monarchies; today, only dictators have it. We all know how much "love and empathy" comes with the rule of dictators – just look at the third generation of the family running that less fortunate part of the Korean peninsula.

If you carry mental programs that say money is evil and rich people "must have earned it dishonestly," those are self-destructive beliefs. They'll effectively block you from making money in the markets.

Money is just a tool that creates opportunities. What you do with it is your decision and your responsibility.

29.2 Big Money Corrupts and Destroys People

If you really believe that — allow me to help.
Go to the link below and transfer that "toxic excess" piling up in your account to me.

If I can help, I always will. :) And if I can save you from moral downfall this way — I feel even more obliged. I'll even endure large sums. :)

https://buymeacoffee.com/sherlocktrades.com

Don't feel guilty — I'll gladly take that burden off your shoulders. If such destructive beliefs are sitting in your head, sooner or later your subconscious will make sure you get rid of that money.
If it even lets you earn any in the first place.

Sort out these programs so that your actions, goals, and deep convictions don't sabotage each other.

29.3 You Can Quickly Make Big Money in the Markets

In theory, yes — but first define "easy," "quick," and "big."
Then show what you bring to the table as a Trader: what skills and experience you have, how much capital, and what your decision-making process looks like.

Believing in easy and fast profits without a solid foundation leads to irrational decisions. Those lead straight to "expensive lessons" — big losses you'll later have to recover (if there's anything left).

Start by adjusting your expectations. Your goals should be realistic and achievable — not fairy tales. Illusions and wishful thinking often end in disappointment.

If you chase them blindly, you might end up wrecked on the rocks.

So what's it going to be? Do you throw your whole ship into chasing a hunch, or do you send out a scout boat first to see whether the Sirens' sweet song of huge profits is real?

29.4 Trading Is a Zero-Sum Game

I hear this "wise" claim a lot and always wonder who keeps repeating it. It's usually not the Traders who actually make money — more often, it's people who like to debate theory.

Fine — I'll answer, even though the topic itself is a bit of a snoozer. The truth is, trading is not a zero-sum game. For Traders, it's a negative-sum game. There's no point overanalyzing it, because that fact doesn't change much. But since the question comes up, here's the breakdown.

Example: Player A goes long, Player B goes short. Both pay costs — spread, slippage, platform fees. Player A loses, Player B wins — but brokers profit regardless of the outcome. So more than one side's loss leaves the players' pool — a slice goes straight to intermediaries.

Your profits must exceed all transaction costs. You can be right about direction and still end up in the red because the spread "eats" your gains. It's normal for brokers to make money — someone has to fund market infrastructure: exchanges, data, derivatives, etc.

Your job is to know exactly what each entry costs and whether there's real potential to net a profit with a proper risk–reward (R:R) — say 1:3 — after costs. If not, don't take the trade — it's bad business for you. In that case, you're not trading for yourself — you're trading for the broker's profit.

29.5 Either Happiness or Money

I've never heard a voice from the heavens or received stone tablets commanding me to choose between happiness and money. That's just another absurd mental program pushed by people who — judging from this slogan — either don't have money or would prefer that we didn't, so we hand ours over to them. :)

There are plenty of poor, unhappy people, and plenty of rich ones who are also unhappy. In my opinion, it's easier to be happy with money than without it.

o paraphrase a famous Polish singer, Maryla:

"It's better to cry in a Porsche than in a beat-up old wreck."

Check what programs are running in your own head, and try to figure out where they came from. One line from the Bible has stuck with me — something I sometimes heard in sermons back when I still went to church:

"It is easier for a camel to pass through the eye of a needle than for a rich man to enter the kingdom of heaven."

I honestly don't see how the size of your bank account could affect your chance of getting into Heaven.

Judging by how "modest" the Vatican looks, I doubt my humble balance qualifies me as "rich." :)

To sum up: I see no evidence that money gets in the way of anything. Be a good and wealthy person. That's the best combo — goodness and the possibilities that capital brings. That's the path I choose, fully convinced it's the right one.

29.6 I'm Not Smart Enough for This

If you say, "I'm not smart enough for this," you might turn out to be right. Not because you actually lack intelligence.

Not everyone is cut out to be a Trader, and it's not just about intellect. It's also about mental toughness, resilience, analytical skills, math skills, and plenty of other traits.

Maybe you've just got a bad mental program running — and breaking it is all it takes to become a great Trader. But you'll only find out once you start learning and make your first trades.

If you want to, get going and see if this path is for you.

29.7 Crude Oil Pays Well...

So you made a nice profit on crude oil once, and now you think oil "likes you"? And you figure that if you're patient, it'll pay you again? Good luck with that. If you start building beliefs and expectations like that, you'll end up paying — and paying dearly — to discover it was all just an illusion. This is just another myth Traders like to repeat. Any instrument can bring you good profits or slam you with losses.

I recommend sticking to highly liquid instruments. Personally, I suggest gold futures (GC), crude oil (CL), and Dow Jones futures (YM). Back in the day, I also traded Euro FX futures (6E).

In practice, I get the best results when I limit myself to 2–3 instruments at most.

It's better to focus on fewer markets, learn their quirks, how they move, when the sessions open, and when key data comes out.

30 Is Trading an Honest Profession?

The world is one big marketplace — some sell, others buy. Exchanges are the arena that make this possible. I'm talking about stock exchanges, ETFs, and futures — for example: gold (GC — CME COMEX — Gold Futures), crude oil (CL — CME NYMEX — Crude Oil), Dow Jones futures (YM — CME — E-mini Dow Futures), or currency futures like EUR/USD (6E — CME — Euro FX Futures).

To an outsider, it looks like a game — like walking into a casino and betting red or black — either you win or you lose.
Nobody claims casinos are dishonest. Everyone knows the house always wins in the long run, yet Las Vegas still dazzles with its neon wonders. People accept the rules; they know what they're signing up for — they walk in, lose, and walk out smiling.

In our language, there's an unfortunate quirk: the vocabulary is limited, so trading is often called a "game."
A "game" is associated with fun and gambling. But as Johan Huizinga pointed out in Homo Ludens, "play is a voluntary activity that takes place within certain limits of time and space, according to freely accepted but absolutely binding rules."

For a professional Trader, trading is neither fun nor a string of random outcomes. There's no room for dishonesty here.
If you entered the market, lost money, and feel cheated, I have only one piece of advice: grow up. This isn't a game.

You, as a Trader:

- You risk your own capital and face the consequences. It's your money — you have every right to decide what to do with it.
- You don't manipulate the market — you're too small to move anything. You can't cheat anyone or mislead them. The chart will look the same with or without you.
- Your profits come from technical analysis and reading the chart correctly. That's just as ethical as betting on a horse race when you actually know horses and jockeys.

- Trading the market, you promise nothing to the other side. You don't sell fairy tales; you don't convince anyone to enter or exit. You have no contact with other participants — you can't deceive them because you don't even know them. It's a fair game with clear rules.
- Your trades and your capital actively support the market because you provide liquidity. Someone can sell only because you're buying. Without Traders — especially Day Traders — markets would be far less liquid, which would mean many people couldn't even execute their trades because there'd be nobody on the other side.

Trading, in this sense, is entirely ethical and fair.
If someone thinks otherwise, they shouldn't step into the market and then complain when reality doesn't match their theories.

People often think in simplistic terms: someone enters the market, loses money — and right away: "I was cheated," "they rob people," "this is unfair."
But ask yourself: why did that person enter the market in the first place? Wasn't it to "beat" others and walk away with their money?
In my view, trading — where only Traders face each other — is one of the most honest professions you can imagine.
But...

30.1 Where Does a Trader Encounter Dishonesty?

On the classic markets — stocks, futures, and so on — a Trader like you or me has no way to scheme or act dishonestly.
But that doesn't mean everything on these markets is fair.

In 2010, we saw the legendary **Flash Crash** — the Dow Jones Industrial Average dropped about 9% in just 10 minutes. The trigger was a single errant sell order On top of that — according to U.S. regulators (SEC and DOJ) — a British Trader contributed by using so-called "spoofing," i.e., placing fake orders to manipulate prices for profit.

Within 20 minutes, the market almost fully recovered to prior levels.

While an errant order can be chalked up as a mistake, deliberate tactics like spoofing are a textbook case of manipulation and dishonesty. If you place a buy order and genuinely intend to buy — that's fine. But if you place a buy order only to bait the market and cancel it as price approaches your order — that's manipulation.

The Crypto Market... Since 2017, I've completely stopped caring about cryptocurrencies and similar inventions.
At first, I thought Bitcoin might be a breakthrough — a real alternative to fiat money. If you listened to the early Bitcoin crowd, it really sounded like a financial revolution.

At some point, I realized it was all about greed — just another bubble, like the Dutch tulip mania, only this time global because we have the internet.

Let me pitch you a deal. You can buy a magic key that gives you access to a record on servers run by strangers, but the record itself has no owner — no one even knows who started the whole thing. With that key, you can add a new transaction to this chain of data. For the privilege of owning one BTC, you pay $100,000. A bargain, they say, because apparently it'll be worth a million soon.

So you pay the price of two solid cars for access to a piece of data in a chain stored on servers.
Is that fair? Yes, as long as no one hustled you into it, sold you fairy tales about profits, or tried to convince you that the price will skyrocket tomorrow.
If it was your own decision — it's a fair deal. Your money, your choice.

Humans are a funny species — they can assign enormous value to something that in reality has none, beyond the price driven purely by speculation.

I know people who trade crypto and get great results — better than in traditional markets. It doesn't matter to me. My priorities are different. What counts for me is peace of mind, the comfort of stability, and knowing that tomorrow the gold, oil, and stock-index markets will still be open.
I also like that the exchanges are closed on weekends. :)
I'm fine with my profits — my peace of mind is all I need. :)
I don't want more at the cost of stress and uncertainty.

Crypto exchanges? That's where you see dirty plays like **pump-and-dump** — junk coins pushed by celebrities or groups of speculators who jack up prices just to dump them on the naïve.

On the stock market, that kind of thing happened 100 years ago — but never at this scale and never this brazen.
Today's stock exchanges push such players out, though on low-volume stocks you can still sometimes run into similar setups.

For me, it's simple: I don't want to invest in something worthless or trade it. I prefer classic markets — stocks, commodities, sovereign currencies — things backed by something real.
I'm fully aware that fiat money — just like crypto — is nothing but digital records on bank servers. Only about 7% of global money exists as physical cash.

But fiat money has power behind it: the government, the laws it makes for itself, the police, the military, tax authorities, debt collectors... That's what creates "trust." :)

Techniques like artificially pumping prices and bailing out before the peak are classic dirty tricks aimed at taking money from the herd of naïve investors. You can interpret it however you want — for me, it's not a fair game.

What else do I consider utterly unfair?
When someone knows perfectly well that their **words shake the markets** and then tosses them around like dice — with zero responsibility.

Picture a "fictional president" of a major country.
Today he announces: "We're imposing tariffs!" — the market goes crazy, and investors panic. The next day he shrugs: "Actually, no... maybe another time." And the charts stagger like drunks again.
Some lose, others win — everyone dances in the chaos triggered by one man.
Would you want to live in such a world?
I would... but only if that president were my buddy, texting me things like: "Go short — I'm about to drop something to the press," or "I'm reversing — go long." :)

Absurd? Of course. And relax — this is just a literary example.
Any resemblance to real politicians or recent events is purely coincidental.
The point here is simply to show how powerful words can be in the markets — and how easily we could all become pawns in someone else's game.

30.2 Speculation!

That word triggers a lot of emotions — usually negative ones. I checked the internet's definition: speculation is the act of buying or selling assets in anticipation of a price change, aiming to profit from that change rather than from the actual use, ownership, or fundamental value of the asset.

In its pure form, speculation is fair.
And speculators? If they stick to speculation "in pure form," they're 100% fair. The big players who can create markets and manipulate them — that's a different story. The 2008 crisis made that pretty clear.

If someone, for example, deliberately hoards silver just to artificially push its price higher — to levels it would never reach on its own — that's manipulation, not speculation.
We're not oil barons — we're not going to corner the market by buying millions of ounces of silver, only to go bankrupt in the end.

Speculation, as a mechanism, is simply a free-market tool to self-regulate prices. That's exactly why **the free market remains the fairest way to determine value**.

30.3 The Free Market

Speculation, exchanges, Traders — they're all inseparable elements of a world built on a free market. Left on its own, the market will eventually reach a fair price.

I don't have a Nobel Prize in economics — so take this as my opinion, not an absolute truth. Even price manipulations by speculators are, in my view, a lesser evil than a regulated market where the government dictates prices. Of course, the world is more complex — there are exceptions. For example, fighting monopolies in the pharmaceutical industry is, to me, an absolute necessity.

Medicines are an "ethically sensitive" product because health — and often human life — depends on them. For most people, health and life are the highest values.

The irony is that for corporations, human health and life become just another commodity, something to profit from. The more, the better — regardless of whether this business model causes people to suffer or even die. Sure, there are exceptions in every industry... let's not go deeper into this one, since I know it a bit too well.

Take the case of a company that produces a drug effective against a disease — let's call it "Aid...". Hiking the price by 5,000%, from $13.50 to $750 per pill, should not be allowed.

If $13.50 was already profitable, raising the price by another $736.50 — knowing people must buy it to stay alive — is a clear ethical problem.

Another case: a drug for "Wils...". It used to cost $1 per pill, then suddenly shot up to $300 — that's a 30,000% increase. Annual treatment runs into hundreds of thousands of dollars. Pay or die. On one side — human life, on the other — corporate greed.

Go further — across the entire sector: if the patient isn't paying directly but the insurer is, why not raise prices endlessly?
Since the patient doesn't feel the impact firsthand, companies push prices up to levels that make health insurance a luxury. That systematically destroys access to treatment for ordinary people.

In such cases, the free market should not be the ultimate value, and greed should not be rewarded or indulged.

Compared to trading your own small account, the question of whether it's "honest" starts to sound absurd.
For me, trading your own account is one of the most honest ways to make money.
But to keep it fair, let's also look at the extreme case of large-scale speculation...

30.4 Speculators vs. Politicians

George Soros's trade against the Bank of England on Black Wednesday (September 16, 1992) made him about $1 billion. The pound collapsed. The U.K. lost. Did Soros do something wrong? How do you judge that ethically?

In my view, Soros was just one cog in the free market. The pound was going to fall anyway — its valuation was overvalued, propped up by bad policy and the state of the economy. Soros only accelerated the inevitable and exposed the weakness of the system. Instead of blaming him, I'd give him a medal and ask:
"How do we make sure the government doesn't waste money and doesn't cling to illusions of currency strength?"

Don't ask about the ethics of trading — ask what politicians are doing with our money. Watch the documentary **Inside Job** (2010) — a great lesson. Also watch **The Big Short** (2015) — it shows the mechanics and motivations. I don't want to get carried away, but what I see in our part of Europe looks like just another cash grab from citizens.

Politicians want people poor and dependent on the system.

Minimum wage hikes? They sound good – if you don't know basic economics. For companies, it means higher costs, so they cut jobs and raise prices on goods and services. The government celebrates because tax revenue goes up. Unfortunately, inflation rises too, purchasing power drops, and the very people who were supposed to benefit – actually lose.

Green subsidies? A bad joke. They take money from people just to "give it back" to others. The result? Subsidized products get more expensive because nobody questions costs anymore – it's "free money."
I know this industry – the only winners are the companies and producers, while, in theory, the ordinary citizen is supposed to benefit. Where's the logic? Heat pumps, panels, subsidies? Some of these things actually harm the environment.

Business subsidies? 60% of those ventures fail within 5 years. That's not investment – it's buying illusions with other people's money. People don't ask whether the business makes sense – they just ask how to get free cash. Of course, there are exceptions, but should everyone pay higher taxes for the sake of exceptions?

There are far bigger issues in this world than the ethics of a small Trader.

Finally: if you really want to find dishonesty, look at POLITICS. That's where money is printed and bribes are handed out under the cover of "caring for citizens." It's politics that enables banks and corporations to create global economic slavery.

I hate these topics. I feel a huge injustice about them – and at the same time, complete helplessness against the system. The only real solution? To have enough money so that, after paying everything the system demands, you can still live the way you want.

31 As a Trader You See Life Differently

As a Trader, you see life differently. Of course — everyone has their own perspective — but here's how I see the world now that I live off trading.

31.1 An Analytical View of Reality

I look at many aspects of life like a chart — I analyze them in terms of costs, risks, growth potential, and the point where it makes sense to place a Stop Loss (SL) if things don't go my way. Less sentiment, more profit — and I don't just mean financial profit.

For example, I've got a car I bought simply because I liked it. It's almost 20 years old, with a 5.7-liter Hemi V8, all-wheel drive — and it's a wagon. I paid a solid market price for it — not cheap. Bringing it to the condition I wanted already cost me about as much as the purchase itself. I'm afraid I'll have to put a bit more into it since a few flaws remain.

Does that make sense? A new car in that class would cost at least three times as much, and its depreciation over just 3–4 years would exceed everything I've invested in the old one. On top of that, repairs on modern high-end cars are very expensive because the engines are packed with electronics and eco-gadgets.

I don't need a car for ~37,000 miles a year anymore, and whether it's the seaside or the mountains, a V8 Hemi will haul my family and me without a problem.

It was a calculation: what do I want to get, what functions should the car fulfill, what emotions should it give me, what's the cost of entry, how much could I lose, and what are the alternatives.

Assuming the car stays with me for 10 years and I keep putting some money into it, the monthly cost of ownership will be about $200. After 10 years, I'll still have the same car — only more of a classic, nearly 30 years old. The V8 will still bring a smile to my face, and I'll still want to drive it.

Another 10 years of use would bring the monthly cost down to around $30 — even assuming a major repair comes up.

And I could always sell it. :)

Funny thing is, driving a big V8 costs me less than driving a Tesla charged at paid public chargers.

A car isn't just a utility. Its value isn't only in getting you from point A to point B — otherwise it would've been cheaper to take taxis for 10 years.

It's about the feelings and emotions you can't put a dollar price on.

For me, it was a great deal.

In an old comedy sketch, there was a great line:

"How much you make is one thing — but tell me:
how much can you lose?"

That's the key shift in perspective — looking at choices through the lens of how much you can lose.

Not just money, but also time, energy, and peace of mind.

The second factor is profit. Do the money and time you put in give you a return that's really worth it? Is the risk–reward ratio (R:R) satisfying?

A Trader, before starting anything, automatically estimates risk, potential losses, costs, and profits. Often it turns out that some projects aren't even worth touching — the profit is tiny, the costs are high, and in the end they'd probably end up in the trash anyway. Stop Loss too wide, R:R too poor, no realistic Take Profit (TP) in sight.

31.2 Looking at the Place You Live

Most of the time, when my wife and I thought about life, we felt tied to one place — work, our business, our kid's school, and so on. People are chained to their location because their income depends on it.

All you need is the internet and a few extras — like big monitors — and you can work from anywhere in the world. That's the beauty of it. That's what gives you a sense of freedom.

Yesterday (June 1, 2025), my country elected a president I'll be embarrassed about for the next five years. Is that a serious problem for me? No. I don't even live there anymore — we decided life would be better farther west. In about two years, there'll be another round of parliamentary elections — and again the risk that the kind of people I'd gladly pack into a rocket and launch to Mars will take power...

Luckily, I'm a Trader.

If I see that this chart is a long-term bear market with no chance of a breakout in my lifetime — I'd be stupid to sit in that position. So I pick another country instead.

31.3 Relationships, Connections, Friendships

Time is the one thing you can't buy back. If I waste some grains of rice from my bowl, I'll never get them back. That's why I have few friends — the ones I have bring me profit, not losses.

It's not about money. It's about the feeling that it was a good meeting, that the time wasn't wasted.

Sometimes it's about having fun, sometimes about an interesting thought. Sometimes it's enough just to sit quietly together and watch the sunset.

My advice? Cut costs fast.

Don't let anyone waste your rice on worthless things.

If you don't know what you did yesterday or last week, it means you didn't do anything important. If you met people and the next day you don't even remember it, it means it was just killing time.

Isn't life too short for meaningless things?

31.4 Tight SL and Quick Loss-Cutting

Probably the most important thing I've gained from trading is approaching life the way I take a position — with a strategy.
In trading, the one thing you can control with some precision is your losses.
That's why a tight Stop Loss (SL) is essential.
If something in life can result in a big loss while the potential reward isn't attractive, the risk–reward ratio (R:R) is weak — better to cut costs and not waste time.
There's no point in even entering that kind of position.

31.5 Good R:R, High TP — I'm In

If the reward is high, it's worth taking the risk — sometimes the goal is worth every penny, and then some.
The best long position I' ve ever taken has lasted for over 25 years – its dividends have grown beautifully, and the R:R is off the charts; call it 1:∞.

The most valuable things in life can't be bought with money.

32 The Source of Your Success or Failure

Here's the source of your success — or failure.
A professional Trader is the sum of technique and psychology.
Opinions differ... Some say success in trading is 10% technique and 90% psychology. Others argue it's 30% technique, 70% psychology.
One thing is certain — humans are rational beings, but reason usually loses when emotions kick in.

You've probably seen news stories where someone regrets committing murder and explains they were in such an emotional state that they couldn't think, acting purely on instinct.
Listen to Traders who blew up their accounts — or don't. :)
I'll tell you how it is.

At the start, you're smart, disciplined, proud of yourself. Then boredom, fatigue, and a need for action creep in — so you throw a bit more fuel on the fire just to feel alive.
Or you try grid trading — hey, the market keeps moving up and down in a range, so this should work.

In the end you forget all about your strategy, you trade like a monkey at a slot machine with its brain switched off, and you watch the chaos like a bad movie with a donkey as the lead actor.

It's not your strategy that's the weak point — it's your head.
Even if your strategy is weak, as long as your Money Management (MM) is solid, you'll have plenty of time to tweak it, improve it, and raise profitability.

But if you've got a raging monkey and a T-Rex in your head, no strategy will save you.
First, grow into a Trader — only then play the game.
Start by knowing yourself...

33 Who You Are — Personality Analysis

33.1 Once I Attended an Interesting Training Session...

Structogram is a method based on Paul D. MacLean's research. It divides the brain into three main areas, each linked to different behaviors and personality traits:

- **Red** (brainstem) — instinct, action, need for security
- **Blue** (limbic system) — emotions, relationships, feelings
- **Green** (neocortex) — logic, planning, strategy

Turns out I lean green. :)
Looking back, I see the personality traits for trading differently — and the conclusions they lead to.

Another interesting model is **DISC**, built on four basic behavioral styles:

- **D** — Dominant — confident, decisive, fast, loves challenges
- **I** — Influential — social, enthusiastic, inspiring, emotional
- **S** — Steady — calm, loyal, helpful, stable
- **C** — Conscientious — precise, logical, analytical, perfectionist

You can play around with tests like these out of curiosity and to learn more about yourself.

33.2 Key Personality Traits of a Trader

- Ability to act and make decisions despite risk and emotions.
- Ability to analyze technicals despite strong emotions.
- Gambling tendencies — taking high risks, breaking Money Management (MM) and risk-management rules.
- Ability to control emotions and reset after intense experiences.

I once read about a study of gamblers in Las Vegas who were also struggling with drug addiction. Researchers selected a group of such gamblers.

The group was kept long enough to feel withdrawal and crave their next dose. In that state, they were given a small amount of money to see what they'd do.

Most chose the casino.

The vision of winning — the dream and illusion of wealth — were stronger than drug cravings. Their thinking was probably, "If I play and win, I'll have enough for drugs — and for more gambling."

That test showed just how dangerous and powerful gambling addiction is — and trading sits dangerously close to gambling.

We don't see many Trader-gamblers because trading is a lonely game at home — and when such a gambler blows up their account a few times, they just quit this not-so-fun game.

Casinos are better at draining money from — let's say — "unfortunate players." :) For me, casinos have no charm.

I know every game has a statistical edge for the house.

What's the point of playing when the house will always take my money in the end?

In the market, nobody complains if you count cards and build a statistical edge. That kind of game makes sense. :)

33.3 Two Extreme and Dangerous Attitudes

33.3.1 Trader Type 1 — a Volcano of Energy, Knowing No Fear

Most often, a new Trader is hyped about trading and wants to jump right in to taste the thrill of easy money.

It's addictive, just like gambling. No time to study — those beautiful opportunities are slipping away...

You've got to trade because only by trading do you learn.

If that were true, a future surgeon wouldn't spend years studying and practicing — he'd grab a scalpel and run straight into the operating room to start cutting people open.

A Trader without knowledge, technical preparation, and mental readiness is like a child running blindly through the fog with a scalpel.

There's a 99.99% chance he'll hurt himself. I harp on this because I don't want you to waste years learning the hard way that this is a tough profession with no shortcuts.

You have to build new principles within yourself — often the exact opposite of what you've learned your whole life.

The result of chasing shortcuts is that, sooner or later, your account flashes the ugly message: "Margin Call."

That's the signal that the game is over — and that you need to add more capital...

But is that really the right conclusion?

If you've lost, do you really need to deposit more money?

"Insanity is doing the same thing over and over and expecting different results." — a saying often attributed to Einstein.

If you've lost, don't deposit more money and don't repeat the same mistakes. A loss is a signal — information that something in your trading isn't working as it should.

It's a sign that **you need to stop**, take a step back, look at everything with a cool head, and figure out where you're going wrong. Every mistake I know I've made is written down in this book. So if you find yourself in such a situation, go back to it and find the weak points in your strategy.

I suggest starting your analysis with risk management. Don't worry — when you finish learning, the market will still be there, running as always. If the markets ever stopped working, it would mean you'd need a machete to fight for your life — because the world as we know it would be over. Luckily, that's unlikely if you live in a stable country. And if not, becoming a profitable Trader lets you live where life is better.
It doesn't have to be the country where you just happened to be born. I myself don't live in my homeland anymore.
The charts are an endless story, and you can join it when you're ready.
And of course — when you've funded a new deposit. :)

33.3.2 Trader Type 2 — The Eternal Student, The Analyst

Some people get excited about trading and making big money in the markets.

They're people of action — but their "action" ends at preparation. This is the analyst type — loves the vision of wealth, feeds it with endless study, but shies away from risk. This eternal student is thrilled by the idea, but fear of risk and loss keeps him from ever trying, from ever experiencing what he dreams of.

If the thought of staking your own money — and possibly losing it — stresses you out, that's a warning sign. Maybe it's better than mindlessly risking your entire account, but both paths lead to the same result: you don't trade, you don't earn, and the dream of being a professional Trader vanishes.

Most often, we fear loss for two reasons:

- Losing money simply hurts too much.
- We're afraid that if we take a trade and lose, we'll prove to ourselves (or others) that we were wrong.

Some people really hate it when the market shows them they were wrong. If a loss hits your ego — that's a lesson you need to work through.

In the first case, ask yourself whether you're trading too large a position. Maybe you just need to size down so that a full SL doesn't sting. Losing $100 can be stressful, but if you shrink the position so it's only $5 — that's just a coffee in town. :)
Once you feel your strategy works, you can gradually increase both your position size and your Stop Loss, as long as you stay within your comfort zone.
It's like adjusting a thermostat: if you max it out right away, it's uncomfortable. But if you raise the temperature gradually, you barely notice when it gets really warm.

Adjust your position size
to your own "financial thermostat"...

The second case is tougher. :)
In my view, it's best if almost nobody knows what you do.
People I'm not close to only know that I work remotely, online — and that it's too boring to talk about. Only three people know that I'm writing a book, and I'd like it to stay that way.
This way I don't have to prove anything to anyone, and I don't need to buy a half-million-dollar car just to show the neighbors that the "gambler" actually wins.

Any outside pressure can be destructive. The only ones who know what I really do are my family and one friend — we've known each other for years, and thanks to me, he also became a Trader. :)
Even in Trader circles, I don't talk much. I prefer to listen, draw conclusions, and avoid the risk of my ego craving applause.
If my ego starts demanding flashy results to impress others — that's not about money; it usually ends in excessive risk-taking.

And I don't need impressive results. I want steady, reliable outcomes that let my capital grow calmly.
I don't want to be recognizable — it would mean unnecessary pressure, image-building, and a bunch of things I'm simply not interested in.

You need to look inside yourself and figure out what's holding you back in trading. Maybe we're alike and I just described exactly how you feel — or maybe not at all. And that's OK too.

I don't even know if I'm the "right fit" for this job.

Given how many years it took me to work on myself — probably not. It doesn't matter who you are. If you want something badly enough, you can change and adapt. It's only a matter of time, effort, and wisdom. You have to discover what needs fixing and what you still need to learn.

And ask yourself this one fundamental question:

Do you want to be right... or do you want to make money?

On the market, you can't always be right. To do that, you'd have to be a fortune teller and predict the future.

I don't know a single fortune-teller Trader.

But I do know Traders who consistently beat the market and make money. You won't win every single trade — that's guaranteed.

But do you really need to win every time to be a winner?

If your ego demands perfection, you've got a problem.Teach your ego that trading isn't a single shot — it's a long game of strategy.

Trading is like chess — it's made of many moves. Along the way you lose pawns and pieces, but only one thing matters: that in the end your king stays safe, and the opponent hears "checkmate."

By the way — "check" even sounds like the noise of cash coming out of an ATM, so the comparison fits. :)

You won't profit on every trade — what matters is that your equity curve climbs over the long run.

Think in stats. What counts is keeping losses and drawdowns small, in line with your strategy, while wins are big enough to push equity higher.

Think of trading as a game of many moves. Your task isn't to win every battle — it's to win the whole match.

Your Ego should focus on the end result, not the emotions after each trade. Your goal is to build a repeatable, effective strategy. Only that gives you a chance for stable profits.

A Trader's work is discipline.

It's keeping yourself from drifting off your strategy. It's catching, every day, the moments when your ego tries to take the wheel.

It's constant analysis, testing new concepts, building stats, reviewing your trades, and learning to recognize the patterns that give you an edge.

From the outside, it looks like a Trader just stares at charts.

In reality, his brain works like a processor — analyzing, calculating, checking.

In the end, you get one of two outcomes:

"I'm not trading because everything I see is inconclusive."

or:

"All the signs point to LONG — a hammer at the end of a correction, with solid volume, SL aligned with my Money Management (MM). I'M IN!"

And then the market does its thing.

If the analysis was good — often, though not always — there's profit. And that's the beauty of it.

Managing a trade in line with your analysis is pure pleasure.

Over time, you move your SL to breakeven, then below the most recent corrections, until a sign appears that the market is shifting — e.g., a supply candle. You close manually or set your SL just below the signal — and the trade is done.

You compare risk (SL) to profit — the R:R comes out 1:5.

Congrats — you just executed a perfect trade.

The opposite scenario:

You take a trade, the market hits your SL — you've got a loss.

You take 5 trades, all 5 stop out, and then one trade brings a 1:5 R:R win — you're back at breakeven.

And being at breakeven... that's not a bad result. :)

That's what this game looks like.
Lose small, win big — and your account grows.
Don't focus on single trades — they're just pieces of a bigger puzzle.
What matters is whether the whole strategy makes money.

And here's one more important thing...
What do you do when your SL gets hit?
If you entered, it means you saw a signal — say, a LONG.
You got stopped out — fine, but that doesn't mean your analysis was wrong.

Keep watching.
If your read on direction was right, the market may soon give another signal. Maybe it retests the low once more — maybe a few times — but if the level still holds, wait and look for an entry again.

Don't take it personally.
Sometimes the market needs one more retest before demand wins.
Then you go LONG again.
At the top, the reverse — you look for a SHORT.
The market will never let you get bored. :) It will always create new opportunities to trade and make money.
You just have to give it time. :)

33.4 New rules, often the opposite of yours

- Don't take risks, because by risking you can lose...
- You need certainty and stability to live a happy life.
- Rules are made to be broken. Who'd want to follow rules all the time?

And the Trader's reply: you can win only by taking risk in line with your Money Management (MM) and your strategy.
Stability is an illusion.
Stable profits from trading are real — and you can build a happy life on them.

Those who break the rules in trading end up bragging on FB about the one time they hit it big — conveniently leaving out that a moment later they blew up their whole account.

Think about your core rules and life maxims — and what I'd say back.

You've already read enough of my thoughts to probably picture me in a Sherlock cap, answering your questions.

And if you want, you can even argue with me — in your head. :)

33.5 What a Trader has to do is basically simple

- **You sit** down at the chart, fire up your broker's platform, and analyze the market.
- **You see** a setup that — based on your analysis — is an entry, so you take the trade.
- **You watch** what the market does and manage the position until it closes.
- **You close** with either a profit or a loss and look for the next entry.
- **You repeat** this for hours — some days I open the charts in the morning and shut them down more than a dozen hours later, taking only short breaks.

It's tough, but if you love analysis, understand the market, and feel how the chart "talks" to you, you do it with passion.

It's like being a compulsive gambler who spends the whole day in a casino and... systematically wins. :)

Can there be anything better? :) Simple, right? :)

Visualize each of these steps. Add emotions: greed, the urge to beat the market, acceptance of loss — and you'll see that what looks simple quickly becomes difficult.

Think about what would be hard for you and how you'd deal with it.

Just don't overthink it, because as soon as you start, you'll face a whole herd of questions and problems anyway. :)
Act. Learn. **Trade**...
But at this stage — **only on a demo account**.

You know those cases where a young guy studies a trade for five years in school, and on his first day at work he realizes he knows nothing and has to learn from older colleagues?
That's why you should study and **trade on a demo account in parallel**. You'll get the feel of the job. By trading, you'll better understand what I — and other market practitioners — are talking about. By trading, you'll see your own weak spots and find ways to fix them.
The key truth is this:

If you can't make money on a demo account — how on earth would you make money in live trading, with emotions added in?

I know of cases where someone made money on a demo account but couldn't handle live trading.
I don't know the opposite — someone blowing up a demo account and then suddenly becoming profitable with real money.
The first case: solid technique but weak psychology.
The second: a typical amateur who just wanted some fun, lost money, and decided it's pointless.
He moves on to something else.

Thanks for leaving your money with us — come back to the table anytime. :)
On LasBrokeras Street, amateurs are always welcome.

34 How to Look at Statistics and Where the Profit Is

Imagine you're a lousy beginner Trader.
You trade a small position, and your maximum Stop Loss (SL) is 30 points — that's a $10 loss.

If you take a trade on a smaller-candle setup, your SL is only 15 points — so you'll lose $5. Some trades will move your way, so you can move your SL to breakeven.

SL/R:R	-1	-½	0	1:1	1:2	1:3	1:5
1	-10$						
2		-5$					
3			0$				
4		-5$					
5					20$		
6	-10$						
7							50$
8		-5$					
9		-5$					
10			0$				
11	-10$						
12		-5$					
13		-5$					
14				10$			
15	-10$						
16			0$				
17						30$	
18			0$				
19					20$		
20		-5$					

On 20 trades:

4 times you took the full loss (–$10)
7 times you lost half the SL (–$5)
4 times you broke even
5 times you booked a profit between $10 and $50
Looking at that scoreboard — how do you feel?
Only 5 wins out of 20 trades — 11 losses and 4 breakevens.

34.1 Does This Trader Even Stand a Chance?

A Stop Loss (SL) of $10 with 1% risk means the Trader has a $1,000 account. Let's assume he's not running around the desert with a Kalashnikov, but patiently taking 5 shots a day.
That makes 20 trades in **4 days**.
If he shows up to trade consistently, 5 days a week, that's 100 trades a month — five times that table.

Now think: with that many losers and only a handful of small winners, is that good, bad, hopeless? Should the rookie pack it up and look for a "real" job at the supermarket?

Take another look.
What you're actually seeing in that table is a $55 profit.
From a $1,000 account, that's 5.5% in 4 days — or 1.375% per day.
Remember the simulations from earlier chapters?
How much do you need per day, per month, per year for the results to impress? Back then, I assumed 1.5% per day and 15 trading days a month.
If this Trader traded 5 days a week — like a regular 9-to-5 worker — then even without scaling position size or risk, he'd earn 5 × $55 a month — that's $275 on a $1,000 account.
Round it down — let's call it $250 a month.

That's still a 25% return per month.
I don't know a bank that pays that kind of interest — not in dollars, not in euros.
A year of discipline with those "lousy" results — and at the end, a pleasant surprise. :)

If you still don't believe trading can give you money and financial freedom — honestly, I don't know what else could convince you that you can become a millionaire. :)

Month	Start balance	Monthly profit	End balance
1	1 000 $	250 $	1 250 $
2	1 250 $	313 $	1 563 $
3	1 563 $	391 $	1 953 $
4	1 953 $	488 $	2 441 $
5	2 441 $	610 $	3 052 $
6	3 052 $	763 $	3 815 $
7	3 815 $	954 $	4 768 $
8	4 768 $	1 192 $	5 960 $
9	5 960 $	1 490 $	7 451 $
10	7 451 $	1 863 $	9 313 $
11	9 313 $	2 328 $	11 642 $
12	11 642 $	2 910 $	14 552 $
1 year:	13 552 $		

Starting with $1,000, after a year of trading, you're up over $13,000 pre-tax. After taxes and a little splurge as a reward, you kick off the next year with a $10,000 bankroll. No need to draw another table... then again... :)

Month	Start balance	Monthly profit	End balance
1	10 000 $	2 500 $	12 500 $
2	12 500 $	3 125 $	15 625 $
3	15 625 $	3 906 $	19 531 $
4	19 531 $	4 883 $	24 414 $
5	24 414 $	6 104 $	30 518 $
6	30 518 $	7 629 $	38 147 $
7	38 147 $	9 537 $	47 684 $
8	47 684 $	11 921 $	59 605 $
9	59 605 $	14 901 $	74 506 $
10	74 506 $	18 626 $	93 132 $
11	93 132 $	23 283 $	116 415 $
12	116 415 $	29 104 $	145 519 $
1 year:	135 519 $		

Alternatively — after taxes and a big splurge as a reward, you start the new year with a $100,000 account. No need to draw another table... but then again... :)

Month	Start balance	Monthly profit	End balance
1	100 000 $	25 000 $	125 000 $
2	125 000 $	31 250 $	156 250 $
3	156 250 $	39 063 $	195 313 $
4	195 313 $	48 828 $	244 141 $
5	244 141 $	61 035 $	305 176 $
6	305 176 $	76 294 $	381 470 $
7	381 470 $	95 367 $	476 837 $
8	476 837 $	119 209 $	596 046 $
9	596 046 $	149 012 $	745 058 $
10	745 058 $	186 265 $	931 323 $
11	931 323 $	232 831 $	1 164 153 $
12	1 164 153 $	291 038 $	1 455 192 $
1 year:	1 355 192 $		

Drama... You've got to pay taxes on more than $1.3 million.

That hurts.

Three years...

On paper, it looks simple, but in real life, staying disciplined for three years is a serious challenge. Still, think about it — turning a thousand into a million in three years isn't exactly a small reward.

With profits like that, pulling out $5,000 a month for a calm, modest lifestyle is no problem at all.

After another year, you've got $10 million in the account — you can spend $10k–$20k a month and you won't even notice it in your balance.

One more year and you might not even feel like working that hard anymore.

If I were 20 again, with today's internet and trading opportunities — and with what I know now — I'd sit at the computer five days a week, eight hours a day. After three years, with my stats, I could relax for the rest of my life.

The only thing is... I'm not sure I would have met my wife then.

So maybe it's better not to mess with time travel. :)

34.2 Villages From Excel Tables...

The most important takeaway, in my opinion, is this:

IT IS POSSIBLE!!!

You don't need genius-level trades or spectacular results to make money in the markets.

In one of those tables, just five average wins were enough to lift the stats to an average of more than 1% per day.

When you look at such tables — or build them yourself — and see how tiny amounts turn into hundreds, thousands, then millions, and eventually cosmic numbers, the feelings that come up are beautiful, motivating... and deceptive.

These calculations are true, real, and achievable — with one caveat: you're human, and humans are weak.

My uncle used to say:

"I have a very strong will... but only for a short while." :)

My father used to say I had "flash-in-the-pan" enthusiasm — meaning whenever I find a new goal, I get excited... then drop it just as quickly and forget it.

Apparently, that was a flaw.

From my perspective, my father just wanted me to achieve something. To start something and see it through to the end. And that was a fair point.

The thing is, I was a teenager back then — I didn't know who I wanted to be or what I wanted to do.

There was no Facebook, YouTube, Instagram, TikTok — not even a stock exchange in our country.

So how was I supposed to discover my goal and purpose back then? :)

Those Excel tables are real, but they miss one factor — you. They don't account for the human element and its weaknesses.

If you want to turn $1,000 into a million in three years — you can. The question is: are you ready to put in the work every single day, for hundreds of days and thousands of hours?

Will you be able to tame the emotions that will shake you during this multi-year marathon? Can you maintain discipline and stick to your strategy that long?

It's only possible if you build the right habits.

If you think it's easy, start and try. You'll see for yourself how it works for you — and whether it's really that simple, or if it takes serious work on yourself.

For me, one thing is clear:

Spending your whole childhood studying, then finding a job between 20 and 25, keeping it for 40–45 years, and retiring at 67 — that's madness.

I wasted almost half my life before I realized I wanted to live differently. You've got the chance to hear what's screaming in my head and think about what you really want from life.

Recently, my wife told me she met one of our daughter's friends.

He finished school, joined the army, and was later assigned as a paramedic at a hospital.

Around 40, he'll be able to retire with a military pension.

And he'll still be able to work as a paramedic — because that gives him satisfaction.

That's a great life plan.

Not for me — but definitely for him. That's the point: to find a life plan that fits your needs and your nature.

Every plan takes work. Every plan has its dark sides. And no plan is just "easy and pleasant."

Pursue your path stubbornly, and don't let go.

The saddest thing you can experience is that moment, with the last grains of rice slipping away, when you realize you could have lived your life better...

Be relentless and, with stubborn persistence, search for your purpose and your own path to a good life.

I only got that purpose within reach at 50.

I know it's late.

I know many have lived their lives better than I did.

Maybe I'm not a master of life or the king of the world – but I'm satisfied with myself.

And even a little proud that I was so stubborn in the search... and that I finally found it.

Maybe I'm not the best example, because many have done it faster, smoother, and more effectively – and those are the people worth learning from.

Still, I believe I have something to share.

My path to purpose can be an inspiration to you.

Just don't make as many mistakes as I did. :)

You can reach your goal faster. :)

I'm rooting for you.

35 Stop Loss — The Foundation of Risk Management

There are two types of Traders:
Some always set a Stop Loss (SL), and others never do — because they prefer to close a position manually when they feel the loss is already big enough.

A moment ago, you saw a table where 11 of 20 trades ended in a loss and 4 broke even.
The final result was still positive — only because the Trader strictly followed Money Management (MM) rules and consistently honored the SL. I don't believe it's possible to achieve that by manually closing losing positions.

35.1 I Always Set an SL

I use a custom MT4 panel to execute trades; it automatically sets both SL (Stop Loss) and TP (Take Profit) the moment I open a position.

That's a U.S. index.
The SL size might look massive — 5,000 points sounds serious — but it's just a difference in how the panel and the broker's platform calculate points.
The broker quotes prices with two extra decimal places compared to the panel.

I don't want to bore you. :)

In practice, those 5,000 points are just 50 points.

That's a bit more than my strategy normally allows, but even then, right after entry I usually cut the Stop Loss (SL) to about 40 points — or less — depending on which candle I place it under (low or high) and how much breathing room I need.

On other instruments — like crude oil, gold, or EUR/USD — I use smaller SLs in points (but the cash risk is the same).

It all depends on the typical volatility of the instrument.

But that's a topic for another book. :)

Why am I so focused on having the Stop Loss (SL) set the moment I open a position?

Because the one thing we can truly control is losses.

Of course, a price gap can happen — so the loss may end up bigger than planned — but over a long series, with hundreds of trades, the average should stay within acceptable limits.

What can happen if you enter a position first and only then set your SL?

- The market can suddenly drop 100–200 points — and you take a loss that's too big. That triggers stress and might lead to stupid decisions.
- Your computer can crash.
- Your internet connection can cut out.
- Your broker's platform can freeze.
- You can have a power outage.

In any of those situations, I know one thing:

My position is secured with an SL, and I won't lose more than I allow. If the price moves my way, a Take Profit (TP) set at 10:1 will close the trade automatically. If the price moves my way, a Take Profit (TP) set at 10:1 will close the trade automatically.

I'll have time to switch from fiber internet to mobile data, fire up a second computer, and log in to the platform.

No stress.

My orders always have a protective SL and a solid TP in place. So even if everything around me crashes — I have nothing to worry about.

Trading without a preset SL can turn into an expensive lesson.

35.2 SL at –53 Million PLN (Over $14,000,000)

On April 13, 2025, Rafał Zaorski posted on X.

https://x.com/rafal_zaorski/status/1911486280052916243

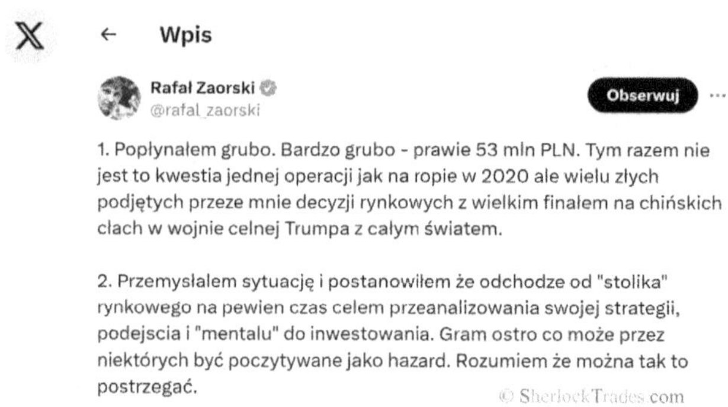
Wpis

Rafał Zaorski
@rafal_zaorski
Obserwuj

1. Popłynałem grubo. Bardzo grubo - prawie 53 mln PLN. Tym razem nie jest to kwestia jednej operacji jak na ropie w 2020 ale wielu złych podjętych przeze mnie decyzji rynkowych z wielkim finałem na chińskich cłach w wojnie celnej Trumpa z całym światem.

2. Przemyslałem sytuację i postanowiłem że odchodze od "stolika" rynkowego na pewien czas celem przeanalizowania swojej strategii, podejscia i "mentalu" do inwestowania. Gram ostro co może przez niektórych być poczytywane jako hazard. Rozumiem że można tak to postrzegać.

Rafał is from Poland, my home country — that's why I follow what happens there.

He described how one of his trades ended. It was a complex process involving multiple positions.

The result?

A loss of almost PLN 53 million. That's a massive amount.

I don't want to judge whether the trade itself made sense or whether the size of that loss was reasonable given Rafał's capital.

What I want to show you is this: once you step into this game, you can lose big.

That's why, before you even start, you must define your rules — your risk level, your limits, your strategy — and refine many other elements if you want to have a real chance at success.

You probably don't ever want to see numbers like the ones Rafał showed in his post on X show up on your account.

I'll be back ...

"Każdy przecież początek to tylko ciąg dalszy,
a księga zdarzeń zawsze otwarta w połowie." WS

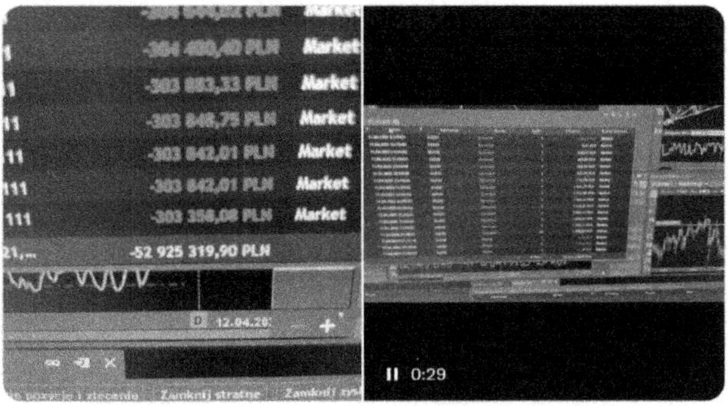

8:26 PM · 13 kwi 2025 · **1,8 mln** wyświetleń

1 tys. 377 5 tys. 1 tys.

Because Rafał shared not just his wins but his losses, we can learn — without paying the same price for the lesson.
Rafał, if you ever read this... I'm rooting for you. May the market be kind to you, and may everyone get what they deserve.

35.3 My SL Got Hit, and I Could Have Had a Profit...

This is a very common thought among beginner Traders: "If I hadn't set an SL, I would've made a profit because the market reversed right after stopping me out."
Even the best entry gets taken out sometimes. The market will always do what it wants — not what we think it should do. If your analysis says a level is a turning point on the chart, it only means it likely is. And that's the key phrase: "with high probability."
This game is not about always being right. It's about one thing: making money trading.

You can be wrong on six trades out of ten and still come out ahead. All you need is for the four winners to more than cover the losses.

That's why it's so important for our trades to keep losses small. That's why it's so important for technical analysis to help us find levels with a high probability of a reversal, where the **potential** profit outweighs the risk many times over.

If I see a setup on the chart where the potential profit is at least three times my SL, and all the conditions of my strategy are met — I take the trade. Because it's the size of the SL that tells me whether the setup is worth entering.

If my analysis tells me that, with high probability, it's going to be a long, but the required SL is beyond my Money Management (MM) limits — I skip it. You don't need to catch every opportunity. It's enough to catch the really good ones.

When I see a setup that looks great but would force me to use too wide an SL — I skip it. I keep watching, because if a big move is about to unfold, it's worth waiting. If I stay alert, then in that move — as Elliott taught — there should be a first wave.

After that comes a correction, the second wave. At its end, maybe a nice geometry shows up, maybe a candle with a clear volume signal. And if not — then maybe the third wave will break the first wave's high, and that could be the spot to get in.

The key is to find opportunities with big profit potential and low risk — not to chase everything that looks promising.

In trading, you've got to be picky. :)

35.4 The "Katyusha" Effect

During World War II, the Soviets used rocket launchers called Katyusha (Russian: Катюша). The psychological effect was powerful — the rockets were terrifying: the noise, the fire, the sheer barrage quickly broke the enemy's spirit.

Their actual combat effectiveness, however, was limited.

Accuracy — terrible. Reloading time — long. And yet they went down in history because they made such a massive impression.

Your Checklist:

- Trend – Is the trade in line with the trend on the time frame you're trading?
- Scenario Checklist – Does the chart situation meet the conditions of the scenario you've defined?
- Entry Signal – Did a clear entry signal appear exactly where, according to your scenario, you expect the move to continue in the direction of the trend?
- Tight SL – Is the size consistent with your Money Management (MM)? Does the number of points make sense relative to the current daily range on the chart?
- High R:R – Does your R:R give you an edge? Are you projecting at least three times the risk in potential profit? Is there room for a big move and a high TP?
- We Trade – If the analysis shows this is a great spot that fits the strategy and all parameters align, we trade.

You don't want to create an amazing impression... you want real results. Katyusha generated high costs for modest actual gains. If not for the psychological effect, it would've been a failure in my view. You have to be different. Fewer shots, carefully chosen targets with high R:R, and lower risk thanks to solid MM and a properly set SL.

That's how your trading should look.

36 Money Management — How Not to Go Bankrupt in a Day?

36.1 The Book Is Unnecessary If You Follow Four Rules

Sounds simple, right?
Over 300 pages become unnecessary if you stop doing stupid things and stick to these four rules.
Why didn't I think of this earlier...

36.1.1 Find the Right Chart Analysis Technique

It sounds trivial, but for someone just entering the game, it can be a real challenge.
On Facebook, I sometimes click investment ads — so the FB algorithm assumes I'm into that topic and keeps throwing more at me. It's scary how many ways a new Trader can waste time and money by buying into some "genius" simple idea for quick market profits.

I promised not to go deep into that in this book — and I'll keep that promise. **First**, because there are plenty of effective techniques out there, and I don't want to bore you with mine if you already have your own method and are only interested in the psychological side. **Second**, because it's too broad a subject to combine with psychology in one book in any meaningful way.

If you're completely green — start by researching the best Traders in history and seeing what techniques they used. These are methods that actually gave them an edge — and they proved it.
The next step is to understand whether a given technique is actually usable for you. If someone uses a system built on complex knowledge, data, and analyses, it may work for them — but for you it could be useless.

When I was searching for my own technique, I wanted a complete, closed system — one that doesn't require magical interpretations or access to secret signals.

I wanted something I could truly understand, that made mathematical and economic sense, and that I could master well enough to use consistently for decades.

Eventually, I chose a technique based on VSA — Volume Spread Analysis. This approach focuses on analyzing price action in combination with volume.

If you want to know more, read about people like:

Richard D. Wyckoff (1873–1934) — American Trader and analyst, considered a pioneer of the ideas underlying VSA.

Tom Williams (1931–2016) — British Trader who in the 1980s formalized VSA, turning Wyckoff's concepts into a candlestick analysis system that incorporates volume.

To be honest, Wyckoff's name is legendary and widely recognized, but what Tom Williams created and shared is a real goldmine of priceless, practical knowledge.

Search the title of his book — "Master the Markets" — and you'll quickly find a PDF.

Tradeguider
https://www.tradeguider.com › mtm_251058 PDF
Mastering The Markets
... markets. Tom Williams, a veteran trader and author of this work, has been energetically applying his expertise to profit from t...

"Master the Markets" — Tom Williams.

It's funny how people say various gurus have "changed lives." Sure, it's nice to read someone like Osho — his perspective on many issues is spot-on.

But if I had to name one person whose work truly changed my professional life, it would be Tom Williams and his VSA methodology.

For me, it was like a Copernican revolution.

Honestly, I don't really care whether the sun circles the earth or the other way around — day still follows night.

Which chart analysis technique you choose is entirely up to you. You need one you really understand.

Will I ever take on the challenge of writing a book about the methodology of technical analysis — I don't know yet. It's a huge amount of work and countless hours in front of the screen.
I do mention it at the end of this book, though.

36.1.2 Build Algorithms and Checklists for Trading

For trading to be a science and not an art, it has to be repeatable and statistically validated. And for it to be repeatable, you need clear criteria. That means every market entry has to be clearly defined and verified with a checklist.

If conditions A, B, C, D, and E are met — then you trade according to MM. Once you've developed specific entry scenarios that trigger your positions, you can start collecting statistics.

If you play out 100 trades with scenario "X" and it turns out that:

- 70 ended in losses,
- 10 breakeven,
- and only 20 made a profit,

then you can see for yourself that flipping a coin gives you better odds.

But if your system shows, for example:

- 60% winning trades,
- 10% breakeven,
- 30% hitting SL,

then check the average R:R and calculate the technique's edge.

Make yourself a simple table. Assume a full SL is $10 — you're trading small; no need to go crazy. Your average R:R is 1:2, which means you win twice as much as you risk. After 100 trades, that system would add $900 to your account.

Keeping stats is worth it. It shows you where you're heading and keeps you disciplined.

36.1.3 Define Your Money Management Rules

This is probably one of the most important points — and yet it can be summed up in a single line. :) Only a chatterbox like me needs more space to explain it. :)
First:

Risk only what you can afford to lose.

Since you're reading this book, I assume you're not making rookie mistakes anymore... right?
For the sake of example, let's assume you have $1,000 and your base SL (Stop Loss) is 1% — $10.

- **Size of SL (Stop Loss) in $**

Whether it's dollars, euros, or any other currency doesn't matter.
What matters is that you clearly define the maximum loss you're willing to take on a single trade.

I recommend starting with a demo account and setting your SL at 1% of capital.
After 50–100 test trades, if your method shows clear positive expectancy, switch to a live account and reduce your SL to 0.25% of capital.

Then, after another 100 trades, analyze the results:

- if it's still working well — increase to 0.5%,
- then to 0.75%,
- and ultimately to a maximum of 1% of capital per trade.

I don't recommend going higher, but it's your money.
For me, 2% is the absolute ceiling, though there are "tough guys" who run a 3% SL.
I'm not in a hurry — I'd rather trade calmly, without excessive risk or stress.

• **Size of SL in Points/Pips**

The SL value in dollars is one thing, but on the chart, SL is expressed in points, ticks, or pips — depending on the instrument.

Let's say you set a $10 SL (1% of your account). You trade as a Day Trader, so a position opened, for example, at 2 p.m. today will be closed before you go to sleep. $10 is a reasonable risk compared to your capital. The problem starts if your analysis shows that this $10 translates into 300 pips, while the market volatility in recent days has only been 100–200 pips.

You've set your SL so wide that a stop-out would mean a move equal to 1–3 days' range. But you plan to close the trade today.

If you're also expecting R:R 1:3, it means you're hoping for a 900-pip move in one day. That's a stretch... but you get the point?

Your entry must be at a potential starting point for a bigger move. That move has to deliver a profit at least three times your SL.

If your SL is $10, and its distance is, say, 30 pips — then there's a realistic chance the trade will close today and pay off nicely.

• **Why 1%?**

Because theoretically, you'd need to lose 100 trades in a row to blow up your account. It's highly unlikely you'll be consistently that wrong.

This setting is safe and gives you enough time to notice that something in your technique isn't working before you suffer a major capital loss. Once you master your strategy and the stats confirm you can afford to risk more — that's your call.

• **Why at least R:R 1:3?**

Because if you aim for smaller profits, the math may leave you at breakeven or even below.

And you're not putting in all this effort just to end up at zero.

Here's a simple calculation:

- Win rate: 50/50 (winning and losing trades)
- Average R:R = 1:1
- 50 losses × $10 = −$500
- 50 wins × $10 = +$500

You're at breakeven, provided you cover fees.

With an R:R of 1:1.5, you'd be up $250 (25% profit on $1,000 capital over 100 trades).
The SL amount in dollars is non-negotiable — at least for me. :)
A fixed percentage (e.g., 1%) of capital per trade is the cornerstone of Money Management.

- **What about SL in pips?**

SL in pips, ticks, or points? That depends on volatility.
On a daily chart where one candle runs 100–200 pips, I'd set SL around 20–30 pips.

And those 20–30 pips must equal $10 of risk — which means you size the position in lots (or fractions of a lot) off that..
If the daily candle runs 300–500 pips, I'd still keep a $10 SL, set around 40–50 pips.

Do a test:

- Open last week's chart.
- Check where your analysis suggests an entry.
- Run a simulation — see which SL would have held and how much profit you could have made by following your rules.

And one more thing...
If you don't know how to calculate position size for, say, a $10 risk with a technical SL of 30 pips, contact your broker's support team.
Let them earn a bit of those commissions. :)

Or experiment on demo:

- set an order of 0.01 lot with a 30-pip SL
- see how much that is in $
- if it's, say, $5, then you can trade 0.02 lot — because then 30 pips = $10

Simple, right?

Remember!

Always check and test on demo first. If it doesn't work on demo — it won't work with real money.

And if it works on demo — start light, with a 0.25% SL.

If it keeps working — scale up gradually.

Don't push your mind into emotional overdrive.

Get comfortable at 0.25%, then dial it up slowly.

If you overdo it, the kettle will boil over.

36.1.4 Recommendation 4 — Never Break This Chapter's Rules

It sounds obvious — yet so many people break them, as if they wanted life to hand them a souvenir kick.

A kick that reminds them breaking the rules is a bad idea.

Have a different opinion?

The market will always take your money.

36.2 How to Survive a Losing Streak

In my country, we say fate throws logs in your path.

These are life's obstacles — either you overcome them or you quit.

And as a Trader, I guarantee you'll face plenty of them.

And they're the real test of whether you can succeed in this game.

Weak people — when they hit a real obstacle — usually give up.

After all, it's the easiest excuse to quit.

When you encounter an obstacle on your path, you have no control over the fact that it's already there.
It's already in front of you — that part has happened.
What matters now is your reaction.
What do you do when faced with an obstacle, a problem, something that blocks you?

I run my analysis program:

- Is this a warning sign?
- Maybe this path isn't the right one?
- And if the path is right and the goal is behind the obstacle — then I care only about one thing: how to get past it at the lowest possible cost.

The faster and cheaper, the better. No point obsessing over obstacles.
A losing streak is just another obstacle.

So you need to run the analysis program:

- How long is this streak?
- Has something like this happened before?
- Has the market changed?
- Maybe volatility has increased and my SL in pips is too tight?

If you identify the cause, you know what to do.
If you can't find the cause, but you've been sticking to your rules — cut your SL from 1% to 0.25% and keep trading.
When your stats improve — increase SL to 0.5%, and later back to 1%.
Write down what happened.
Maybe it was just a random string of unlucky trades.
Or maybe your approach just needs tweaking.
Not sure why trading isn't working for you today?
Switch instruments. Or take the day off.
Tomorrow's a new day. Maybe the market will be kinder. :)

36.2.1 Set Your Safety Rules

If you've hit a losing streak — do you really want to keep it going, or do you want to cut it short?
In my view, it's always better to stop and analyze what's happening.
A losing streak eats away at your emotions.
You might feel the urge to get revenge, win back the losses... and suddenly dream up a "brilliant" idea to break your Money Management (MM) rules.

Be careful.
This is exactly the moment that separates a professional from a rookie who's just itching to pay for another painful lesson.
That's why you need to design your own safety rules.

Examples?

- Take a one-hour break if you lose twice in a row with 3 full Stop Losses (SL).
- Take the rest of the day off if you feel emotions are taking over.
- The 3-bullet rule — you can take three trades a day.
  Only three.

Only three trades a day means you really have to pick your shots.
If you hit at least 2:1, you earn an extra bullet.
This way you protect yourself from a flood of weak trades.

If you spot a recurring problem in your trading — create a vaccine for it. Preferably before it spreads.

37 How to Increase Your Trading Profit Fivefold?

I know, you'd love it to be easy and for me to hand you a magic fix right now.
Fine. I'll share the secret with you — but this is a serious book, so it won't be some miracle method ripped from a Social Media ad:

"You know nothing, you have nothing — buy this for only 47,90 $ and in a week you'll be a millionaire genius.

They laughed when I started, and now they're borrowing money from me."

If for even a split second you thought that ad had something for you — stop being naive.
If you want to increase your profits, you'll have to put in real work.

37.1 The Foundation of Every Method to Boost Profits

Think of it like your car.
Under the hood you've got a steady 5.7 HEMI, V8, 340 horsepower.
My 5.7 AWD was so lively that in the first week after buying it — out on the road it leapt up and... took out a pheasant for me. :)

That car has exactly what I expect.
I look at it and I smile. I start the engine — the V8 growls.
I hit the gas and it jumps forward like a wild stallion.
Every drive puts a smile on my face.

And yet, it doesn't stir up much emotion in people — it's an old car. No stickers shouting that it's a big V8. No roaring, "broken" exhaust that makes the whole neighborhood turn their heads. Nobody envies me — nobody pays much attention.

And most importantly — it didn't cost hundreds of thousands of dollars.

It fits my approach to managing living expenses.

Price-to-joy ratio: perfect.

Lots of fun at low cost.

So let's take this "patient" as an example.

37.1.1 Motivation

0–100 km/h in about 6.5 seconds.

At over 2 tons, that's decent — nothing spectacular.

It's a bit like trading: your results are stable, but you want more.

Why do you want more? Are you racing someone?

Some guy in a little Japanese car with a big turbo beats you at a stoplight?

Do you have a goal and just want to get there as fast as possible?

What are your priorities?

Think carefully about what matters most to you.

Could chasing profits beyond what you've already achieved just feed an emotional need — while putting your core life goal at risk?

For me, the most important goal in trading is:

- earning a living
- building a calm, secure future

I don't know what your goal is.

For me, increasing profits is great — as long as it doesn't threaten my core goal.

Any method that boosts profits without increasing risk is worth considering.

Higher profits at the cost of higher risk?

No thanks.

37.1.2 The Basis for Increasing Profits

Let's assume you're a Trader, you're profitable, and you want more. You've got your calm 5.7 HEMI and you dream of turning it into a furious SRT — or even an extreme Hellcat or Demon.
Over 800 horses. Zero to 100 in 2.3 seconds. That's what you think you need.
The question is: why? What's the motivation? What's the goal?
Let's assume you've made a conscious decision: "I want more."

Where do you start?

- You check out available tuning kits.
- You look at the performance of those who've already modified this machine.
- You search for a workshop that can do it right.

Before you rebuild the engine... you need to check the baseline.
Is everything solid enough that adding power won't end in a blown engine and a totaled car?
To know that, you need data.
Sensor readings. Measurements. Parameters.

And it's exactly the same in trading.
If you're doing it consciously, you have:

- a Trader's Journal
- trade summaries
- performance statistics
- info on R:R and the volatility of your equity curve

The data shows whether **there's room to grow** — or whether every tuning attempt will just blow up your account.

Without stats, you don't know:

- how much you're really risking
- what's working
- what changes when you introduce new rules
- which tweaks actually deliver good results

Without it, you can't safely get better results.
Of course, you can do everything "by feel" — because "you just sense it'll work."
Just remember:
Flying a jet through fog without instruments, you can slam straight into Mount Everest — not because you're a bad pilot, but because you ignored the data. I don't like bureaucracy either.
I hate entering numbers, calculating, analyzing.

But you know what I hate even more?

- wasting time, wasting money
- walking blindly, not knowing where I'll end up or what I'll smash my head against

That's why I force myself.
Excel spreadsheets. Trade journal. Analysis.
That's the prerequisite for any tuning.
Do the analysis, collect the data, and see what's safe and what's possible.
Without it, all you'll do is blow up the engine.

37.1.3 Two Tuning Options

- **The best, coolest, dream-come-true option.**

This is for dreamers: you hand your car over to a tuner, pay 35,000 dollars to have everything done properly and safely.
You pick up the car with a shiny supercharger, reinforced transmission, new exhaust — and under the hood, more than 600 horses.
First corner, foot to the floor and... that sudden surge of power sends torque to the wheels that can't hold it on the asphalt.
You lose traction, fly off the road.

If you're lucky, you survive and make enough
to buy a new car. If not, it's game over.

- **Boring, no adrenaline, nothing flashy.**

In this option, you do everything calmly.
Small changes — like a new camshaft, a software update.
The result? Fifty more horses, but still under control.
The car drives much like before, just a bit sharper.
You test, analyze, check if it suits you.
Over time, another idea comes — you analyze the data again, make the next upgrade.
Until you reach the point where you have to decide: stick with sensible improvements, or go extreme — big turbo and full madness?
My suggestion?

Go get your thrills off the charts.

Let that be the reward for steady, profitable trading.
In the market, it's better to introduce changes slowly and safely — step by step. Extreme parameter tweaks usually end badly.
The main goal is to reach your destination without wrecking the machine — or yourself.

37.2 Tuning Stage 1

You've analyzed your data. The equity curve is rising steadily — your average daily growth is 0.3%, and the Stop Loss (SL) on a single trade is 0.25% of capital.

These are safe, balanced results. You can trade like this for years, building capital step by step.
Looking back at the last three months, the longest losing streak was 15 trades. The analysis showed it was a mix of tough market conditions, technical mistakes, and weaker mental form.
You learned from it, and since then your results have stayed stable.

If you now increase your position size by 4x (with the same SL in pips), your risk per trade rises from 0.25% to 1% of capital.
That means in a similar losing streak you could lose not just 4% but 15–30% of your capital — a level of risk that triggers stress and lowers the quality of your trading.
That's why every change must be introduced gradually and carefully observed.

Doubling SL from 0.25% to 0.5% could lift profits from 6–7% a month to 12–14%.
At 0.75% SL, you're looking at around 20% monthly profit.
At 1% SL, about 27%; at 1.5%, over 40%.

But remember: bigger positions mean not only bigger profits, but also bigger risks. That's why your decisions must always be based on long-term stats.

Start on a demo account — make sure your strategy works and you can consistently manage risk. Once you achieve stability on demo, move to real funds, but start with small capital and an SL of 0.25%.
That's a safe level that lets you calmly adapt to trading live.
Only when your results confirm it — scale up your position.

Gradually. No rush.
Ramping up risk too fast can trigger emotions that wreck your plans. On paper you'll be ready, but mentally you won't handle it — so climb slowly, steadily, and eventually your results will surprise you in a good way.

37.3 Tuning Stage 2

A common mistake among beginner Traders is closing profitable positions too quickly while letting losses run.
It should be exactly the opposite. :) You need to cut losses quickly and let profits run. :) If you want to tune your trading, you need a profitable strategy and solid data to compare results before and after making changes.

Introduce changes one at a time and analyze the effects – if you change several things at once, you won't know what worked and what didn't.
Another area worth tuning is how you manage and close positions.
Before I worked on that, I often broke even or closed trades with an R:R between 1:1 and 1:3, averaging around 1:1.5.
After changing my approach and working on position management, my average R:R climbed to 1:3 and higher.
Better position management boosted my profits – and made trading much calmer.

I've prepared Long and Short position management cards and I stick to the plan.

At the end of this book, you'll find a "buy me a coffee" banner – if you appreciate this book, you can buy me a symbolic coffee, and in return you'll get my cards as a gift.
I've got them printed and laminated – I mark on them which phase the trade is in.
I can see what I'm waiting for, when to move SL up or shift it to TP, and when to close if the market starts showing strength the other way.
These cards were the start of the next stage of tuning my trading. Without them I wouldn't have mastered position management as I have now, and achieving high, repeatable R:R results would have been impossible.

37.4 Tuning Stage 3

Solid long-position management naturally forced me to watch the chart closely – during rallies and during pullbacks.
This book wasn't meant to cover trading technique, but since I've brought it up...
I'll share a bit more than I planned.

In fact, this belongs to the mental side of trading, because the way you manage trades is very much a mental game. The right technique shapes the right reactions and mindset. Everything has to align and work together.

So how does this position management look in practice? :)

Let's assume you open a Long position and the price starts rising. I analyze price and volume, so I see that demand is in control — rallies are impulses, and pullbacks are just corrections.

If the chart is clear and the market sends strong signals, I can calmly watch the rise. When a pullback shows up, I see low volume in it, so I know it's just a correction. At the end of that correction, there's often a perfect spot to open another Long.

That's exactly the level where I move my SL — which means I lock in profit from the first entry.

And now two things happen:

- the SL from the first position effectively becomes a TP if the market reverses,
- and I can open another position — within the same move.

If the move has potential — why make money only once?

Of course, I only add when the earlier positions are already secured. It would be foolish to risk 1%, then another 1%, and then another. Breaking MM rules like that always ends badly. Always.

I haven't calculated exactly how much this boosts my returns, but solid chances to pyramid positions usually come every 2–3 days. Instead of banking 5×SL, sometimes it turns into 10–20×SL.

It's worth practicing — because it improves results, builds discipline, and forces focus.

You're not just managing an open position — you're constantly hunting for the next setups.

My position management card shows on one side where to move SL, and on the other it marks potential spots for new trades. :)

Isn't this job great? :)

37.5 Bad Tuning — "Doubling Down"

If you've ever had the idea to add more to a losing position, hoping for a rebound and a quicker recovery — **forget it**.

The cemeteries around casinos are full of people who tried to beat roulette using the "Martingale" system. :)

The rule I follow without exception:
Never add to a losing position. Never!

What's cheap can always get cheaper. What's expensive can always get more expensive. Price is the result of speculation and the forces of supply and demand.
Check the record low of crude oil futures in 2020 — it'll remind you that **sometimes even zero is too expensive.**

For fun, I once tested whether you could beat the casino at roulette. I built myself an Excel sheet, tracked results, and tried to play only long streaks, betting on a change.
For example, if red came up 10 times in a row, I'd bet on black. I analyzed not only colors but also other combos, trying to spot some statistical edge by mixing patterns.
I didn't find one. :) That's why I'm a Trader. :)

Martingale is a "clever" system that only works if you've got unlimited capital and no betting limits.
You start with $1. After 10 losses, you'd need to bet $512 just to recover everything and win... $1. By then you've already dropped $1,023.
By the 20th bet, the stake tops half a million dollars, and your cumulative loss is about the same.

Believe me — if you try to save yourself this way, you'll end up broke.

38 The Myth of What a Trader "Must" Do

38.1 A Real Trader Doesn't Play on Demo — That's for Wimps

The so-called "real" Trader is a tough guy, proudly losing money because, hey, it's just small change — and he'll make it all back on one big trade...

Don't fall for that kind of myth.

The foundation of being a professional Trader is not losing money. This principle is best summed up by the legendary investor Warren Buffett:

"Rule No. 1: Never lose money."

"Rule No. 2: Never forget Rule No. 1."

A real Trader treats trading like a business.

If you can test whether something works — for free, without losses and without stress — why wouldn't you take advantage of it?

Open a demo account with your broker. Take 20, 50, or even 100 trades and check whether your theory holds up, or whether it needs fixing.

On demo you can do whatever your imagination suggests. Blow up the account? No problem — just add another million and keep playing.

But remember: **if a strategy doesn't work on demo, don't expect it to magically work live**. In reality, it only gets harder. Don't want to "waste time" on demo because you think opportunities are slipping away?
OK — maybe you need proof that it's not opportunities slipping away, but your money.
First demo — and proof that the strategy works.
Only then go live.

38.2 The Most Famous and Legendary Trader Started on Demo

If you ask who was the most famous speculator in history, you'll come across the name Jesse Livermore.
As a teenager, he worked in a so-called "bucket shop" — the equivalent of today's Market Maker brokers.
He quickly discovered a talent for numbers and for sensing repeating patterns in the quotes he received via telegraph. There were no candlesticks, no charts, no online quotes — data came in on ticker tape and had to be read by hand.

Livermore jotted his predictions in a notebook — marking the moments that felt like opportunities, then checking whether he was right and how much he would have made or lost.
Only when those notes proved that his strategy produced solid results did he put real money on the line and start trading live.

Even such a legendary speculator first tested on a "demo account" — in his notebook — before risking a single dollar.

He also taught something else: that the hardest skill is to **"sit on your hands" and wait.**

"I never made money in the market until I learned to sit tight and wait. The greatest difficulty isn't trading — it's patience."

38.3 How to Understand Buffett's Rule "Never Lose Money"?

Every trade, every market entry carries the risk of losing money. There's no other option — you're always taking on risk.

- Your market entry must align with your risk and capital management rules.
- It must be in line with your trading strategy.
- It must be based on your technical analysis — you need a clear entry signal.
- It must have a cost — every entry carries the risk of a loss within the limits set by your strategy and Money Management (MM).

Before Warren Buffett bought shares of any company, he conducted thorough analysis — finances, market potential, and long-term outlook. He invested only in companies with a future — ones expected to generate growing profits.

Did he take risks? Yes. Every investment decision carries risk. Not making a decision carries risk too. Look at his track record — Buffett also had losing investments and closed them at a loss. But he never let one position ruin him. He had a plan, a strategy, and knew how to cut losses. He never let his ego keep him tied to a sinking ship.

It's worth listening to Buffett — his results speak for themselves.

Some of my favorite quotes from Warren Buffett:

The best thing you can do after a mistake
is admit it and learn from it.

We don't have to be smarter than the rest.
We have to be more disciplined than the rest.

Discipline and consistency lead to success — not fantasies and flashy trades.

38.4 Trader Must Follow Market News...

I don't read, listen to, or watch the news.
I don't waste my time processing informational noise.
The only thing I care about is **the timing of key data releases** or announcements on a given instrument — because only that moment can move the chart.
I don't care what the news says.
What matters is how the market reacts — and I'll see that on the chart. Timing matters, because that's when the unpredictable can happen.
Why don't I analyze the content of news? Because all the big players get it before I do. They'll react first, and I have no idea what their reaction will be.

What's the market reaction to good news? Prices go up?
Here's the answer: prices go up, down, or nowhere.
Good news might already be priced in.
Its release might just confirm expectations — and then the market takes profits.
Or the news could be good, but not good enough, and investors get disappointed.
There are many possibilities, but the conclusion is always the same:
It's not worth focusing on the news itself, because you can't predict the reaction. Better to just watch the chart.
Is this the only right approach?
I don't know — it's my approach. :)
You do it your way and test the results of news analysis.
Maybe you'll discover something I haven't. :)

38.5 A Trader Must Be a Real Tough Guy

The moment I hear that I "must," a warning light instantly flashes in my head with the word: STOP.
I don't have to do anything.
At most, I can choose to.

Over 2,000 years ago in Greece lived Aesop — remembered for his fables that carried life lessons.

One of them tells the story of the oak and the reed:
"One day, an oak tree — mighty and proud — looked with disdain at the reed growing beside it.
'Why do you bend every time the wind blows?' it asked.
'Look at me! I don't bend. I stand tall, proud, and unshaken.'
The reed replied gently:
'I don't envy you. When the wind comes, I bend. But when the storm arrives, I survive. You, though strong, may be broken.'
And indeed — a powerful storm came.
The oak split and crashed to the ground.
The reed survived — bent, but not broken."

Being a Trader is a profession.
The goal is to make money, not to prove anything to anyone.
Trading is a long-term endeavor. If some part of it demands too much effort, in the long run it becomes too heavy a burden.
That's why I write so much about calm trading — not stressful gambling for huge wins.

It's a marathon, not a sprint.
If you sit in front of the chart and feel the market choking you, it's a clear sign you're breaking the basic rules.
Can you endure that stress for the next 10 years? I'd bet not.
Either you'll quit, or you'll end up with a heart attack.

In trading you need to be tough — tough enough to stick to your rules.

----

39 My Trading Workspace

If you expect my office lined with gold and overlooking the world's priciest districts — sorry, I can't deliver those AI-generated images.

I am who I am, and I ask you not to judge that.
Not because I really care — it's about something else.
When you build expectations, attitudes, and judgments, you only hurt yourself. That's a universal truth that goes far beyond this book or this chapter.
There's a wise saying:
"Don't judge a book by its cover" — although in my opinion, my cover turned out pretty good. :)
And another one:
"Lotus flowers grow in the mud."
Sometimes I wonder why I'm even writing this. :)

I'll show you where I work — at the exact moment these pictures were taken, I was writing the very book you're reading now.
This is where I trade, this is where I spend many hours every day.

I don't like spending money unless it's really worth it. I'm more of a Gen X guy (I think... I'll check later how they classified that).

I like doing things myself, with my own hands. I like coming up with something, testing it, using it — if it works.
That gives me satisfaction.
Sometimes the ideas are great, sometimes just average.
You have to improvise.

The trading space means a lot to me.
I sit there for hours — it has to be comfortable, ergonomic, so that afterward nothing hurts and I feel good.
In my Trader's workspace, I faced two major challenges and one minor one...

39.1 I'll Start with the Simpler One — the Desk

I didn't have to look for a desk — when we closed the company, I kept a few pieces of furniture, including this big, heavy desk. Here's how it looks...

A top-down view — maybe not like an Ikea ad, but I hope that beyond the mess you'll see what I had in mind when choosing it.

- It has height adjustment — I was able to set it so my arms rest freely on the surface, with a relaxed, natural posture instead of a forced one.
- I rotated the desktop so the part with the old monitor stand (which I removed) became my seat side — now my arms rest comfortably on the protruding edges.
- Those blue fabric parts are soft cushions I added myself, playing upholsterer — it may not look perfect, but it's comfortable, and that's what matters to me.
- The desk stands on felt pads, so I can slide it around easily whenever I want.
- I mounted all the wiring under the desk for the computer, keyboard, and mouse, so everything's tidy and nothing gets yanked or snagged.

39.2 The Chair and a Comfortable Sitting Position

I tested many chairs and was always disappointed.
I'm a difficult customer when it comes to chairs, because I expect couch-level comfort — and no office chair ever gave me that.
I couldn't find anything that fit, so I designed and built something myself. :)

It's a seat from the last-generation Renault Espace. :) I wanted comfort and elegance — leather, fabric, all breathable, with manual adjustment so I didn't have to mess with electronics.
It was supposed to be super comfortable... but it fell short.
I figured I didn't want to keep searching for another seat from a different car.
So I decided to upgrade the factory version. :)

I built a solid wooden frame that, thanks to a fabric bottom, slides easily on the floor.
No wheels — the seat doesn't roll away, and that's exactly what I wanted.
The bottom cushion is multi-layered, shaped to the seat profile. I wanted a soft, flat surface.
On top: a breathable coconut-fiber mat, under that 10 cm of foam, and beneath it all — the original Renault seat. :)

The backrest had solid side supports, but they weren't needed — when watching charts, the movement is up and down, not side to side. :)
I adjusted the cushion through trial and error, and once I mounted it, that's how it stayed.
Where I'm from, we say, "temporary fixes last the longest." :)
If I ever get bored, I'll finish it properly. :)
I experimented with the headrest, since it was too far back.
I tried different cushions, but since my neck doesn't get tired, I let it go.

The position is semi-reclined, with arms resting on the desk. That's optimal — part of the weight on the bottom, part on the back.
What I cared about was good blood circulation.
The seat choice was average, but after modifications and DIY tweaks — it works brilliantly.
I know it looks funny, but the comfort is excellent, and I don't have circulation problems in my legs.
On regular office chairs I always had that issue during long hours of work.
Here, the chair–footrest–desk combo with arm support works perfectly.

39.3 The Footrest

It's not very clear in the pictures, but under the desk I've got a large footrest on wheels with thick cushions.

Its surface is about the size of one and a half seat cushions. I adjusted the height so it's about level with the chair seat — together they form an almost flat surface.

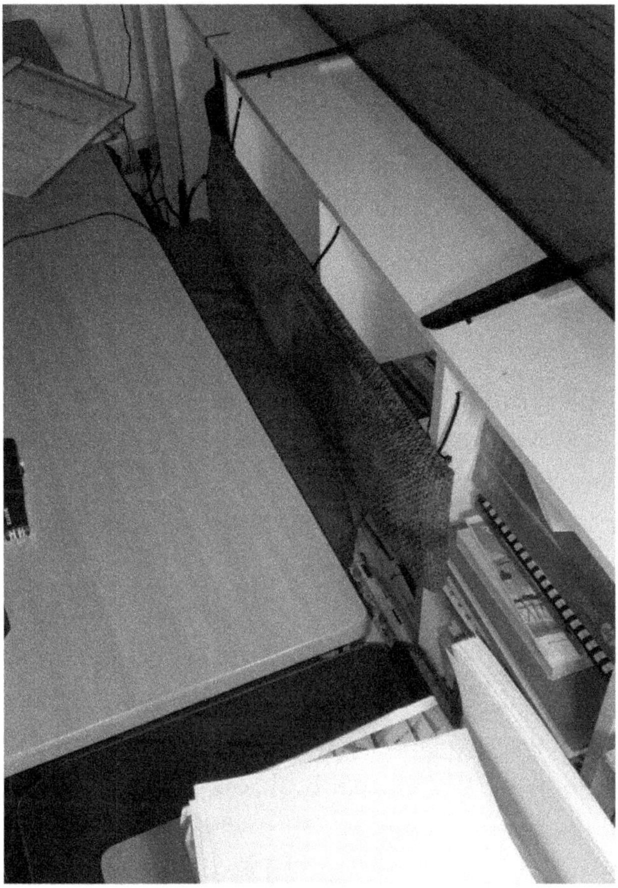

The cabinet that holds the monitor (actually a 75" TV) is just a shelf unit turned on its side — it happened to be what I had, and it fits perfectly. Between the desk and the shelf you can see the footrest cushion, and on the shelf, strapped on with zip ties, I attached another DIY cushion. :)
It's a board padded with foam and a layer of coconut mat, upholstered in fabric.

It works great — when I'm sitting, I can rest my legs on it, which keeps me from sliding lower and lower in the seat, like what happens with chairs that don't have a proper leg rest.

39.4 Computer, Printer, Monitors...

On the left side of the desk, on a stand, sits my desktop computer used exclusively for trading — and now also for writing this book. :)

On the right — an inkjet printer with refillable tanks, cheap to run. I can print as much as I want.
To complete the setup, I've got a laminator and a paper cutter, so whenever I come up with a tool, like a checklist, I can "produce" it right away.

Monitors were always a tricky issue for me.
Whenever I looked at how people set up their workstations, nothing about it appealed to me.
I wanted a screen the size of a wall — no limits on window placement.
About four years ago, after lots of experimenting, I decided to buy a 75-inch TV as my main monitor.
On that screen I can fit everything I want — arrange the windows my way, with no constraints like having six separate monitors.

I went, bought it, plugged it in and... it's amazing.
The comfort of working on such a huge screen is incredible.
I'll show later how the charts look on it, but I can already say: working on such a large monitor is a whole new level of comfort.
The size also means I can stand up and still see everything — no problem changing position.
I once tried a desk with an electric adjustable height, but that's probably better for typical office work.
In trading, you don't really need to write books :) — so raising the desk doesn't matter.

The giant monitor is a fantastic solution.
I'll never want to go back to small monitors — aside from one side screen next to the desk.

That's pretty much how it looks right now.
On the left – a small monitor, around 27", luckily not one of those short panoramic types, so it actually holds a lot.
On that monitor I run the broker's platform to place orders, while all the analysis happens on the big screen.

Around the monitor I keep 15 key cards with the things I always want in front of me.
My friend Chris had to dismantle his trading setup every evening, so he copied all my cards into a file and projected them onto the wall next to his desk. :) Smart guy. :)
It worked great for him – he could change on the fly whatever he wanted to keep handy.
There are endless ways to organize a trading workspace.

39.5 Light, Air Conditioning, Fresh Air

What matters in this room are the windows with blinds — I can block out light when the sun gets too strong.
In summer, it's great to trade with the windows open, because oxygen is fuel for the brain.
When it gets too hot, I close the windows most of the way, leave them slightly open, and turn on the air conditioning.

Without AC, working at the monitor on hot days would be unbearable for me.
Proper lighting is important too — the area around the monitor should be bright, so your pupils narrow and your eyes don't get as tired.
A dark room with a bright screen used to give me headaches after a while.
When I turn on the lights behind me (so they don't reflect on the screen) and behind the monitor, the fatigue fades and the headaches disappear.
Does it look pretty? I don't know. Honestly, I don't care.

The only thing that mattered in setting up this workspace was my comfort.
This is my private space in a separate room, where no one enters except the household.
I don't invite people here, I don't run trainings.
It's my space. I'm showing it to you because maybe something here will help — maybe spark an idea for your own setup.

40 Tools I Use and Why

I'm not saying Sierra is the best tool in the world – I just use it. I didn't do any deep market research. Some of my friends who trade professionally were using it, so I checked it out, liked it, and stuck with it.

Quite often I use tradingview.com to check different things. In my opinion, it's a user-friendly platform where I can easily find stocks, ETFs, and other instruments. I don't have a paid subscription, so the data is probably delayed, but to see whether something is already dropping on the 1-day chart :) – that's more than enough for me.

In my trading, I mainly use two things: the MT4 platform from my broker and https://www.sierrachart.com/ for chart analysis.

40.1 Why MT4?

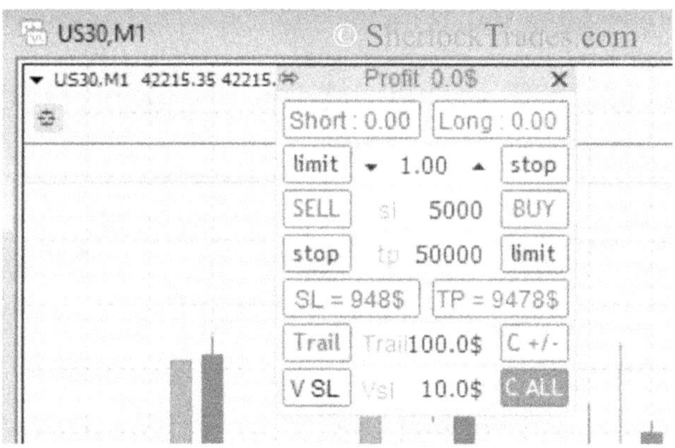

I've tested different broker platforms, and each one has its pros and cons. I'm a minimalist – it has to be exactly what I need, nothing more. I even commissioned my own custom panel for MT4 that covers all my requirements (see chapter 35.1).

Why this choice? Every option has its pros and cons. For me, the decisive factors were leverage and negative balance protection. But that's not really a topic for a psychology book. :)

40.1.1 Always Set SL and TP Immediately

For my peace of mind, it's crucial that every position has an SL (Stop Loss) and TP (Take Profit) order right from the start.
What you see in the picture above is my custom trading panel.

The SL order must be precisely defined and placed at the moment of entry — this panel handles it automatically. I don't have to count points or click around — I just hit buy or sell, and everything is set according to my money management rules.

I use limit and stop orders only in special cases, for example when I trade a breakout of wave 1, anticipating a longer move after a trend reversal. In the screenshot, the SL might look odd (like 5,000 points), but that's for the Dow Jones contract. The broker quotes with two extra decimal places, so instead of overcomplicating things, I just set it to 5,000 — which in reality equals 50 points. That's still more than usual — after entry I manually adjust the SL line into the 25–40 point range.
I don't use wider SLs because I assume the move will be about 100–150 points. Without an R:R (risk–reward ratio) of at least 1:3, the trade makes no sense to me.

40.1.2 Automatic Position Sizing as % of Deposit

The panel has two options for position sizing. You can set it manually — then the lot size stays fixed — or in the settings you can specify that the SL should equal, for example, 1% of your capital. Then — depending on the number of points you've set for the SL — the program automatically calculates the appropriate position size.
I usually set the position manually, immediately seeing the cash amount of the SL. Calculating 1% of the deposit is trivial — with good stats, I size the position so the SL is roughly 1.5%.
After entering a trade, I fine-tune SL placement, and it usually turns out the actual risk is under 1% — sometimes a bit more, like 1.2–1.3%. On average, the SLs that get hit on my trades are about 30 points on YM. And here I am rambling again. :)

40.1.3 Other Features I Wanted to Have...

At the top, there's a "profit" display — the total profit or loss from all open positions on a given instrument. That's useful during longer moves when I'm holding several positions — I can instantly see how much I'm making overall.

Below that, there's a Short and Long counter that shows how many lots I currently hold in each direction.

The SL and TP amounts shown in dollars are super convenient — no need to calculate anything, I can immediately see the potential loss or gain.

The Trail function lets me set an automatic trailing stop — for example, $100 behind the price. If I've got a decent profit and want to grab a cup of tea, I just switch it on. If the price keeps moving, the stop moves up and locks in more profit.

V SL is a virtual Stop Loss — separate from the SLs set on individual trades.

Let's say I've got several trades open with a total profit of 250 USD. If the chart starts looking shaky, I can set a V SL at 150 USD, and if the total profit drops to that level, all positions close automatically.

I don't use C+/-. That button closes all winning or all losing trades — not something I find useful.

C ALL — I do use when there's a strong signal in the opposite direction of my trades and I want to close everything at once manually.

When it comes to opening and managing trades, I don't need anything more.

40.2 Why Sierra Chart?

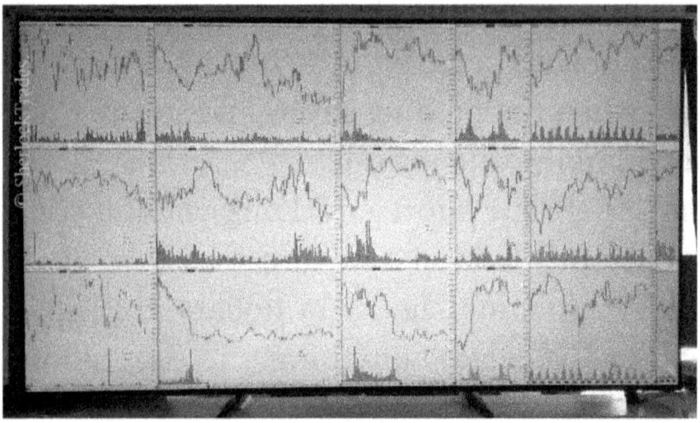

This is what my charts look like live on the monitor.
Sierra lets me set up everything exactly how I want. For a fee, it gives me real-time data plus all the measurement and markup tools I need.

Right now on my 75" screen I'm tracking three instruments: E6, GC, and YM.
From left to right I've got the timeframes:
1m, 5m, 15m, 60m, 240m, and 1D.

The 5-minute chart takes up the most space, and the 1D the least — basically just the tail end of the last two weeks.
This setup lets me see everything that's happening on these instruments at a glance. That's what my workstation screen looks like...

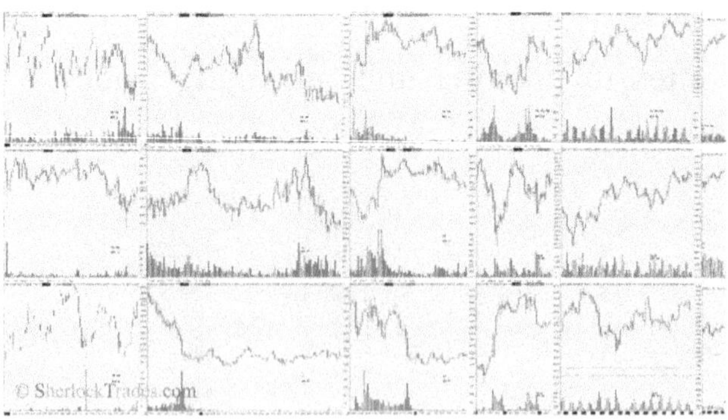

I can zoom in on any chart, analyze it in detail, add annotations, and so on. What's key — markings from higher timeframes automatically show up on lower ones.

Sierra — in my opinion — isn't easy or intuitive, but it's learnable. Even if you're 50 and weren't born with a smartphone in hand. :)
In the book you probably can't tell, but live my eyes are about 150 cm from the screen and I can clearly see every candle, every wick, and every volume bar.
If I were to change monitors, I probably wouldn't go bigger... maybe 80" would still be fine, but 100" would be too much.
Even now, when I look at the top right corner, I'm at the edge of being able to catch fine details sharply.
Although, knowing myself, when this monitor dies I'll probably buy a 100" anyway — I always prefer bigger... but that would be the absolute max.

40.2.1 How Much Does Sierra Cost?

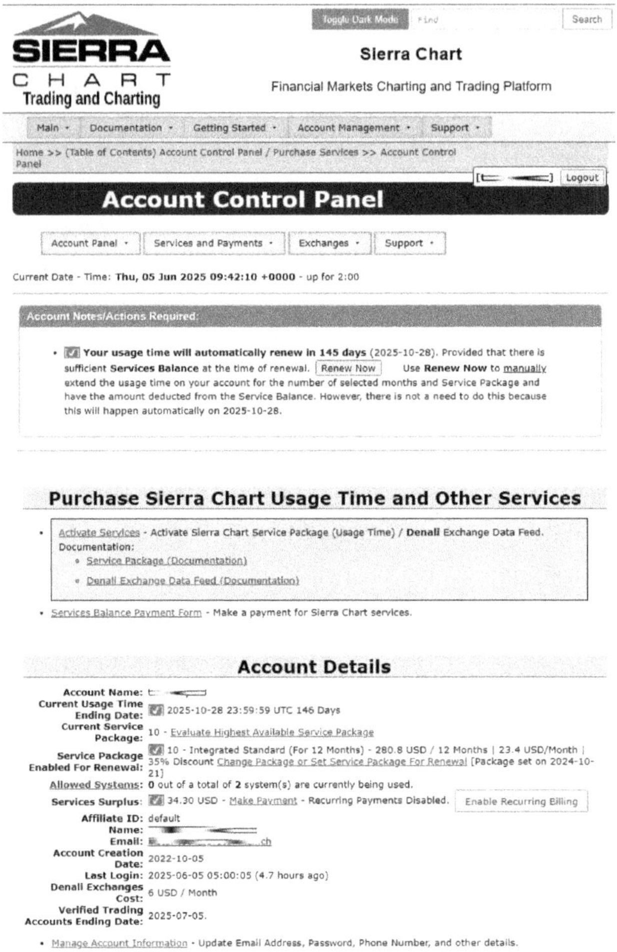

Here's what I'm paying right now in 2025.
If I pay Sierra once a year, it comes out to about $280 — just under $24 a month.
On top of that, Denali data is $6 a month.
To get these rates, you need to be an individual Trader and link your Sierra account to a broker accepted by the platform, like IB.
So for $30 a month you've got a tool that lets you analyze charts like a pro.

I won't go into the details here — that's material for another book on chart analysis, strategies, and so on.

I'll just say this: mastering all the settings and putting my tools into the shortcut menu took me about two days, and yeah, I complained a bit about how complicated it was.

Sierra is a universal tool, which means it comes packed with so many options and functions that you really have to dig to find the ones that fit you best.

Once I set everything up the way I wanted, I couldn't imagine switching to another charting platform.

What I have now does everything I need. I can zoom, mark, and measure charts at any scale, with pinpoint precision.

At this point it feels like an extension of my hand. :)

Compared to MT4, it's like an old bicycle versus a sports car.

41 Rituals and Habits — Daily Routine

This is a section you need to write for yourself.
There are no fixed rules saying you must do it this way. You have to listen to yourself and design a daily routine for trading days.

Why routine?
Because routine automatically triggers the emotional state you want to be in.
When you sit down at the table and know food is about to appear, your body starts producing saliva, you lick your lips...
Nothing is on the table yet, but you're already ready.
This is a well-known phenomenon — the so-called "Pavlovian response."
Ivan Pavlov, the Russian physiologist, received the Nobel Prize in 1904. He's most famous for his experiments with dogs trained to associate a specific stimulus (like a sound) with food — the sound alone triggered a physiological reaction.
If you've ever had a dog, you know the reaction when you touch the food bowl...
That's exactly why it makes sense to create a ritual before starting your trading session — it automatically puts you in the state you want to be in when you sit down to trade.

I'm working on adding a regular morning walk with poles along the river to my ritual — up at six, moving for an hour.
I know it's a great idea, but sometimes I just don't feel like it.
I'm sticking with it because I know it's good for me. Then a shower, meal planning, and prepping everything so I don't have to break away from the charts later.
Coffee, a bottle with juice, vitamins, minerals...
Checking messages — does anyone need a reply.
A quick look at market news — just in case the world ended while I was asleep.

A few words with friends and then I start reviewing charts.
I clear out old markings from yesterday, analyze the situation, and mark the levels worth watching more closely.
My ritual is a calm entry into the rhythm of market analysis.

Sometimes there's an errand — groceries, the mechanic, whatever.
Today I went to change the oil — unfortunately the mechanic bought the wrong kind, so tomorrow my ritual starts after I get back from the shop.
Having to go somewhere is not a problem.
I don't feel pressured to sit from morning till night and squeeze the charts like a lemon.
I approach it without pressure.
Whatever the market gives — I'll gladly take.
If it's generous, I'll stay until evening. If it's moody, I back off and wait until it calms down.

The more relaxed I am about trading, the better I do.
Relaxed doesn't mean without rules. Rules are sacred.
But it also doesn't mean you need to play on your knees. :)

Create your own rituals and train your inner self so that at the sound of the bell you're focused and ready to trade.

In the last century, Austrian psychiatrist Viktor Frankl, who created the concept of "paradoxical intention," taught that too much tension and pressure block natural action. Letting go frees the mind to work more naturally, often making it easier to reach your goal.
In trading, it's worth easing into the market — without pressure, without artificially pumping emotions or stress.

42 How to Double This Book's Value with Two Clicks?

I honestly have no idea how, but... :)

If I had to guess what could increase the value of this book for you, it would definitely be your own work with it: notes you'll come back to until you achieve what you've decided is important for you.

When you read it again sometime later, you'll see it differently and draw other conclusions — because by then you'll already be a different person.

What else?

I'm planning to launch a YouTube channel where I'll publish my analyses — market situations that I believe were both interesting and predictable based on the chart.

The purpose of these videos is, on the one hand, to show where to trade, and on the other, to explain the "mechanics of the market," so the chart isn't just a bunch of lines but a readable story showing cause, effect, and the process of price formation.

Of course, it's not all sunshine — you can't explain or predict everything on a chart. But the goal of a Trader is not to predict or explain everything.

The goal of a Trader is to patiently wait for the moment when the market behaves clearly and in a purely technical way.

In those moments, we can take trades with low risk and high probability of success.

It's exactly those trades that build strong stats. You can subscribe to my channel — once it's live, you'll decide for yourself if it's valuable for you.

https://www.youtube.com/@SherlockTrades

Honestly, the growth of this channel is up to you.

If you enjoy my book and I get a comment, a review, or even a small tip — I'll know it was worth the effort. I mention "Coffee" because for me it's a signal that the content really helps you — it's not about the dollar.

I don't know how you perceive what you're holding in your hands. After all, this wasn't written by a professional author or a PhD in psychology. Without your feedback I won't know if it made sense.

Time will tell. :)

I'm an optimist and don't give up easily, so YouTube videos will definitely come — I'll start working on them once the writing and publishing of this book are done.

More than half of trading success lies in what's in this book. What's still missing is the other leg a Trader needs to stand steady — the craft of chart analysis and trading strategies.

Friends who've read and reviewed this book keep urging me to start writing the next one right away — on technical analysis.

They probably don't realize how much time and work this one took. Let me put it in Trader's terms: that's a very wide Stop Loss with a completely unpredictable risk–reward ratio... and right now I'm not sure it's a trade worth taking.

If this book on trading psychology is well received and I see positive feedback, I'll know it was worth writing — that it helped someone and makes sense as my contribution to making this world a little better. Then I'll sit down, invest a few months, and write a book on technical analysis — with my approach to the market, entry strategies, and trade management.

If you'd like to be the first to get the info, leave me your email on the website:

https://sherlocktrades.com/books/AT

I promise — zero spam. Apart from the signup confirmation, you'll only get two messages: one when work on the book starts, and another when it's finished and ready.

43 EGO

I'm just an ordinary Trader who's managed to succeed on my own small, private scale. Maybe not entirely "ordinary," because after many years of mistakes I finally joined that tiny percentage who make money consistently. :)

I want you to know that I'm just a regular guy. I don't have a huge EGO constantly demanding more and more.

If right now the thought flashed through your mind: "I'd like to be known, famous, I don't want to be ordinary" — then you've just caught a thought worth pausing over. Behind it there may be a serious issue to work through.

In life — and especially in trading — EGO is your enemy.

- EGO doesn't want to admit mistakes. But trading is a constant cycle of admitting mistakes, learning from them, and... making the next mistake.
- EGO wants to be right. A Trader's job is to make money — not to be right.
- EGO holds on to a losing position because "maybe it will turn around," and closing it would mean admitting defeat.
- EGO takes wins and losses personally — but in the market it doesn't matter, because the market doesn't even know you exist.

EGO is like a nasty little program running in your head — like a tumor. If you let it grow, it can take over your whole life. It will start feeding you goals that serve it, but not you.

And you'll be the one paying the price.

EGO has no single, precise definition — but everyone knows exactly what it is.

Take care of yourself, your happiness, and your own interests. Not some made-up self-image.

----

44 Exercises for Focus and Attention

If you use a search engine, you'll find a whole set of methods to improve concentration and sharpen attention. There's so much out there that you'll surely find something that suits you.

Below I'm listing what I've tested and know, and at the end — what I actually practice myself. If any of these exercises interest you, you'll find plenty of material online on how to do them properly.

I don't want to bore you with theories. I don't know what will work best for you. What I do know for sure — it's worth finding your own way to calm the mind and build focus.

When you sit down at the charts, your thoughts might still be scattered by what happened earlier — tasks, problems, emotions.

You need to cut that off. Quiet the mind.

Focus only on one thing: charts, analysis, strategy, trading.

- **Trataka** (yogic tradition)

Description: Staring at a candle flame without blinking until the eyes start watering.

Purpose: Quieting the mind, increasing focus.

Origin: Ancient yoga (hatha yoga, raja yoga).

- **Exercise with ticking clock** / noise / movement

Description: Focus solely on one auditory or movement stimulus (e.g., a clock's second hand).

Purpose: Training selective attention.

Origin: Military schools, Zen techniques, NLP.

- **Counting backwards** (e.g., from 100 by 3s)

Description: Counting down from 100 in steps of 3 (100, 97, 94...).

Purpose: Engaging active concentration, loading working memory.

Origin: Cognitive psychology (Baddeley, Stroop tests).

- **Sensory loop** (mindfulness)

Description: Focus in sequence on: 5 things you see; 4 you hear; 3 you feel; 2 you smell; 1 you taste.
Purpose: Anchoring the senses in the present moment.
Origin: Modern psychology (MBCT/MBSR – Jon Kabat-Zinn).

- **Closing the mind** (thought pause)

Description: Imagine stopping every thought – as if you hit the "pause" button.
Purpose: Breaking the stream of thoughts, controlling attention.
Origin: NLP, Zen meditation, special forces training.

- **Mindful looking** (at an object, artwork)

Description: Observe one object for 3–5 minutes, mentally describing every detail.
Purpose: Training perception and visual focus.
Origin: Gestalt psychology, Montessori education.

- **Body scan**

Description: Mentally shifting attention through the body – from feet to head.
Purpose: Grounding in the "here and now," stress reduction.
Origin: Buddhism, MBSR (Jon Kabat-Zinn).

- **Fix & Breathe** (visual fixation with breath)

Description: Sit still and fix your gaze on one point (e.g., a dot on the wall). Breathe slowly through your nose, counting each inhale and exhale up to 10, then start again. If a thought arises, just return to counting.
Purpose: Synchronizing visual and breathing focus, calming the nervous system, training resistance to distractions.
Origin: Zen practice, sniper techniques, focus training in sports.

In the room where I have my trading setup, on the right-hand wall hang two paintings — spontaneous works by my daughter. On one of them I've pinned a small card with a black dot.

I don't know if this is the perfect method — it's more like a mix of a few approaches. I sit comfortably, slow my breathing, and once I reach a calm state, I focus on just one thing — the black dot in the center of the painting. I keep my eyes fixed on it, stay aware of my breathing, and once I hit full concentration, I start noticing everything around it with my peripheral vision. When I feel fatigue, I close my eyes and try to recreate the dot and the surrounding image in my mind. This exercise works for me like closing the door to a room.

Everyday matters stay outside — and I'm here, one-on-one with the charts.

Of course, it doesn't always go perfectly, but I try to minimize other thoughts, mute my phone, avoid messages, and stay away from Facebook. I stick to a simple rule: it's better to do one thing well than several things poorly.

44.1 Multitasking — Miracle or Myth?

I often hear people claim they can handle several things at once and therefore get work done faster.
In my opinion, the mind doesn't work like that — and research on the subject is very clear.

Doing several things at the same time significantly reduces efficiency and quality.

If you're trading, maybe scrolling through TikTok or other distracting apps isn't the best idea.

Don't believe it?

Try playing a video game while watching a movie. If you focus on the game, the movie becomes background noise — it takes part of your attention but won't let you really understand what's going on.

Distractions lower the quality of your trading.

You have to choose — either you treat this seriously and dedicate yourself to it fully, or you do it at 80% because you'd rather watch silly clips or chat about nothing that seems "important" at the moment.

I once tried trading while chatting with a friend about the market. It was fun, time passed quickly... and neither of us made much money.

Maybe some people can do it differently, but in my experience, **trading requires focus and calm**. Since you're already sitting at the charts, skip all the distractions and entertainment. Otherwise, you'll have a good time, but the results won't make you feel good.

Approach this like a real full-time job. You're at your station on the line, focused only on what's happening. No phone, no side chatter. You're in your own money factory.

Focus on your work, or you'll get fired for lack of results — or for running out of funds in your account.

----

45 Does Being Generation X or Y Define You?

How do people get divided and labeled depending on their birth year? Is there some truth in it? What conclusions can we draw?

45.1 Baby Boomers

Birth years: approx. 1946–1964

Key motto: "**Work is a duty, not a passion**."

Weaknesses and limitations:

- Difficulty adapting to technological change — often feel lost in the digital world.
- Strong attachment to authority and hierarchy — makes it harder to accept modern flat structures.
- Tendency to judge younger generations through the lens of their own values ("back in our day...") — builds intergenerational barriers.
- Lack of flexibility — expect stability and clear rules, which are hard to achieve in a world of constant change.
- Workaholism — equating self-worth with work often leads to burnout and lack of balance.

45.2 Generation X... my generation... the best one :)

Birth years: approx. 1965–1980

Key motto: "**I'll handle it myself**." — Of course. :)

Weaknesses and limitations — none... that's what we think. :)

- Skepticism and distrust — raised during times of transformation, they often don't believe in "the system."
- Tendency toward isolation and individualism — reluctant to ask for help, often closed off.
- Lack of developed soft skills — focused on hard skills, sometimes struggle with relationships and feedback.
- Underestimating younger generations — often accuse them of lacking discipline and being entitled.

- Resistance to new ways of working — technology is fine, but remote work, automation, or "coaching" are viewed with skepticism.

As Lech Wałęsa once said [25] — "there are positive pluses and negative pluses." My generation? Only positive pluses. :)

45.3 Generation Y (Millennials)

Birth years: approx. 1981–1996

Key motto: "I want a job that helps me grow and makes sense."
Weaknesses and limitations:

- Low tolerance for stress and criticism — raised in a world of praise, they struggle with pressure and failure.
- Torn between ambition and reality — high expectations, but quick to quit when faced with obstacles.
- Job-hopping tendencies — they lose continuity of experience and depth of skills.
- Dependence on feedback — they need constant recognition, which weakens their inner motivation.
- Information overload — they consume tons of content, often only superficially, which lowers focus.

45.4 Generation Z

Birth years: approx. 1997–2012

Key motto: "I want it fast, now, and my way."
Weaknesses and limitations:

- Very short attention span — raised on TikTok, Stories, and multitasking.
- Strong dependence on technology — without their phone or internet, they feel paralyzed.
- Blurred boundaries between private and public — often don't distinguish digital life from the real one.

- Struggle with routine — expect everything to be dynamic and tailored to them.
- High emotional sensitivity — the world of likes/shares/hates creates anxiety and insecurity.
- Lack of patience for the process — they want results instantly, not understanding the value of hard, tedious work.

Oh... I know this generation. Raised with care, yet the world still managed to spoil them a bit. :)

45.5 We Are Herd Animals

We strive to belong to some group — even just mentally — and we shape our traits according to its patterns.

Even if you think you don't belong to any community around you, you've just signed yourself into the group of outsiders.

The traits of the Baby Boomers, Gen X, Y, or Z are not just literary fantasy.

People are shaped by the times they grow up in.

I'm from Gen X, and I really see how different Gen Z is from us.

Do your own analysis — look at the traits of each generation and try to define what your own brings.

Not to judge who's better or worse — but to spot the traits that might hurt you in trading... and eliminate them.

When you sit down at the charts, there are no "fruit Thursdays." You've got to take care of everything yourself.

Trading doesn't teach, doesn't forgive, doesn't help, doesn't refund your money "because you feel bad."

It doesn't matter which generation you're from, what expectations, ambitions, or grievances you have.

If you want to pull money out of the market — you need to be good enough. This isn't a fight with someone else for something.

It's just you and the chart.

Either you can cash out from it like an ATM, or you'll just keep feeding it your money.

How beautiful and pure that is...

Everything depends only on you.

No bluffing, no faking, no excuses, no finger-pointing, no arguing that "it wasn't fair," that "someone should do something," or that you're entitled to something just because you feel you deserve it.

If you win — it's 100% your credit.

If you lose — it's 100% your responsibility.

If you want to improve something — it's 100% up to you.

And if you want to file a complaint against the market, write a letter to the same address you used to send to Santa Claus as a kid.

Beautiful, fair rules.

Zero excuses.

Do you know why I keep talking so much about responsibility and that everything depends only on you?

Because you need to understand that once you finish this book and step onto the trading floor, you'll be there alone.

It's not a fairytale land with wolves or other monsters lurking around.

There's nothing good or bad out there.

Everything you encounter **is inside you — and it will play out inside you.**

You can build an oasis of calm within yourself, where you'll spend a few hours a day and from time to time feel a thrill of excitement.

Or you can just as easily build a battlefield inside yourself and walk away from the market with PTSD.

And no, I'm not exaggerating.

46 Don't Work on a Better % Result in Trading

Work on Better Quality Trades.

Your result is just the effect of quality.
Focus on the cause, not the outcome.
Want to make more money?
To get there, you take dozens, even hundreds of decisions and trades that ultimately form your account balance.
So what do you think needs to change for you to see more money at the end of the day or week?

- Does the quality of your entry matter?
- Does the quality of managing a position affect how much you take out of it?
- Does the decision on when to exit change your result?
- Does solid analysis cut out bad trades and help you hit better ones?
- Does capital and risk management affect the outcome?
- Does your mental state, your Trader's mindset, make a difference?

The answer will always be the same:

Only quality can truly improve your financial results.
Only quality is worth focusing on.

Everything you dream of — money, freedom, success — is just a side effect of the quality of your trading.

You can try to "rip dollars" out of the chart, wrestle with the market, jump in and yell at the screen telling the chart what to do...
And you'll end up the day as exhausted as a farmhand after plowing behind an ox.
Meanwhile, all the real effort should go into analysis and the decision to take a trade.

Once you're in the market, you're just an observer.
Like an air traffic controller in the tower — you give the signal for takeoff, check if the plane has the right conditions, decide when it should make a loop and when it should approach for landing.
If the sky is clear — you clear the next flight.
If there's a storm overhead, other pilots are panicking, and the runway is buried in snow — you calmly say:
"In this weather, I don't fly," and go grab a cup of tea.
When the weather improves — you'll fly.

You trade only when you have an edge — because your analysis confirmed it.
You don't trade because you "have to."
You trade because you see a solid opportunity.

47 No Progress on the Account — The Solution

Are your results leaving you unsatisfied?
Do you even know how to judge what's "a lot" and what's "a little"? So, what are your actual results? If they hover around break-even or slide into the red — of course that's frustrating.
But if you're averaging 1–2–3% per day — that's actually pretty good. Ask yourself whether your expectations might just be unrealistic.
Pulling off a double-digit profit in a single day?
Possible once in a while, but rare. That should never be your benchmark.

For comparison, Larry Williams pulled off 11,376% in a single year. Sounds impossible? Let's do the math.
A trading year is roughly 250 sessions. To hit that kind of return, you'd need to generate 1.9% profit per day, reinvesting your gains. The next day you'd play a bigger position — because your capital is larger — and hit another 1.9%. After 250 days, your $10,000 grows into over a million.

Target Calculation: Daily Return Needed to Grow $10,000 to $1,100,000 in 250 Days

Formula:

We use **compound growth**:

$$\text{Final Amount} = \text{Initial Capital} \times (1 + r)^n$$

Where:

- **Initial Capital** = $10,000
- **Final Amount** = $1,100,000
- **n** = 250 (trading days)
- **r** = daily return rate (what we want to find)

Rearranging the formula:

$$1,100,000 = 10,000 \times (1 + r)^{250}$$

$$(1 + r)^{250} = \frac{1,100,000}{10,000} = 110$$

$$\ln(1 + r) = \frac{\ln(110)}{250} \approx \frac{4.7005}{250} \approx 0.0188$$

$$1 + r \approx e^{0.0188} \approx 1.019$$

$$r \approx 1.9\%$$

Conclusion:

You need to make ~**1.9% profit per trading day**, compounded, to grow **$10,000 into $1.1 million** over **250 trading days**.

1.9% per day sounds small?
I thought so too. I figured the math program must have glitched a bit.
So I plugged the numbers into Excel — and sure enough, it checks out.
That shows the scale of what's possible, but also how unbelievably hard that level is to achieve.

In my view, if you can average 1% per day over the long run, you're in the absolute elite.

47.1 Small Changes, Huge Differences

You might think the key to success is your trade setups, and that's where all your attention should go.
Now imagine something different:
that you don't need to learn anything new to improve your results.
Here's a comparison for you...

Daily Return	Daily	Every 5 Days	Every 21 Days
0.5%	34,795 $	34,371 $	32,840 $
1.0%	120,322 $	114,674 $	96,869 $
1.5%	413,533 $	371,897 $	261,268 $
2.0%	1,412,677 $	1,173,909 $	653,207 $

Comparison of capital growth at different compounding frequencies. The table below shows how capital changes after 250 trading days — assuming you start with 10,000 USD and hold a steady daily return (0.5%, 1%, 1.5%, 2%).

The key factor is how often you reinvest your profits.

Daily compounding
Each day you trade with the position size based on your current balance.
Example: yesterday you had $10,000. Your SL at 1% equals $100.
Today you made 1%, so now you've got $10,100 — your SL at 1% is $101. Seems like just a dollar more... but over the year, this "playing with pennies" makes a massive difference.

Compounding every 5 days

So, once a week you recalculate your position as 1% of balance and stick with that for the whole week.

Compounding every 21 days

So, once a month you recalc your position and trade with that size for the entire month.

See? You don't need to "discover" anything new, and you don't need fresh entries.
All it takes is a simple plan to regularly adjust your position size.
Cost: zero. Workload: minimal.
And the effect? Pure magic. :)

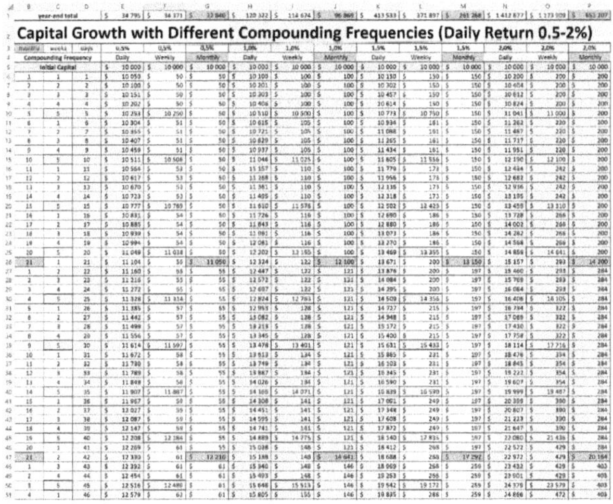

I enjoy building tables and spreadsheets — it's a very useful skill in a Trader's work. If you haven't yet gotten comfortable with spreadsheets, I strongly recommend catching up on that.

Once you start trading, you'll quickly have data worth organizing in tables. Over time, you'll start drawing concrete conclusions from them.
That's the foundation for trading consciously and for refining your technique, tactics, and risk management.
Definitely worth it.

47.2 Check How the Growth Curve of Capital Changes Depending on Daily Return and Position Recalculation Frequency

Capital growth curve with 0.5% daily profit.

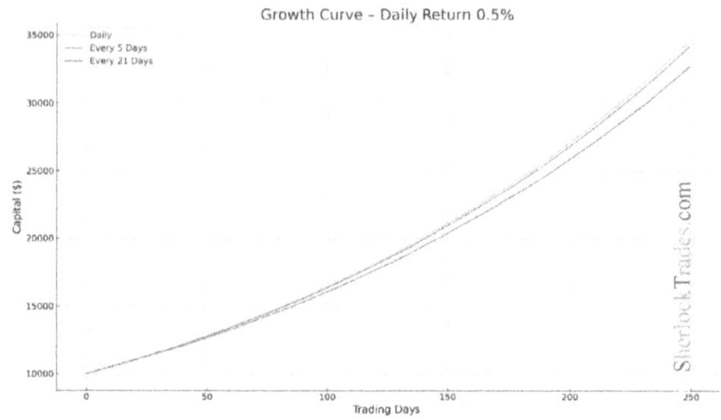

Capital growth curve with 1% daily profit.

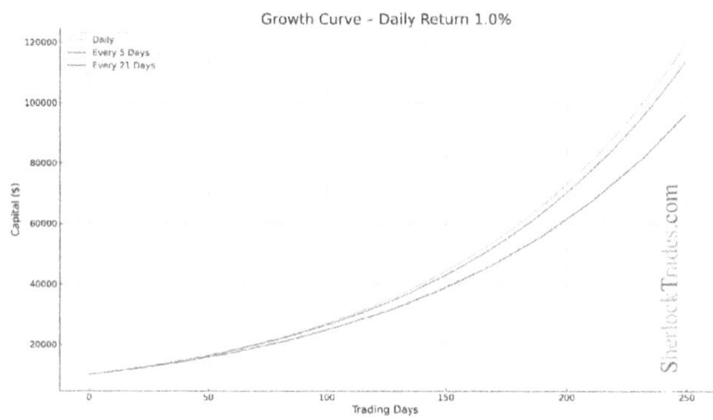

Capital growth curve with 1.5% daily profit.

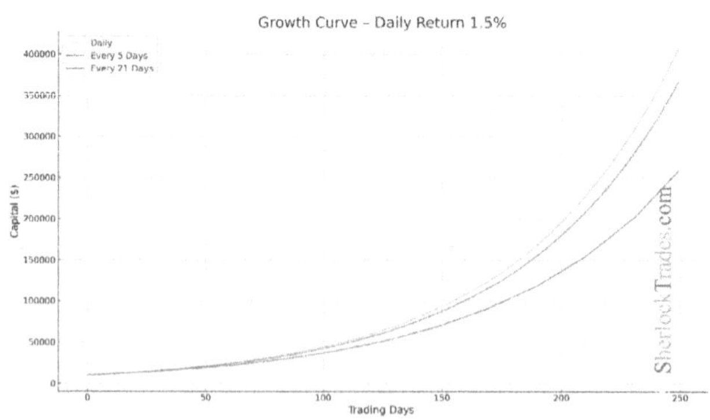

Capital growth curve with 2% daily profit.

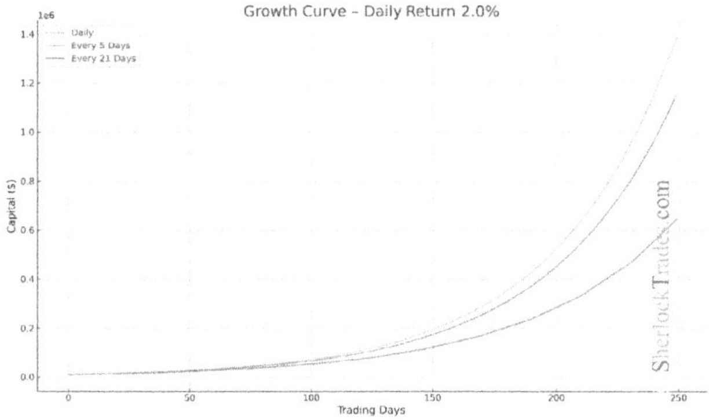

You can see the difference over a year, but what happens over, say, 3 years?

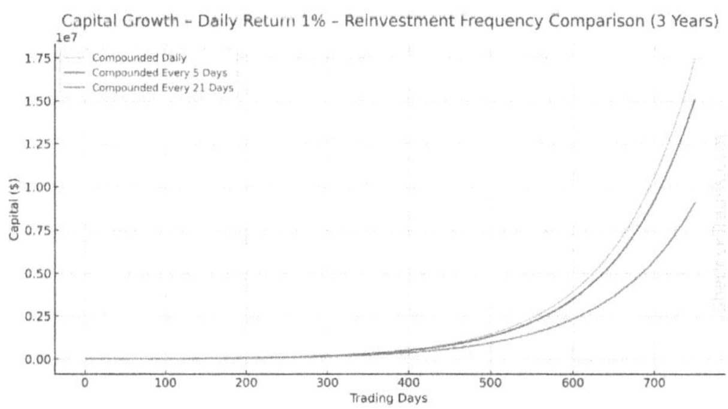

1e7 on the scale means "1" equals 10,000,000 USD.

The difference in the final result depending on how often you increase your position (daily, every 5 days, or every 21 days) is roughly 9 million, 15 million, and 17.5 million USD respectively.

If you simulated this over 10 years, the final values would be hard to even write down because of the zeros, and the difference between compounding every 21 days versus daily would reach x 8.86.

Interesting stuff — fun to think about massive gains — but these tables don't take into account the human factor: our mistakes, weaknesses, lack of consistency, emotions, or the simple need for rest.

You can dream of astronomical results, but life will quickly set the record straight.

Remember: Larry Williams pulled off over 11,000% in one year, but he didn't repeat that performance in the years that followed. If he had, today he'd be worth several times more than Elon Musk — and he isn't.

So keep this in mind: go step by step and stay consistent.

If your stats are positive, it's only a matter of time before big money shows up.

If you start rushing, pushing risk higher — you'll get a lesson.

Be like the turtle. You've got time. Stay consistent with your goal. After a year or two of steadily making a "modest" 1–1.5% per day, your financial life could become unrecognizable.

Then you can play smaller positions and aim for lower daily percentages — and still be pulling in more than you can spend.

And once you've got serious money, it starts to fade into the background.

What gains importance is the **quality of your life**.

47.3 The Value of Perfect Trade Management

On my desk — right next to my entry checklists — I always keep two cards for managing positions.

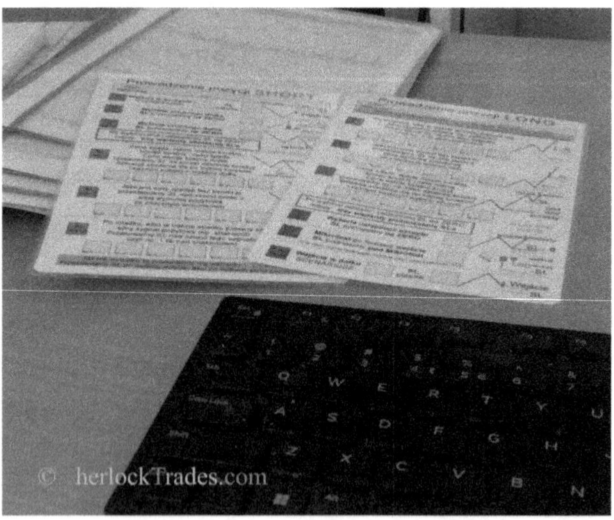

These cards marked the start of my serious trading journey.

I designed them years ago and still use them today.
Sure, I've got newer, better-designed versions, but out of sentiment I still stick to the old ones.
You can also create your own cards — tailored to your strategy and rules — and actually use them.
Why does it matter?
Because a sheet like this is a precise, repeatable algorithm for action that, over the long run, delivers better results than gut-feel decisions.

When price moves up, you're long and in profit, emotions kick in.
You start "seeing the profit," and the fear of losing it grows.
The result? You close too early. Then you watch the price climb further after a small pullback.
Instead of pulling 1:10 out of the market, you settle for a weak 1:2.
Cards give you clarity:

- When you can move SL to break-even,
- When and how to lock in profits,
- How to trail the position in line with what the market is showing.

With such cards, you can also review past trades and check whether you could have managed them better.
The most important part: you must have some kind of rules for managing positions. Without rules, there's no consistency. Without consistency, results are just random.

If you'd like to get my new position management cards — there's a simple way: they're linked to my "Buy me a Coffee" account. Anyone who wants to support my work gets a thank-you link to download the cards.
You can print them, laminate them, and use them for years.
Or you can create your own, based on mine, tweaking the rules to fit your style of trading.
It's truly a great tool — I highly recommend it.

Use my cards or make your own from scratch.
What matters is that you actually use them — so your trading stays systematic and consistent.

https://buymeacoffee.com/sherlocktrades.com

Why is this so important? Let me explain...

47.4 Consistency and Statistics Are the Door to Big Money

Imagine you don't have the funds for a bigger deposit with your broker and you're practicing on a demo account or trading a few hundred dollars. Suddenly, you get handed a million in cash.
You can do whatever you want with it.
You think: "I'll throw it into my broker account. 1% a month is 10,000 dollars — that's a nice salary."

You deposit it... and what do you feel?
Let me guess: paralyzing fear. You've got no strategy, no proven playbook, no stats from 50 or 100 trades, and no clearly defined MM.
All you've got is a vague idea of technical analysis and maybe you've skimmed something on psychology.
That million... it's about to change owners, because you're not ready to trade money on that scale.

Now imagine another scenario:
For the past six months (or longer) you've been practicing on a demo account or with a small live account. You've been learning, drawing conclusions, analyzing your mistakes. You've built stats, you've got checklists, printed setups of your best trades. You know exactly what your R:R is, where you set your SL, how you manage positions, and what your monthly results look like.
You've got a ready-made system — a money-making machine — in your head and on paper.

You put in $100 — it turns into $120.
You put in $1,000 — it turns into $1,200.

This isn't gambling — it's a repeatable process.
You're not playing roulette, you're not throwing a million on red. You don't feel fear, because it's just a larger stake inside a tested system. Without that kind of preparation, you'll never be able to handle big capital. Sure, you might get lucky — a bull market, everything goes up.
I've seen plenty of those "lucky guys" — and just as fast as they made money, they lost it all. You don't want that experience.
Become a professional Trader and be ready for big money.

I remember a call from my buddy Patryk in 2017.
I'll skip most of his words — it was nothing but curses.
He had closed a position that at its peak was worth nearly a million dollars. He closed it when there was less than 20,000 left in the account. A leveraged Bitcoin trade. Didn't work out.

Did he stick to his rules? No.
He kept telling himself: "Just a little more, then I'll start playing safe." First at 100K. Then at 500K. The goal was a round million, and then... then it was supposed to be safe.
It didn't work. He never got back to a million. Not even to 100K.

When I asked him what he'd have done if he actually saw a million on the account, he said: "I'd probably think it's too little and aim for 10 million."

I asked: "And then 100 million?" — he just laughed.
He broke the rules. After that, it only went downhill.
Today, Patryk doesn't trade anymore. Either you play by the rules all the time, or sooner or later you'll tell yourself: "Just one more time..." and then again... and again — **until you blow up.**

47.5 If You Really Want to Earn More, You Must...

First — treat trading like a professional and stick to your rules. Analyze your trades, refine your chosen method of chart analysis, build rules, checklists, playbooks, templates — everything that gives you consistency in the game.

Second — learn to gradually "turn up the thermostat" in your head. Each of us has a certain level of financial comfort.
For one Trader, losing $10 is no big deal, but $100 already feels different and triggers emotions.
For another, $1,000 is just a casual position, but when the SL means $10,000 at risk, stress starts to creep in.

Soon you'll read about the concept of habituation.
I also mentioned earlier the EST training, where people confronted their traumas, relived them, and got used to them — until they stopped being so painful and overwhelming.

That's how the financial thermostat in your head works. You have to gradually accustom it to higher amounts you're trading with. :) You're used to certain sums in your pocket. A certain risk feels acceptable, while a higher one sparks emotions.
And emotions limit your ability to analyze and think logically.
Give yourself time. Notice at what level you start feeling tension — but not panic yet.
If that level is, say, $200, then reduce your position size so your SL is around $150–180. Trade without pressure.
In a few days, raise it. Then raise it again. Over time, you'll get used to higher stakes. A sudden jump in size can backfire — don't speed up too quickly, or your brain will panic and you'll end up in trouble.

48 Habituation — Pros and Cons

Habituation is one of the basic psychological and neurobiological phenomena. It means the gradual fading of response to a **repeated stimulus** that brings neither new information nor threat. You know this from experience:

- A clock in the room — at first you hear the ticking, then you stop noticing it.
- Perfume scent — strong at first, then it disappears.
- Repetitive noise — like street sounds that stop bothering you after a few days.

Back in college, I lived in an old townhouse right next to the tram tracks. At first, I heard every tram and felt the floor vibrations. After a while, they ceased to exist in my perception.
Today, I hear birds singing outside my window.
Sometimes I feel like they're holding bird conferences — but I only notice it when I take a break from the charts and look into the distance to rest my eyes.

48.1 Why Is It Worth Knowing About This Phenomenon?

The downside of habituation is indifference — for example, during study.
Surely you've experienced reading a few pages of material... and then realizing you don't remember a word of it.
To learn effectively, you need variety: a dialogue with yourself, questions, and attempts to challenge your own viewpoint.
When you "argue" with yourself on a topic and beat your own counterarguments — you've won. :)
Remember EST training?
Exposing yourself repeatedly to fear helps you get used to it.
Over time, it loses its edge.
But let's be clear — this doesn't mean you should walk through bad neighborhoods and provoke gangsters. :) Or fight fear of heights by walking on a tightrope between skyscrapers.

Sometimes your subconscious is right to scream: “Don’t do this!” — and then it’s worth listening.
That’s our natural warning system. We just need to teach it new rules in the context of trading, so it doesn’t paralyze us with false alarms.

48.1.1 Habituation in Trading — Pros:

- Reduces stress in recurring situations — what once triggered strong emotions becomes normal.
- Lowers sensitivity to external stimuli — like news.
- Analyses become partly automated — you enter the stage of “unconscious competence,” which frees up your mental processor.
- The mind filters out noise — allowing you to spot what matters. Like red lights shining through the fog: certain candles “speak” to you: “Look here!”

48.1.2 Unfortunately, There Are Cons Too:

- Too much exposure to risk can numb you.
- Anxiety is an important warning signal.
  If you don’t feel it — have rules in place to protect you.
- Too many stimuli and routine weaken concentration.
- You can’t stay fully focused for 8 hours straight.
  Focus when signals show that something’s happening.
- Automation can go too far.
- You start acting on autopilot, ignoring critical signals.
  That’s like trading after a sleepless night — it just won’t work.
- Getting used to losses can be dangerous. It’s better if they still “hurt.”

48.2 Newbie vs Experienced Trader:

A new Trader reacts emotionally to every candle and every price move.

An experienced Trader has seen it all thousands of times, waits calmly for his setup, goes through the checklist, and only then switches to full focus when it's time to hunt.

What's worth doing?

- Minimize stimuli: muted chart colors, dark mode, blue-light filter, no alarms.
- Multiple alerts on different instruments just created chaos for me — half the time I didn't even know what they were for.
- If I miss something — so be it. Peace of mind is more important.

How to protect yourself?

- Regularly check if you're operating too automatically.
- Change your window layout, colors, or rituals from time to time — it helps restore awareness.
- Our brain is a slacker — it cheats to avoid effort, so you have to cheat it back.
- The only way to make sure nothing gets skipped is... a checklist.

Trading is like launching a plane.
You definitely don't want to take off without fuel just because you couldn't be bothered to check the checklist.

A checklist really serves three purposes:

- It takes the load off your mind, since you don't have to constantly remember which criteria must be met and what needs to be verified.
- It minimizes the risk of errors from overlooking something that's part of your strategy.
- It ensures consistency, which is the foundation for building stats and analyzing performance.

It's absolutely worth creating and using checklists.

49 Emergency Procedures

Writing about habituation almost put me to sleep...
Luckily, I remembered something that gets the blood flowing:
ALERT – FAILURE!
Imagine you're in the middle of a trade and suddenly... well, you get the idea.
Make a list of possible failures and set up procedures for each one.
What can happen without warning?

- Computer crash – how will you monitor your open position?

If you follow my rules, you've got SL and TP in place, so you're covered. But what if you still want to check something?

- You want to call your broker – do you know the number?

How does verification work? Do you have the required data and passwords? Or is it all stored on the computer that just died?

- Internet outage – do you have a backup connection?

Here's how I handle it:
I switch to my phone's cellular data from a different provider – even from another country – full diversification.

- A sudden "domestic drama" at the door – someone shouting they can't find the cotton pads. :)

What do you do?
Think this through in advance. Prepare a notebook with emergency procedures – it'll save you stress.
Here's what I keep:

- two configured computers, encrypted drives, etc.
- a ready-to-go phone – actually two of them,
- backup access to platforms and data,
- everything important runs on a UPS backup power supply.

Basically, I don't panic — worst case, I miss something and SL takes out the position. So be it — one failure won't change my long-term stats.

For me, SL is the key — I always set it with the order.
That's why I can afford the attitude: "System down?
Then I'm on break."
And you know what?
There are worse things in life than an unplanned rest. :)

49.1 A Vaccine Against Well-Meaning "Friends"

Most of us have heard wise advice along the lines of:
"Don't do that, it's dangerous — people only lose money on this stuff."
"Listen to your uncle, he'll tell you — he was in the war, he's seen worse."

And so it begins...
Someone is trying to push their programs into your head without the slightest idea of what you actually do.
And you — just to avoid making a scene — sit and listen, while in your mind you're recalling who scored in the last match.
Honestly? I don't have a magic fix for this.
I like a simple life.
If someone does something stupid and it concerns me — I cut it off.

I set a boundary.
I explain that we won't be discussing this topic — politely or firmly, depending on the person. Case closed.
No one who doesn't have experience even close to mine is going to tell me anything about trading or making money in the markets.
I'm not interested in debates or convincing anyone.
I don't have questions or doubts — I've got stats and I've got my account balance.

That's enough.
Listening to other people's beliefs is like dumping garbage straight into your head.

I don't see the point of talking about how much you earn each month.
In Poland, the best answer to the question "So, how's life on the stock market?" is:

"**Don't even ask**.
Just stress and throwing money at it. Sometimes I wonder where to borrow cash for it... maybe if I traded bigger..."

That ends the conversation.
The other person senses it's a setup for borrowing money — so they immediately change the topic.
I get peace of mind, and they don't think I'm some clever guy who "makes easy money" and can be tapped for some of that "easy" cash.
Everybody's happy. :)
I don't like telling fairy tales, so usually I just don't talk about my work.

Now it'll be easier — I'll say I became a writer and published a book. :)
Great conversation topic.
And if someone asks:
"So, how's the writing... any money in that?"
Answer:

"**Don't even ask**.
Just stress and throwing money at it. Sometimes I wonder where to borrow cash for it..." :)

50 Good and Bad Rewards, Good and Bad Vibes

50.1 Hunger and Thirst for Reward

Motivation to act and reach goals is driven by rewards.
Even if you're a tough guy and the goal itself keeps you going, it's still nice to give yourself a little reward along the way.
I recently talked about this with my daughter and suggested an idea that — in a slightly different form — I sometimes use myself.
She's got exams at university, and in those moments it's easiest to do anything but study. The usual distractions and time-wasters appear — TikTok, Instagram, FB, X, etc.

Everyone has their favorite way of wasting time.
Funny thing: when a goal really grabs us or feels truly important, we handle motivation just fine. The goal itself becomes the reward, and distractions simply don't stand a chance — we're fully absorbed by the plan. But studies — as it turns out — don't always have that kind of pull. :)

So I offered her a solution with two benefits:

- First: the reward is attractive.
- Second: its attractiveness comes from a deficit we create ourselves — and that creates an extra benefit.

I suggested blocking social media during the day and only letting herself scroll in the evening, once study time was done.
No social media during the day means more focus and fewer of those constant interruptions like: "I'll just take a quick look, maybe someone replied."

This creates hunger for the activity, while also reframing it as a reward. The system saves time, builds motivation through scarcity, and delivers a reward at zero cost.
In my view, a solid option — but it got shot down... well, that's Gen Z for you.

Personally, I use a similar trick. What I deny myself during the week are movies and series. I love a good film, I love a good show — but they're time-consuming and not very productive.
So I made a rule: no watching anything during the week.
On the weekend — whatever I want, as much as I want. I can — but usually there are more interesting things to do anyway, so I don't end up watching that much. :)
As a result, I choose more carefully and only watch things that are really worth it. And if the weather's bad on the weekend — catching up on films becomes the perfect reward.
Not watching movies during the week gives me more time, better sleep (since I'm not up late), and builds anticipation, making the weekend reward even more attractive.

All upside, no downside. :)
Plus, postponing the "reward" works like detox — the habit weakens with delay. After a while without SM or movies, the urge to waste time on them nearly disappears.
I start to realize it was never that important — honestly, just a waste of life. Interestingly, the delayed reward gradually stops feeling like a reward at all.

It's like the magic fades — what once felt tempting and special loses its shine. Something shifts in my brain's neural network, and suddenly, FB isn't a "reward" anymore, but a waste of time.
Beautiful. :)

50.2 A Win That's Really a Curse

Think back to when you did something stupid — like taking a position way too big, or averaging down into a loser, only to dig yourself deeper. That's a terrible trading approach.

In roulette there's a strategy called Martingale — "you can't lose." In reality, it's a fast track to bankruptcy. Adding to a losing position, hoping the market will bounce back and save you, usually ends badly. Yes, the market will turn — just not in time.

Remember, we're talking about trading here, mostly short-term. This isn't long-term investing where you can sit around and wait.
Here's the punch line.
If you do something wrong and **take a loss — that's good**.
That's a lesson. You've learned, and next time you won't repeat the mistake.

But if you do something wrong and the market "rewards" you with a profit — that's a curse.
What happens next? You repeat the same mistake, because "it worked last time." You increase your position.
The market doesn't turn. You add again, because "now it has to."
And then it does turn — just after your broker shut down your positions and "turned off the lights."

You got rewarded for bad behavior, and that shaped you.
Sometimes it's better to lose and learn than to "win" and pick up a destructive habit.

50.3 Good and Bad Vibes

"Vibes" might sound a bit mystical. :)
Picture a guitar: six strings, and you pluck just one at the edge.
After a moment you mute it — but the other strings, untouched, are still softly resonating.

Vibes spread. Things around fall into resonance. Suddenly — instead of calm — you've got disturbance.
You know those people whose very presence sends your blood pressure through the roof?
I stopped watching political news, even online, because it instantly made my nerves vibrate in all the wrong ways.
Why should I get worked up about some mediocre guy winning an election in a country where I'm just a guest?
Does it help me? Can I profit from it?
If there are no upsides, why bring on downsides — wasting time, energy, and nerves?

When you sit down at the charts — what thoughts and emotions from daily life are cluttering your head? Do you feel harmful, unnecessary vibes from things you shouldn't even be following? Maybe it's time to clean those parasites out of your environment. Here's how I picture the good vibes around me as a Trader:

You walk through the city, and behind you marches the power of your knowledge and experience.
The Bull and the Bear are your allies — you feel their strength.
You walk with confidence, because with buddies like that, nobody's messing with you.

You're the one in charge here...

Or the other version:

I don't even know if it's worth describing...
You're not striding forward — you're, to put it mildly, RUNNING AWAY! :)
So what kind of environment do you want?
What kind of vibes do you let in?

Do you really think you can calmly analyze charts and make smart decisions with a pack of yapping dogs snapping at your heels?
No way...
You need to bring order to your surroundings.
Trading is like swimming across the English Channel — you can do it free and light, or with a concrete ball chained to your leg.
Your choice.
If it were me, I'd clean house and cut out everything unnecessary that drags me down.

50.4 Listening to Experts and Fortune Tellers

You've built knowledge, mastered your techniques. Everything works, you're making money. And then suddenly the thought sneaks in: "Maybe someone's got a better idea. Maybe they know more than I do?"
Option one:
"Maybe I should listen — after all, it's always worth hearing out smart people..."
And just like that — you've stepped into the trap.
There are only two ways this goes: either others are smarter and you're the fool, or you're smart enough and it's not worth listening to them.
Which one do you choose?
If you're honest and objective, you'll admit — of course there are people smarter than you. So logically, it seems worth listening.
You switch on the financial news — some guy in a suit, with a professor's title, talking about indicators, signals, forecasts...

You've got no clue what he's saying and feel like a farm kid dropped into the middle of Manhattan.

And just to be clear: my grandparents were farmers, my roots are rural, and where you come from doesn't make you better or worse.

So you listen to this guy on TV, figure he must be right — because he explained it so professionally.

You do what he suggested. You lose money.

And then you sit there wondering: what just happened...

Option Two:

You're the smart one, and it's not worth listening to others.

Is that true? No...

But so what, if that's the right attitude.

Feeling smart — it gives you strength.

Not listening to others — often a good idea.

We're not the smartest people in the world — neither you nor I.

Doesn't matter, because only one thing counts: can you sit down at the chart and grow your capital consistently.

If yes, then you're smart enough and you don't need anyone whispering advice.

Hey, guy on TV — you've got good tips?

Then open an account, put in your own money, and trade at your own risk.

Listening to others wrecks your analysis — and it's your analysis that brings you profit.

Taking cues from "specialists" who earn their living from appearances and smooth talk? Pointless.

Picture this: a super expert tells you the S&P 500 will crash hard within a month. And he's right.

What do you do with that?

You don't know if the drop comes today or three weeks from now.

You don't know if there's a new high before the fall.

You don't know how long it will last.

Even though the information is true — it could ruin you.
Now picture this: the futures price of a widely used commodity collapses almost to zero.
Not theory. Something you use in daily life.
A price like that looks impossible.
I don't know what analysts were saying back then, because I don't listen to them.
I suspect they were spouting the kind of nonsense you'll never find in a textbook, because "such a thing can't happen."
And yet...

Check what level the May WTI crude oil futures contract hit in April 2020.
I wasn't trading oil back then, and honestly, I don't know how I would've reacted. I could show you the chart... but you're supposed to be a Trader.
Find it yourself. Because if it happened once — it can happen again.
If you treat trading seriously, you're already digging into what happened then.
And if not — at least write it down to check later.

50.4.1 Test

You know I've written about this before. Did you check it then?
If yes — great. If not, then realize one thing: maybe you enjoy reading this, but once you're done, you'll remember just a couple of smart sentences... **for a moment**.
A week later you'll slip back into your old routine, and nothing will change.
Is that really what you want?

Is your life so perfect that you're afraid to "mess it up" with a change?

Or maybe it's just fear, laziness, or something you don't want to call by name — because it's uncomfortable when someone says it out loud.

I don't know you, I'm not judging you, I don't want to change you. All I try to do from time to time is shake you a little — because maybe that's exactly what you need to make a positive change.

It's you who decides whether something inside you needs to change.

And it's you who makes that change happen.

My role? To give you the spark to act.

50.5 What Do You Think of Yourself?

We've been talking about vibes, about external factors.

But what kind of vibes are buried deep inside you?

Do they give you strength, or do they drain it?

I've written quite a bit here about forgiving others — in the context of our nation's history and the work of Professor Bartoszewski.

Forgiving others sets us free...

But what about forgiving yourself?

Most of us have made mistakes.

So have I — and plenty of them.

Mistakes, when possible, need to be fixed.

You need to draw conclusions from them.

You can't brush them aside — but **you also can't build altars to them in your heart and worship them like relics**.

----

*If you've messed up — **fix what you can,***
***then forgive yourself** and let the lesson*
shape you into a better human being.

It's not mistakes that define you — it's how you get back up afterwards. You've got the rest of your life ahead of you — make sure you can look at it with pride.

Forgiving yourself and building something good will give you strength. Only strong people achieve something truly great.

51 You've Got the Manual, But Prefer to Wallow in the Mud?

Picture this: in a magic car showroom you buy a car. It's a piece of junk for 100 dollars – but the dealer throws in a book with the keys. On the cover: "Manual."
Only it's not a regular manual – like where to top up washer fluid or how often to change the oil.
This one's a magic manual.

It lets you gradually, almost magically, transform the car. Follow it step by step – first the engine turns new, a week later the seats are renewed, a few months in the paint starts to shine, and three years later that $100 wreck becomes a million-dollar limousine.

Could you actually pull that off? **Do you really want it?**
The book you're reading right now is that magic manual.
It holds dozens of topics that can make your life extraordinary.
It's all up to you – whether you'll use it, or dismiss it as too much work and once again get tempted by some $3,000 course that promises millions from the sky without lifting a finger.

I've done what I could.
The good news: now it's all in your hands.
Nobody will stop you – except yourself.
The future is waiting. It can be beautiful. It can be yours.
You just have to earn it.

If you don't succeed, it means you didn't try hard enough, didn't put in the work — and you've just learned that the world doesn't pay out rewards for laziness.

Forgive the bluntness — but if you don't get this, you've wasted your time reading this book. And I'd regret that you bought it, because it was never about the sale, only about the result.

I want that crazy feeling that my work on this book made the world just a little better.

That even one life got better.

That's my goal.

I've mentioned before — I'm not a writer.

I didn't study how to craft books.

I'm a Trader with the soul of a philosopher and analyst — someone who often reflects on the meaning of life.

In this book I touched on many topics that, in my opinion, matter. Some I presented better, some worse.

I'm not perfect, but **I gave it my all.**

What you take from this book is entirely up to you.

If you just skim through, never pause to think about the deeper meaning of each chapter, never notice what I really wanted you to focus on — well...

You got the manual.

It's not a masterpiece where every thought is handed to you on a silver platter, magically seeping into your mind just by carrying the book in your briefcase.

The manual is what it is — but it's your life.

If you don't put in the effort to figure out what it really means, then even a "better" form wouldn't change anything. Because you simply don't want it.

I could politely motivate you, gently push you toward your goal, pat you on the head...

But this is about life. And life isn't a fairy tale.

It's over 8 billion people fighting every single day for survival. Fight for your own — because no one else will do it for you.

Let me give you another real-life example.

On one of the Polish FB groups, people were diving into a Japanese method of technical analysis — Ichimoku Kinko Hyo.

The problem? There was almost no literature on this technique in our language. Even in English there wasn't much. Translating from Japanese is no small feat — it's not exactly a common skill in our part of the world.

But we cared. So we gathered a group determined to get the original books that described Ichimoku in detail.

We pooled money, a couple of guys handled the logistics — and in the end, everyone who chipped in got beautifully bound volumes on Ichimoku.

When people truly care, they'll go to great lengths to get the knowledge needed to reach their goal.

And you? What effort and sacrifices are you ready to make to achieve your dreams?

To close, here's a lighter story.

A family gathering. "Uncle Know-It-All" listens as a young man talks about learning trading and wanting to play the markets.

Uncle: "Forget it, it's full of crooks and thieves, they'll just take your money and that's all you'll get out of it..."

A few years later — millions in the account — the young Trader meets his uncle again.

Uncle: "I knew you'd make it! If I were younger, I'd have gone into it too and become a millionaire!"

Some achieve success. Others just talk about it...

52 SUMMARY

52.1 Psychology Is the Key to a Trader's Success

Almost everything discussed in this book applies just as much to a Trader as to any other person. By growing as a Trader, you grow as a human being. In my view — that's a positive change.

Success in trading depends more on the ability to control emotions and act rationally under their influence than in most other professions.

You can be a master of technical analysis, a brilliant lecturer, an expert giving credible, well-argued opinions — and still fail completely at trading.

It's the ability to stick to your strategy under emotional pressure that separates successful Traders from those who leave their money in the market.

That's the foundation.

You've got it in your hands — so **what will you do with it?**

52.2 A Healthy Mind in a Healthy Body

A healthy lifestyle directly impacts trading performance.

Regular sleep, a balanced diet, exercise — and not the finger workout on the TV remote :) — plus avoiding stimulants all help with focus and emotional control.

I won't compete with lifestyle guides — there are plenty of those.

I'll just show you what I use myself:

52.2.1 A Workspace Suited to My Needs

I've described it earlier, but in the context of health I'll add a few things.

Long hours of sitting are harmful.

You need breaks, you need to move — these are basics you already know.

But there's something less obvious.

I enjoy good movies. Often I watch them more than once — like The Intouchables, the French film from 2011.
If you don't know it — I highly recommend it. A true story, full of humor, meaning, and great music.

Philippe, one of the main characters, is paralyzed. In one scene, Driss — his caretaker — puts on his compression stockings.
Funny, but also thought-provoking.

Look up medical compression stockings
— that tip might just save your life.

Long sitting hours mean **risk of circulation problems, blood clots, embolisms.**
The richest man in my country died from an embolism — it was a complication after surgery in his case, but it shows how serious the problem is.

When you sit for hours in front of a monitor, some veins can be pinched, blood flow reduced or blocked.
A proper chair and footrest help a lot, but they may not be enough.
Don't underestimate this issue — the consequences can be severe.
After all — once we've earned those millions — we want to have time to actually enjoy them. :)

52.2.2 Eyes

Our main tool is our vision.
I'm not a doctor, I won't prescribe supplements. I personally take herbal mixes "for the eyes" — maybe it's the ingredients, maybe it's belief, maybe both.
Exercises? I try every 15–20 minutes to look at a tree 10 meters outside my window and watch the birds.
Green calms you down, and looking into the distance relaxes both eyes and mind.
I also look around the room, squint my eyes, and focus on a painting with a black dot in the middle.

52.2.3 Tennis Elbow

It's an inflammation and microdamage of the tendons where they attach to the outer part of the humerus (the outside of the elbow).
Repetitive wrist and finger movements — typing on a keyboard, using the mouse — especially with the wrist bent or under tension, are the main cause.
When your wrist "hangs" in the air or lacks support, the extensor muscles are constantly engaged, overloading the tendons.

Even without movement — just holding your arm in one position for too long (isometric tension) — can lead to micro-injuries.
Add to that no breaks, poor ergonomics, overusing one hand (e.g., only the right one), wrong desk height, no wrist rest — all of it makes the problem worse.
That's why I keep a pair of small, rubber-coated 5 kg dumbbells next to my desk. They're comfortable to grip, and whenever I want a break, I pick them up and do a few quick exercises.

52.2.4 Sleep

I go to bed no later than 11:00 p.m. and wake up naturally, usually between 6:00 and 7:00 a.m.
At that time, in European hours, not much is happening on the markets. Things really wake up around 8–9.
That's when you can often catch an interesting position for a few hours — or even for the whole day.

52.2.5 Sports

I'm not a sports fanatic — it's an area I keep trying to improve. But I do enjoy Nordic Walking, which I highly recommend. The poles take weight off your legs, engage the upper body, and let you go farther, faster, while feeling your whole body worked.
Add cycling, a stationary bike, a bench, and dumbbells... I know I should train more, I want to train more — but I keep finding "more important things." So I'm not the best example.

52.2.6 Diet

I'm not a fanatic — I mix elements of keto, low carb, and carnivore. Few vegetables, only the low-carb ones with a low glycemic index.

Most often I eat one meal a day, sometimes two — keeping a 20:4 eating window (intermittent fasting), meaning I eat between 8:00 a.m. and noon, then only drink fluids.
With low sugar intake, that's no problem. From the "three white poisons" — **I cut out sugar and flour**, but not salt. I use natural, unprocessed salt, free of chemicals, rich in minerals and trace elements.
Salt is a preservative, improves taste, and is a key ingredient in electrolytes — and without electrolytes the human body just... shuts down. :)

52.2.7 Drinks

Coffee, tea, sometimes unhealthy energy drinks — **I know they're bad**, so I try to limit them.
On the healthy side, I've got my favorite 1.2-liter steel bottle. Every morning I mix vitamins, natural juices, supplements in it. A healthy daily dose of fluids.

I recommend the idea — clean filtered water, minerals, vitamins... and if needed, a bit of taurine or powdered caffeine — your own "energy drink on demand" to sharpen focus... or at least kick up the blood pressure. :)

I advise against stimulants — you need focus, but not overexcitement. It's much better to build concentration through natural methods.

Trading is a long-term game — we need to take care of "our guy," because without health, nothing else has value.

52.2.8 No TV or Internet News

We haven't had TV at home for more than 10 years. Step by step I cut down political news until I finally quit news portals completely. And guess what — life goes on! I just made a deal with one friend that if a war breaks out, he'll let me know.
We still keep a TV, but it's only for movies — no ads, no politics, no time-wasting junk.

Ads are like a toxic drip feeding other people's needs into your brain.

Watching ads means letting someone implant foreign ideas in your head that drain your time and money.

Money is time. Ads steal both.

It's all about mental hygiene — don't load your head with informational garbage.

52.2.9 Peaceful Environment

We live in a small town. Everything is close by, no traffic jams. What's happening in the big city? I don't know, and I don't care. What matters is safety, shops, and peace.

If we want more, it's just 30 minutes on the highway to a big city with millions of people.

52.2.10 People

For me, family comes first — mutual support, love, understanding, acceptance. Simple, yet rare. I'm lucky.

Friends? A few. For me, they're special people — quality over quantity.

Acquaintances? Don't need them. Sounds antisocial, I know — but I cut off the media, so "sorry, I didn't know" how things are supposed to be. I don't care what people outside my circle are doing, and I don't want to waste time on it.

I wrote this book to share my thoughts, knowledge, and experience. I want people around me to live well and happily — but that doesn't mean I want to dedicate every day to everyone else.

I'd have no time left for myself.

52.2.11 Privacy

I value it deeply.

It gives me peace, saves time and energy.

That's the result of my life philosophy and knowing what really matters to me. I won't go into detail here — this isn't that kind of book.

52.2.12 Peace of Mind

It comes from all of the above. If you know what you're doing here on Earth, if you've thought through your foundations, if you don't feed on media drama — life is calm.
Some might call it boring — but they're not Traders, they don't write books, and they don't analyze how their own minds work. They don't ask which needs and desires are real and which are just the Matrix. They don't look for ways to improve their lives and find real happiness.

52.2.13 Strength, Humility, Modesty, and Cutting Down Ego

Strength is a strong sense of self-worth — you don't need applause or approval.

Humility is respect for other people's views and opinions.
I'm not the smartest, I'm not infallible, I make mistakes like everyone else.

But humility doesn't mean letting others tear us down. It doesn't mean accepting imposed authorities and blindly following their rules. Everything has limits — respect your own boundaries.

Modesty... given my definition of humility, maybe I shouldn't even write about it. :) I value honesty, sincerity, restraint, and empathy more than modesty.

Ok, but modesty does mean something to me.
For me, modesty is respect toward others and not believing I'm better than them. Judging and comparing yourself just to look "superior" — that's sick and weak.

True modesty is treating everyone as equals. Sometimes I might even see someone as better than me — that's my call and my right. If someone's achieved great things, I can quietly respect them for it. Just don't confuse achievement with human worth.
Some have accomplished a lot — and yet I wouldn't even want to meet them.

Ego. There are many definitions.
For me, Ego is the image you build of yourself.
When I talk about cutting down Ego, I mean not building an inflated picture of yourself as someone special, above others.
For me it's like creating a cult of personality in some twisted totalitarian state.

I'm just human. I haven't saved the world. I try to do something good, but in the end it's just one drop in the ocean.
Sooner or later, the last grain of rice will fall from my bowl. A few decades later, no one will remember me — just like billions before.

There's no point in getting excited about your own greatness — we're just dust in the universe. We'll be gone without a trace.
Ask your Ego if it has a different opinion. :)

52.2.14 Happiness and Joy

We should live in a way that makes life good for us and for others — or at least doesn't get in their way — while enjoying it ourselves.
If someone has a problem with our life, maybe it's worth changing the environment — or just buying them out and plowing their field.
The key is not to get too worked up and not waste time.

52.2.15 Enough, Right? I Went On Again

This isn't one of those "5 Steps to Become a Super Trader" books. I don't know any easy way. I've touched on many topics, and it's up to you whether you'll develop them and put them in order in your head — or just let them slide.
If you've reached this page, there's a good chance you'll achieve something.
I'm considering creating a shortened workbook version of this book. If you're interested, leave your email, and I'll let you know once it's ready.

http://www.sherlocktrades.com/books/mental/workbook

52.3 MM More Important Than TA

You already know that psychology is the "most important factor."
You know that health and a well-trained mind are the foundation.
You also know that risk and money management matter more than Technical Analysis and the typical beginner's questions:
"Where do I enter? When do I enter?"

It's all laid out here like cards on the table.
All you need to do is read the book several times, take notes, work through the topics, find methods that fit you, maybe get some extra training in NLP, raise capital for your first deposit, pick a broker, and master tools like "Sierra...".

Just make sure you're holding good cards – because not everything that looks like poker actually is.
Now you can start your path to a new life. :)

Right... I also promised that simple, secret recipe for a million. :)

53 „Top Secret”

This chapter is only for those who actually read the book.
If you're trying to cut corners and skipped chapters, you've just fallen into your own habit trap. Sometimes shortcuts work, but most of the time it's those who do **the hard work that earn the real rewards**. If you didn't read the whole book — do your homework first, then come back here — because in a moment you'll discover what really hides under the term "shortcut."
I promised, so here are the details of the method:

„No luck. No hype. Just 1 month. 1 million”.

This is a strategy that, in one form or another, has been tested by millions of Traders. It's so effective that those who've pulled it off usually stay quiet — because if you stumble upon something like this, you'd rather keep it to yourself.

But I promised to share everything I know, and I keep my word. Alright, let's get down to business — maybe later we'll do a Q&A or something. **Focus now**, because the devil is in the details.

Step 1 — Open a new broker account. Arrange with your broker that as soon as the balance hits 1 million USD, everything gets automatically closed.
That's the key element of this method. **1 million** is the level that, according to this concept, means "**enough**."

Of course, you can set any other limit. Your money, your rules.
Got the account? Great.

Step 2 — Deposit 10 million dollars and start trading on the first day of the month. By the last day of that month, the balance will show 1 million — or more, if luck is on your side.

The trading technique doesn't matter here.
Burning 90% of capital can be done any way you like — slowly, quickly, whatever. :)

I'm writing this at 1 a.m. Normal people are asleep — I guess I just needed a break from serious topics. :)
I hope my sense of **humor** didn't let you down in this book. :)

As always — if what I've created here gave you more value than the price you paid, I'll be glad if you buy me a coffee.
Small gestures like that really give me the energy to keep sharing knowledge.

https://buymeacoffee.com/sherlocktrades.com

Did I mention that as a thank-you for a coffee I'm giving away my new position-management cards? :)

I'm launching a YouTube channel. I've already learned video editing :) so I've got the amateur tech side covered. :)
Once I wrap up editing this book and release it on ebook platforms, I'll start preparing analyses of interesting chart setups — of course using the same technique I trade with.

Add my YouTube channel to your subscriptions so you won't miss any practical content and valuable insights.

https://www.youtube.com/@SherlockTrades

Friends asked me if, after a book on trading psychology, I'll also publish something on **technical analysis and trading strategy**.

Hard to say — I thought writing this book would take me just a few evenings, but it turned into over 1,600 hours: text, graphics, editing, corrections... and I haven't even started the translations into other languages yet.

Apparently that's still fast, but probably only because I wrote about what was already in my head. I didn't have to invent nonsense just to fill pages. And even then, I don't think it's perfect — but chasing perfection can kill the whole point of the work.

With technical analysis it might be harder: less narrative, more hard facts, and every word can carry weight.

I'm not sure if pulling 2–3 months out of my life is a good idea.

I'll see how people react to this book — whether they like my style, my approach, and my format. That will be my main motivation.

I'm not a craftsman churning out books for royalties to pay the bills. If this book sells well, if I see good reviews from around the world — **that will give me wings**.

And if the response is weak — it means there's no demand for my style of writing, and there's no point in forcing it. I know it's blunt, but I'm not a politician and I don't waste time telling stories just to win applause. I'm not doing this for the money.

Money matters to me, but in this case it's only a measure of whether what I do has value for others.

I like it when my work has meaning and bears fruit.

Leave your email there — you'll be the first to know if a book on technical analysis and strategy is coming.

https://sherlocktrades.com/books/AT

54 Is This It?

Is this the end of my journey writing my first book?
A bit sad, because it's been an amazing ride.
Almost makes me want to do it again. :)
After all... I didn't kill off the main character, so who knows. :)

I still have a chance to sneak in a piece of a Trader's life philosophy into the footnotes :) **but this really is the end of the book.** I wonder if you can say that a person is worth as much as the book they've written...
Some actually wrote a book, others made their whole life into one.

To finish, I'll remind you of words the whole world knows — and yet they're worth repeating:

"Never give in, never give in,
never, never, never, never-in nothing,
great or small, large or petty — never give in
except to convictions of honour and good sense"

Winston Churchill. October 29. 1941. Harrow School.

Never give up if the goal is good and important.
Never abandon your dreams. Never.
I'm rooting for you. And now...

55 Footnotes

I was wondering whether to even add footnotes, because to me everything seems obvious.
Then I remembered the early days — how many things were unclear to me back then. I don't know if I'll manage to catch everything in the text that might need explaining, but I'll try to point out what could be confusing. As for the rest — Google surely knows and will gladly help. :)

I'll do my best to make these explanations not dry and boring. :)

[1]
Smart Money — in trading this means the big players (funds, institutions, banks) who have enough capital to move the market.
They don't trade like the crowd — they accumulate during declines and sell in times of euphoria. Their actions aren't directly visible, but they leave clear footprints on the chart.
The key is to observe where volume shows up, how price reacts to it, and whether you can see a process of accumulation or distribution. This topic is worth exploring when learning technical analysis with VSA — Volume Spread Analysis.
Back to text — [1]

[2]
A Trader is someone actively trading financial markets — not investing for years, but profiting from shorter price moves.
Trading is a process — analysis, decision, entry, position management, and exit. It's work, not just "clicking buttons."

A Day Trader is a specific type of Trader: trading within a single session and closing all positions before the day ends.
Day trading is built on discipline, resilience, precision, and fast decision-making.
In my view, it's the best but also the toughest form of trading.

Technical Analysis is a method of evaluating the market based on charts — without looking into financial reports or news. It assumes that everything important is already reflected in price. Traders analyze candlestick patterns, support and resistance levels, trends, volume, or indicators (like RSI, MACD).
The goal isn't to predict the future, but to recognize the probability of certain scenarios.
In practice: you're analyzing the crowd's behavior, not the market itself.

Mental — Trader Psychology is the second pillar of effective trading. It covers everything going on in the Trader's mind: emotions, beliefs, discipline, reactions to stress and losses.
A strategy can be perfect, but if you break down mentally — hitting the button out of revenge, fear, or boredom — the market will crush you. Trader Psychology is the skill of controlling yourself in moments that test your weak spots.
Back to text — [2]

[3]
Money Management is the way you handle capital while trading. It covers position sizing, setting stop losses, choosing leverage, and splitting risk across trades and strategies.
The goal isn't to maximize profit, but to control risk and survive in the game. Even with a 40% win rate you can make money, if you manage capital properly.
Without MM — even the best setup ends with blowing up your account.
Back to text — [3]

[4]
"**Blowing up an account**" is trading slang meaning a complete loss of funds in a broker account — balance going to zero. It usually happens to beginners who start without a plan, without risk management, and with emotions at the wheel.

Many experienced Traders have blown up their first account — a brutal but common lesson in humility at the start.
Back to text – [4]

[5]
"It's a brutal game with no sentiment and no mercy."
The market has no mercy — because it has no consciousness.
A common mistake among beginners is attributing bad intentions to the market, as if it were a player against us. In reality, the market is the impersonal sum of thousands of participants' decisions — and the chart is just a mathematical record of those decisions.
We're not visible to it, we're not a target — we're invisible cogs in a massive machine. If you lose, it's not because the market "sees you" or "wants to catch you," but because you make mistakes: misjudging the situation, trading too big a position, not having a plan.

The real threat isn't the market itself but often the middleman — for example, an MM broker creating its own quotes with a vested interest in your loss. That's why it's crucial to understand how your broker operates and pick one that isn't betting against you.

It's worth comparing your broker's chart to the actual exchange-traded futures contract it's supposed to mirror. You'll see whether the charts align — or whether odd candles magically appear on the broker's feed at turning points, wiping out clients' SLs.
Quite often, the futures chart holds the level — but at the MM broker it suddenly breaks. :)
An alternative to an **MM** broker is an **ECN** broker (Electronic Communication Network).

ECN broker:

- Connects Traders directly with other market participants (banks, funds, other Traders).
- No conflict of interest — the broker isn't counterparty to the trade.

MM broker:

- Takes the opposite position to the client — acts as counterparty.
- May manipulate quotes.
- May offer lower costs than ECN.
- Usually faster execution of small orders, but always with potential conflict of interest.

Another option, without the risk of chart manipulation, is using brokers that provide **direct access to exchange-traded futures.**
I recommend digging into broker types — their pros, cons, costs, and capital requirements — before sending in your money.
Back to text – [5]

[6]
Mentoring programs in trading are paid, usually long-term forms of learning directly from experienced Traders. It's not about an online course or an ebook, but close cooperation, trade reviews, Q&A sessions, and so on.
The goal isn't only to learn a strategy, but to understand the thinking of a professional and to develop your own approach.
These programs are usually expensive and don't guarantee success.
You can figure everything out on your own, but sometimes money well spent shortens the road to your goal. Sometimes it's worth it... sometimes not.

If I had had a book like this one earlier, plus the one on technique that I haven't written yet, I wouldn't have had to spend so much time in training. :)

In my case, it turned out that I don't really use what I learned in mentoring, but I can't say it wasn't worth it, because the training led me to my own analyses and to finding methods that suit me, which I implemented, still use, and they work.

What's more, I taught my methods to a friend who is doing well with them. I didn't discover anything new, but I managed to combine known methods into a consistent system.
Back to text – [6]

[7]
NLP (Neuro-Linguistic Programming) is a method of working on changing beliefs, emotions, and thought habits — developed in the 1970s by Richard Bandler and John Grinder.
It assumes that the way we talk to ourselves and perceive reality influences our reactions and decisions.
In practice, NLP is a set of techniques for changing thinking patterns, breaking through mental blocks, and programming new, more effective behaviors — used in psychology, coaching, and in shaping a Trader's mindset.
Back to text – [7]

[8]
"**Nemo vir est qui mundum non reddat meliorem**"
This is a Latin phrase appearing in Ridley Scott's Kingdom of Heaven (2005). Literally:
"A man is no one if he does not make the world better."
It's not a quote from classical Roman literature but a modern paraphrase in Latin style. In the film it expresses the core idea of responsibility for one's actions and their impact on the world, regardless of era or religion.
In my understanding, this sentence reflects the idea every good person should have: **if you can — do something good**.
It may be on a small scale or a big one.
As much as you want, as much as you can, and as much as those in need deserve.

Do as much as you can to leave the world
at least a little better because you were here.

My view has no religious reference. In my opinion, religions on this Earth have done more harm than good. We can be good people without any religious label hanging over our heads.
Back to text – [8]

[9]
Statement live – in the trading community "statement live" means a real, ongoing record of results from a Trader's live account – not from demo, not from Excel, not from manually edited screenshots.
Usually it's a screenshot from a broker platform (e.g., MT4, cTrader, NinjaTrader) or a public link to a tracker like Myfxbook, FX Blue, FundedNext, showing actual results, trade history, equity, drawdown, etc.
In practice: if someone claims they're making money – a statement live is the only reliable proof. The rest is just talk. This matters especially in the context of training. Buying a course from a mentor usually costs serious money and time. At that point, credibility is everything. Whether he can trade profitably is one thing; whether he can teach it is another.
Back to text – [9]

[10]
Ichimoku Kinko Hyo is a Japanese technical analysis system created in the 1930s by Goichi Hosoda.
Translated, it means: "a picture of balance at a glance."
Ichimoku is a complex yet complete system based on five lines (Tenkan-sen, Kijun-sen, Senkou Span A & B, Chikou Span), which show trend, support/resistance, and potential entry signals.
Simplified, it's built on moving averages from different periods. I studied it for a while – definitely an interesting option.

Price Action is a market analysis approach based solely on price movement, without technical indicators. A Trader analyzes candles, patterns, support and resistance levels, and price behavior in key areas — everything without "decorations."
The principle: price tells you everything — just watch how it reacts to levels, how the momentum looks, whether it's a correction or a false breakout.
Price Action is the backbone of many effective intraday and swing strategies — clean, simple, precise.
I use quite a few elements of Price Action in my technique. But as a whole, something was missing for me.
Maybe it was my wrong approach, but that's how it felt. :)
Back to text — [10]

[11]
VSA — Volume Spread Analysis is a market analysis method created and popularized by Tom Williams — a former professional Trader. VSA combines three elements: volume, candle spread, and chart context to understand the actions of the big players (the so-called Smart Money).
It doesn't generate ready-made signals — instead it teaches you to look at the chart as a footprint of capital decisions. As if Smart Money left fingerprints beneath the chart in the form of volume.
Back to text — [11]

[12]
Equity curve is a chart showing how a Trader's account balance changes over time — after each trade. The ideal curve rises smoothly upward, without sharp drops, but in reality it always contains drawdowns. The only question is how deep those drawdowns are, and whether they're large enough to eventually bankrupt the Trader.
Drawdown is the difference between a local peak and the lowest point of the subsequent decline.
It can be expressed in % or in currency.

It's a true measure of risk — showing how much capital a Trader had to endure or sit through in losses before the account recovered to profit. Even a profitable strategy may have deep drawdowns — the question is whether the Trader's account and psyche can withstand them.
Back to text — [12]

[13]
Drawdown — in trading this is the percentage drop in account value from the last peak to the lowest trough — the moment when a Trader is "underwater."
Drawdowns of 30–50% carry not only huge psychological and financial risk but also hard math: to recover a 50% loss, you need a 100% gain.
If someone has already lost half their capital, chances are they don't yet have the skills to double it back. Drawdown isn't just a number — it's a mirror of risk, showing how badly a strategy (or a Trader) can go off track before recovering. And if it really goes off the rails, the only way back is adding fresh capital. :)
Back to text — [13]

[14]
SL and TP — Stop Loss and Take Profit — are the two basic types of protective orders used in trading:

SL (Stop Loss) — automatically closes a position when price reaches a defined loss level. It limits risk and protects capital from deeper drawdowns.

TP (Take Profit) — automatically closes a position with profit at a pre-set level. It helps lock in gains without emotions and stick to the plan.

SLK — Equity Stop (Stop Loss on total capital).
SLK isn't an order in the platform but a way of limiting the maximum total loss you're willing to accept on your entire capital — not just a single position.

In practice: you keep only part of your capital in the broker account (e.g., 10–30%), while securing the rest elsewhere (bank account, bonds, etc.).
When losses hit your threshold (e.g., -10% of total capital), you stop trading — no matter what the chart says — because your broker account is out of funds.
It's protection against emotional spirals and Black Swans — if the broker goes under, the platform freezes, or you lose your head, the SLK keeps your capital from getting wiped out.
Back to text — [14]

[15]
Black Swan is a concept popularized by Nassim Nicholas Taleb — meaning an unpredictable, rare event with huge consequences that, in hindsight, seems obvious.
In trading, a Black Swan can be a flash crash, war, central bank decision, sudden disaster — something that wasn't in the plan but can wipe out an account "in a minute."
You can't predict them, but you can prepare — limit exposure, use SL, and manage risk as if something unthinkable could hit tomorrow.
Back to text — [15]

[16]
Tommi Mäkinen is a Finnish rally driver, four-time WRC world champion (1996–1999) with Mitsubishi. **Known for his cool head, perfect control, and aggression only when needed**.
For many motorsport fans, he's a symbol of calm under pressure and pure effectiveness, without showmanship or wasted words.
In the world of trading, you could say: he drove like a Trader with a plan — risking only where he had an edge, not where emotions tempted him.
Back to text — [16]

[17]
Emotional Anchoring is a technique from NLP and psychology, based on consciously linking a stimulus (gesture, sound, image) with a specific emotional state — e.g., focus, calm, confidence. Once an "anchor" is reinforced, using it can instantly bring back that state — even under stress, like when entering a trade or handling a loss. A gesture, breath, or word becomes a mental switch."
Back to text — [17]

[18]
EST (Erhard Seminars Training) was a controversial personal development method from the 1970s, created by Werner Erhard. It was based on harsh confrontation with one's own beliefs, traumas, and defense mechanisms, often in the form of intensive, multi-hour group sessions.
The aim of EST was to spark a sudden breakthrough — breaking down the illusions a person carried about themselves and the world. It stirred mixed opinions but shaped later coaching, NLP, and transformational therapy trends.
Back to text — [18]

[19]
Buy, Sell — long and short positions
In trading, "**Buy**" means opening a **long** position — you're betting on price going up. You take a Buy position and if price rises, you profit; if it falls, you lose.
The opposite is a short position.
"**Sell**" means a **short** position — betting on price dropping.
If it falls, you profit; if it rises, you lose.
"Going long" = betting on upside.
"Going short" = betting on downside.
These are the two basic directions in trading — you can make money whether the market rises or falls, as long as you're right on direction.

How do you make money when prices fall?
Shorting stocks — how it used to work.
In the past, to short stocks a Trader had to first borrow them from a broker or another investor (e.g., from the securities account of a financial institution's client).
The Trader borrowed shares and sold them at the current market price. If the price fell, he bought them back cheaper and returned them to the owner, pocketing the difference. If the price rose, he had to buy them back at a higher price, taking a loss.
It was a straight bet on a price drop — profit or loss came only from the gap between selling (entry) and buying back (exit). That required access to brokers or institutions that allowed physical stock borrowing — so shorting was mostly for big players and institutions.
Today, it's often done through futures or CFDs.
Back to text — [19]

[20]
Trigger — in English, a trigger is a stimulus that provokes an automatic emotional or behavioral reaction — often unconscious.
In the Trader's psychology context, a trigger can be, for example, a sudden loss, the sight of a big candle, or the sound of an alert — anything that sparks stress, fear, impulsiveness, or compulsive action.
Awareness of your triggers is the key to emotional control — it's never the trigger itself that wrecks your account, but your reaction to it.
Back to text — [20]

[21]
Shakeout — a sudden, often manipulated move against the crowd's positions, meant to flush out weak players (no plan, tight SLs, impulsive).
A classic shakeout is a sharp dip under support that trips stop-losses on longs — then price snaps back up.
In VSA and Smart Money analysis, a shakeout is a sign that big players are clearing the market before the real move. For a Trader: it looks like a trap — because that's exactly what it is.
Back to text — [21]

[22]
Margin Call — a warning (or automatic action) from the broker that your account no longer has enough margin to maintain open positions.
In practice:
• The broker demands more funds,
• Or forcibly closes positions, starting with the biggest losers.
A Margin Call usually comes from too much leverage, no SL, and oversized risk.
If you get one — your risk management blew up.
Back to text — [22]

[23]
The Nixon Shock refers to President Nixon's August 15, 1971 move to suspend the dollar's convertibility into gold.
This ended the **Bretton Woods** system (where currencies were tied to the dollar, and the dollar to gold) and launched the era of **fiat money** — currency whose value rests solely on trust in the state. For markets, it was a turning point — from then on the global system ran on trust, policy, and perception, not gold.
Got it? The value of money — a central part **of our lives — depends on trust in politicians and bankers. :) :) :)**
This is not a dark joke. It's the Matrix we live in.
Back to text — [23]

[24]
Focus Trigger (FT) in trading is a specific chart condition that instantly snaps a Trader into full focus — the cue that the money game starts here.
It can be, for example:

- price tagging a key technical or geometry level,
- a pattern backed by decisive volume,
- a VSA signal showing Smart Money activity,
- or any setup the Trader classifies as high quality.

An FT isn't a trade — it's the mental "click" when the **Trader stops passively watching and shifts into decision-ready mode.**
Back to text – [24]

[25]
"**Positive pluses, negative pluses**" — Lech Wałęsa
This is the famous (and often mocked) line from Lech Wałęsa — former President of Poland — who in one interview tried to describe a complex situation with the words:

„There are positive pluses and negative pluses."

Absurd as it sounds, what he meant was that everything has both good and bad sides — even if you call them "pluses."
It became a cult quote, used ironically to comment on mixed results or ambiguous decisions — also in the world of trading.
Let me add a few words — just so my view on Poland's politics is on record here.
I don't like politics, but sometimes a man has to..."

Historically, Lech Wałęsa was the legendary leader of "Solidarity" and President of Poland from 1990–1995 – one of the most admired yet controversial figures in Polish politics.

As a worker who led a peaceful anti-communist revolution, he gained worldwide recognition, the **Nobel Peace Prize (1983)**, and the status of a symbol of freedom.

In 1989 he played a key role in peacefully overthrowing communism in Poland, and a year later became the first President of the Third Republic elected by popular vote.

In 1991 Wałęsa addressed the joint session of the **U.S. Congress** – a symbolic tribute to his role in ending the Cold War. He began his speech with the words:

"We, the People!"

It was a deliberate reference to the preamble of the U.S. Constitution – and it sparked a standing ovation.

On the other hand, his career was full of controversies, many fueled by the Kaczyński brothers. Wałęsa had brought them into politics – later he pushed them aside. He didn't know they'd become the "Trojan Horse" in his career.

I won't play the historian here or debate who's a saint and who's... let me hold back my words.

I once quoted the Bible:
"By their fruits you will know them."
For over a decade, the main source of "fruits" in our country has been **Jarosław Kaczyński**. And what are those fruits?
The nation is divided. Half the country sees the other half as the enemy. Families argue about politics at the holiday table.
Little Jarek shattered the nation's unity – weakening the country just to **divide, rule, and cling to power**.

I could list countless wrongs I've seen in Polish politics. Half the people would hate me for it, half would applaud. Isn't that sick? If those are Jarosław's fruits — I don't need to explain whose hand I wouldn't shake.

----

*“**We, the People!**” — Today we're divided and weakened, because someone keeps splitting us just to cling to power.*

One of my few close friends is of Jewish descent. I truly enjoy talking with him — I don't share those genes, but I respect that nation for its mindset and life philosophy.

I know — I've probably just offended half the world. As if outside Poland there were another Kaczyński stirring up hatred, pitting nations against each other, starting wars just to cling to power. Ordinary people die and suffer, while politicians move pawns and fight battles with others' hands.
But that's not the point...

Imagine you have a choice: make a good deal or a bad one. Which do you pick?
You're holding a poker hand — do you fold or play to win?

Wałęsa was a symbol — a strong card. Politically, he could have been used to secure many good deals for Poland. On his own, maybe he wouldn't have managed — but with skilled politicians, he could have opened many doors.

That political capital could have been used for years.
Unfortunately, one small man couldn't stand it. Jarosław preferred to waste that potential, destroy it, smear it — rather than put the country's good above his personal vendetta.
We had poker in hand — and threw the cards in the trash.

I'm telling you this to show **how destructive a human psyche can be.**
How much can be ruined and wasted by emotions.
You are — or want to be — a Trader. You, me, all of us — carry plenty of foolish, destructive programs in our heads. The problem is that in our business, a bad program means a bad financial outcome.
You can have 95% of it — from technique to mental game — perfectly set, and then one tiny background script pops up... and ruins everything.

You've got tough work ahead of you.
You've got to fine-tune your mental software so no hidden script whispers: "I've got poker — I'll bend the rules and grab more" (like pushing for that million... and winding up with 20K trading Bitcoin).
I don't know if I scared you enough or if these examples hit home. I hope they did.
If not — then you already know: it's all on you.
Find your own examples that strike a chord and trigger the effect that works for you.

These are the last lines.

I'm not leaving you alone.
I leave you in good hands — your own.

Make sure this book bears good fruits in your life.
And if it does — maybe someone will write me a positive plus in heaven, if such a place exists. :)
Back to text — [25]

www.ingramcontent.com/pod-product-compliance
Lightning Source LLC
Chambersburg PA
CBHW050521240926
51846CB00003B/644
* 9 7 8 8 3 9 7 6 1 4 0 1 7 *